GCSE AQA
Physics
Foundation Level

This fantastic book has everything you need for a top GCSE grade in Foundation Physics — all the important facts, theory and practical skills for the exams.

There are clear notes for the whole course, helpful tips and plenty of exam-style questions, with all the answers at the back.

We've also included lots of online revision in CGP RevisionHub — it has quick quizzes, summary tests, videos and more, all matched to your book... Amazing!

Unlock CGP RevisionHub

Just scan a QR code in the book to access the CGP RevisionHub.
Or go to **cgpbooks.co.uk/revise** and enter this code!

1940 1004 1747 3776

By the way, this code only works for one person. If somebody else has used this book before you, they might have already claimed the code.

Revision Guide
with new CGP RevisionHub

Contents

How to Revise with CGP RevisionHub 1
What to Expect in the Exams 2

Paper One

Topic 1 — Energy

Energy Stores and Systems 3
Conservation of Energy and Energy Transfers 4
Kinetic and Potential Energy Stores 5
Energy Transfers by Heating 6
Investigating Specific Heat Capacity 7
Power 8
Reducing Unwanted Energy Transfers 9
Investigating Reducing Energy Transfers 10
Efficiency 11
Energy Resources and Their Uses 12
Wind, Solar and Geothermal 13
Hydro-electricity, Waves and Tides 14
Bio-fuels and Non-renewables 15
Trends in Energy Resource Use 16
Revision Summary Test for Topic 1 17

Topic 2 — Electricity

Current and Circuit Symbols 18
Resistance and $V = IR$ 19
Investigating Resistance 20
I-V Characteristics 21
Circuit Devices 22
Series Circuits 23
Parallel Circuits 24
Investigating Circuits 25
Electricity in the Home 26
Power of Electrical Appliances 27
More on Energy Transfers and Power 28
The National Grid 29
Static Electricity 30
Electric Fields 31
Revision Summary Test for Topic 2 32

Topic 3 — Particle Model of Matter

The Particle Model and Density 33
Investigating Density 34
Internal Energy and Changes of State 35
Specific Latent Heat 36
Particle Motion and Pressure in Gases 37

Topic 4 — Atomic Structure

Developing the Model of the Atom 38
The Structure of the Atom 39
Isotopes and Nuclear Radiation 40
Nuclear Equations 41
Half-life 42
Background Radiation and Radiation Dose 43
Irradiation and Contamination 44
Uses and Risk 45
Fission and Fusion 46
Revision Summary Test for Topics 3 & 4 47

Paper Two

Topic 5 — Forces

Topic 5a — Forces, Moments and Pressure

Contact and Non-Contact Forces 48
Weight, Mass and Gravity 49
Resultant Forces and Work Done 50
Forces and Elasticity 51
Investigating Springs 52
Moments 53
More on Moments 54
Fluid Pressure and Atmospheric Pressure 55
Revision Summary Test for Topic 5a 56

Topic 5b — Forces and Motion

Distance, Displacement, Speed and Velocity 57
Acceleration 58
Distance-Time Graphs 59
Velocity-Time Graphs and Terminal Velocity 60
Newton's First and Second Laws 61
Newton's Third Law 62
Investigating Motion 63
Stopping Distance and Thinking Distance 64
Braking Distance 65
More on Stopping Distances 66
Reaction Times 67
Revision Summary Test for Topic 5b 68

Topic 6 — Waves

Topic 6a — Wave Basics and EM Waves
Transverse and Longitudinal Waves 69
Frequency, Period and Wave Speed 70
Investigating Waves 71
Refraction 72
Reflection 73
Investigating Light 74
Electromagnetic (EM) Waves 75
Uses of EM Waves 76
More Uses of EM Waves 77
Dangers of EM Waves 78
Revision Summary Test for Topic 6a 79

Topic 6b — Light and Radiation
Lenses and Images 80
Convex Lenses and Ray Diagrams 81
Concave Lenses and Magnification 82
Visible Light 83
Transmitting Visible Light 84
Black Body Radiation and Temperature 85
Investigating IR Radiation 86
Investigating IR Absorption 87
Revision Summary Test for Topic 6b 88

Topic 7 — Magnetism and Electromagnetism
Permanent and Induced Magnets 89
Electromagnetism 90
Electromagnetic Devices 91

Topic 8 — Space Physics
The Solar System and Stars 92
The Life Cycle of Stars 93
Red-Shift and the Big Bang 94
Revision Summary Test for Topics 7 & 8 95

Working Scientifically
The Scientific Method 96
Communication & Issues Created by Science 97
Risk 98
Designing Investigations 99
Collecting Data 100
Processing and Presenting Data 101
More on Processing and Presenting Data 102
Units 103
Maths Skills 104
Drawing Conclusions 105
Uncertainties and Evaluations 106

Practical Skills
Apparatus and Techniques 107
More Apparatus and Techniques 108
Working with Electronics 109

Answers 110
Glossary 113
Index 118
Formulas 120

Published by CGP

From original material by Richard Parsons

Editors: Sammy El-Bahrawy, Josie Gilbert, Sean McParland, Charlotte Sheridan, Jack Simm, Dan Sreeves, Julie Wakeling and Maddie Wright.

With thanks to Mark Edwards for the proofreading.

ISBN: 978 1 78908 323 1

With thanks to Jade Sim for the copyright research.

Data used to construct stopping distance diagram on page 66: contains public sector information licensed under the Open Government Licence v3.0. https://www.nationalarchives.gov.uk/doc/open-government-licence/version/3/

Printed by Sterling, Kettering.
Clipart from Corel®

Illustrations by: Sandy Gardner Artist, email sandy@sandygardner.co.uk

Text, design, layout and original illustrations © Coordination Group Publications Ltd (CGP) 2025
All rights reserved.

Photocopying more than one section of this book is not permitted, even if you have a CLA licence.
Extra copies are available from CGP with next day delivery • 0800 1712 712 • www.cgpbooks.co.uk

How to Revise with CGP RevisionHub

There's more to revision than just reading this book — you need to understand and remember it too. Read on for how to get the most out of your Revision Guide and RevisionHub...

Here's a handy guide to using RevisionHub.

1) You Need to Learn Your Stuff

This book covers everything you need to know for GCSE AQA Foundation Physics.

1) Read it — but not all at once... break it into manageable chunks.
2) Once you've read over a chunk, try making your own mind maps and flash cards — writing down and thinking about the content will help it to really stick.
3) We've also included some videos to help with the trickier bits — watch out for the QR codes.

2) Check That You Can Remember What You've Learnt

Ta-dah!

If you don't test yourself, you won't know what you don't know. So try covering up a page and seeing if you can write it all out. Then try quizzing yourself using RevisionHub:

Quick Quizzes

- The QR code at the top of each page takes you to a quick quiz of the stuff on that page.
- These quizzes are a quick check of the key facts and your maths skills.
- Revisit questions that you get wrong by doing the 'Your Mistakes' quiz, and there are Paper 1 and Paper 2 quizzes too.

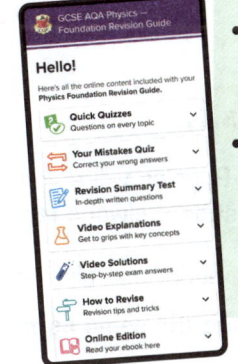

Revision Summary Tests

- At the end of each topic in the book is a fiendish memory test on as much stuff as we could cram in.
- You can do these tests on paper or you can complete them on the RevisionHub — follow the QR code.
- Online, you can also find sample answers, assess your progress, and look back at your results for previous topics to see the areas you need to work on.

3) Make Sure That You're Exam Ready

To see if you're exam ready, try some exam-style questions. Luckily for you, there are loads in this book.

- You'll find one or more exam-style questions at the bottom of each page.
- Use them to check that you can apply what you've learnt to exams.
- There are answers in the back of the book, and many questions also have a video solution for you to watch — you'll see a QR code next to the question.

It's also worth getting your hands on some practice papers and seeing how you score.

> You probably won't stick strictly to this order of steps — for example, you might want to try some exam-style questions as you go, and you'll need to look back at bits of this book if you get a question wrong or are finding a topic hard.

Ready, steady, REVISE...

Yep, revision can seem daunting. Like a looming monster with sharp teeth and smelly breath. If it's making you feel like you don't know where to start, follow this QR code and see what we recommend.

Find the CGP RevisionHub at cgpbooks.co.uk/Mass

What to Expect in the Exams

Before you get cracking with your revision and exam practice, here's a handy guide to what you'll have to face in the exams. You're welcome.

Topics are Covered in Different Papers

For GCSE AQA Foundation Physics, you'll sit two exam papers at the end of your course.

Paper	Time	No. of Marks	Topics Assessed	Maths Skills	Practical Skills
1	1 hr 45 mins	100	1, 2, 3 and 4	At least 30% of total marks	At least 15% of total marks
2	1 hr 45 mins	100	5, 6, 7 and 8		

You're expected to know the basic concepts of energy transfers in both papers.

There are Different Question Types

In each exam, you'll be expected to answer a mixture of multiple choice questions, structured questions, questions that have short, closed answers, as well as open response questions.

For some open response questions, you'll be marked on the overall quality of your answer, not just its scientific content. So...

Always make sure:
- You answer the question fully.
- You include detailed, relevant information.
- Your answer is clear and has a logical structure.

You'll be Tested on Your Maths...

At least 30% of the total marks for GCSE Physics will come from questions that test your maths skills. For these questions, always remember to:

- Show your working — you could get marks for this, even if your final answer's wrong.
- Check that the units of your answer are the same as the ones they asked for in the question.
- Make sure your answer is given to an appropriate number of significant figures.

We've indicated maths skills throughout this book with a handy stamp that looks like this: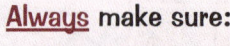

...and on Your Practical Skills

PRACTICAL

Required practical activities are marked up with a stamp like this.

GCSE Physics contains 10 required practical activities that you'll do during the course. You can be asked about these, and the practical skills they involve, in the exams.

E.g. you might have to comment on experimental design (the apparatus and method), make predictions, analyse or interpret results... Pretty much anything to do with planning and carrying out investigations.

At least 15% of the total marks will be for questions that test your understanding of the practical activities and practical skills.

You'll Need to Know About Working Scientifically

Working Scientifically is all about how science is applied in the outside world by real scientists.

For example, you might be asked about ways that scientists communicate an idea to get their point across without being biased, or about the limitations of a scientific model.

You need to think about the situation that you've been given and use all your scientific savvy. Always read the question and any data you've been given really carefully before you start writing.

Topic 1 — Energy

Energy Stores and Systems

Energy is never used up. It's just the way that it's stored that changes.

Energy is Transferred Between Energy Stores

Energy is stored in the different energy stores of an object.
You need to know the following energy stores:

1) KINETIC — anything moving has energy in its kinetic energy store.
2) THERMAL — all objects have energy in this store. The hotter the object, the more energy in the store.
3) CHEMICAL — anything that can release energy by a chemical reaction has energy in this store, e.g. food.
4) GRAVITATIONAL POTENTIAL — any object raised above ground level has energy in this store.
5) ELASTIC POTENTIAL — anything stretched has energy in this store, like springs and rubber bands.
6) ELECTROSTATIC — e.g. two charges that attract or repel each other have energy in this store.
7) MAGNETIC — e.g. two magnets that attract or repel each other have energy in this store.
8) NUCLEAR — the nucleus of an atom releases energy from this store in nuclear reactions (p.41).

Thermal energy stores can also be called internal energy stores.

Energy can be Transferred in Four Ways

BY RADIATION
- This is when energy is transferred by electromagnetic radiation (p.75).
- For example, when energy from the Sun travels to Earth by light.

ELECTRICALLY
- This happens when a moving charge does work (p.27).
- For example, when a current flows through a light bulb.

BY HEATING
- When energy is transferred from a hotter object to a colder object.
- For example, when a pan of water is heated on a hob.

MECHANICALLY
- This happens when a force does work (p.50) on an object.
- For example, a force pushing an object along the floor.

Energy can also be transferred mechanically by sound waves. This is a mechanical energy transfer because a force is needed to create a sound wave.

When a System Changes, Energy is Transferred

1) A system can be:
   - A single object — e.g. a tennis ball.
   - A group of objects — e.g. colliding vehicles.
2) When a system changes, energy is transferred to a different store in one of the four ways above.
3) Closed systems are systems where no matter (stuff) or energy can enter or leave.
4) When a closed system changes, there is no net (overall) change in the total energy of the system.

For example...
- A cold spoon sealed in a flask of hot soup is a closed system.
- Energy is transferred from the thermal energy store of the soup to the thermal energy store of the spoon by heating.
- But no energy leaves the system. The total energy stays the same.

Transfer this information to your exam knowledge stores...

Energy stores pop up everywhere in physics. Make sure you understand them before you read the next page.

Q1 Name four energy stores that energy can be transferred between. [4 marks]

Find the CGP RevisionHub at cgpbooks.co.uk/Mass

Quick Quiz

Conservation of Energy and Energy Transfers

Repeat after me: energy is NEVER destroyed. Make sure you learn that fact, it's really important.

You Need to Know the Conservation of Energy Principle

Energy can be transferred usefully, stored or dissipated, but can never be created or destroyed.

1) This means that whenever a system changes, all the energy is simply moved between stores.
2) This is true for every energy transfer.
3) Even when energy is dissipated (wasted), it isn't gone.
4) It's just been transferred to an energy store that we didn't want.
5) There's more about wasted energy on p.9.

Energy is usually wasted by heating — see p.6.

Forces Cause Mechanical Energy Transfers

1) If a force moves an object, then work is done.
2) Work done is the same as energy transferred.
3) So energy is transferred mechanically when a force moves an object.
4) You might be given a situation, and be asked to describe the changes in how energy is stored.
5) Here are a few examples:

Example 1 — A ball thrown into the air
- A person throws a ball upwards.
- The person exerts a force on the ball.
- Energy is transferred mechanically from the chemical energy store of the person's arm to the kinetic and gravitational potential energy stores of the ball and arm.

upwards force

There's more on work done on p.50.

Example 2 — A ball dropped from a height
- The ball is accelerated by the constant force of gravity.
- Energy is transferred mechanically from the ball's gravitational potential energy store to its kinetic energy store.

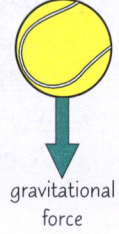
gravitational force

Example 3 — A car slowing down
- Friction acts between the car's brakes and its wheels.
- Energy is transferred mechanically from the kinetic energy stores of the wheels to the thermal energy stores of the wheels, brakes and surroundings.

frictional force

Example 4 — A car hitting a wall
- When the car and the wall touch, there is a normal contact force (p.48) on both of them.
- Energy is transferred mechanically from the car's kinetic energy store to lots of other energy stores.
- Some energy is transferred to the elastic potential and thermal energy stores of the wall and the car.

All this work, I can feel my energy stores being drained...

The four examples above aren't the only ones you can be asked about. Test yourself with this question.

Q1 Describe the energy transfers that occur when the wind causes a windmill to spin. [3 marks]

Q1 Video Solution

4 Topic 1 — Energy

Kinetic and Potential Energy Stores

Quick Quiz

Now you've got your head around energy stores, it's time to work out how much energy is in them.

Movement Means Energy in an Object's Kinetic Energy Store

1) Energy is transferred to the kinetic energy store when an object speeds up.
2) Energy is transferred away from this store when an object slows down.
3) The formula for kinetic energy is:

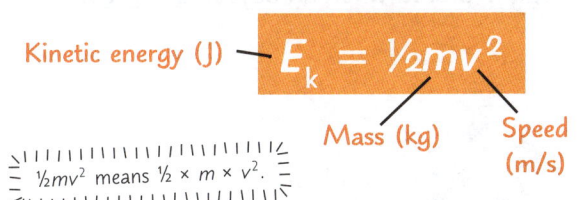

Kinetic energy (J) $E_k = \tfrac{1}{2}mv^2$ Mass (kg) Speed (m/s)

½mv² means ½ × m × v².

EXAMPLE
A car of mass 2500 kg is travelling at 20 m/s. Calculate the energy in its kinetic energy store.
$E_k = \tfrac{1}{2} \times m \times v^2$
$= \tfrac{1}{2} \times 2500 \times 20^2 = 500\,000$ J

MATHS SKILLS

Raised Objects Store Energy in Gravitational Potential Energy Stores

1) All objects raised above the ground gain energy in their gravitational potential energy (g.p.e.) store.
2) You can find the energy in an object's g.p.e. store using:

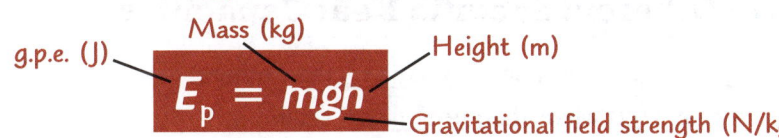

g.p.e. (J) Mass (kg) Height (m)
$E_p = mgh$
Gravitational field strength (N/kg)

Gravitational field strength on Earth is equal to 9.8 N/kg.

Falling Objects Also Transfer Energy

You can also make calculations when energy is transferred between two stores. For example:
- You saw on p.4 that a falling object transfers energy from its g.p.e. store to its kinetic energy store.
- The conservation of energy principle (p.4) says that energy can't be destroyed.
- So for a falling object when there's no air resistance:

Energy lost from the g.p.e. store = Energy gained in the kinetic energy store

GPE → KE

Stretching can Transfer Energy to Elastic Potential Energy Stores

Stretching or squashing an object can transfer energy to its elastic potential energy store. The energy in the elastic potential energy store of a stretched spring can be found using:

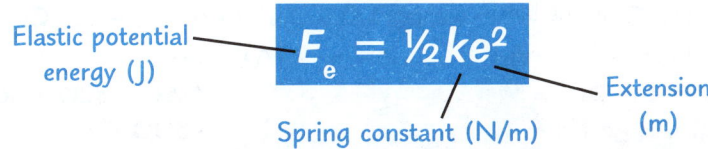

Elastic potential energy (J) $E_e = \tfrac{1}{2}ke^2$ Extension (m)
Spring constant (N/m)

This equation only works if the limit of proportionality has not been passed (p.51).

Make the most of your potential — jump on your bed...

Wow, that's a lot of energy equations. Make sure you're really happy using them before moving on.

Q1   A 2.0 kg object is dropped from a height of 10 m.
Calculate the speed of the object after it has fallen 5.0 m, assuming there is no air resistance.
Give your answer to 2 significant figures. $g = 9.8$ N/kg. [5 marks]

Q1 Video Solution

Energy Transfers by Heating

Heating is just one way of transferring energy, as you saw back on p.3. Also coming up on this page — specific heat capacity. And if you can't handle all that heat, you should probably get out of the kitchen...

Energy can be Transferred by Heating

1) As a material is heated, energy is transferred to its thermal energy store.
2) This causes its temperature to increase.
3) You need to be able to describe the changes in how energy is stored when an object is heated.
4) For example, if you boil water in an electric kettle:

- Energy is transferred electrically to the thermal energy store of the kettle's heating element.
- Energy is then transferred by heating to the water's thermal energy store.
- So the temperature of the water increases.

Different Materials Have Different Specific Heat Capacities

1) Some materials need more energy to increase their temperature than others.
2) These materials also transfer more energy when they cool down again.
3) This all means they can store a lot of energy.
4) The amount of energy stored or released as a material changes temperature depends on the specific heat capacity of the material.
5) Specific heat capacity is the amount of energy needed to raise the temperature of 1 kg of a material by 1 °C.
7) So the higher the specific heat capacity of a material, the better it is at storing energy.
8) The change in thermal energy stored by a material as it changes temperature can be found using:

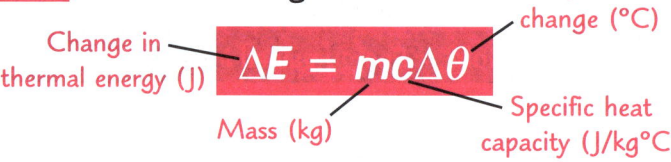

$$\Delta E = mc\Delta\theta$$

Change in thermal energy (J)
Mass (kg)
Temperature change (°C)
Specific heat capacity (J/kg°C)

θ (theta) and Δ (delta) are Greek letters. 'Δ' means change in. 'θ' is just the symbol used for temperature in the equation.

EXAMPLE

A hot block of metal cools from 55 °C to 25 °C. The block has a mass of 0.50 kg and is made from a material that has a specific heat capacity of 320 J/kg°C. Calculate the energy transferred from the block as it cooled.

1) First, calculate the change in the block's temperature.
2) The numbers are in the correct units. So put them into the equation.
3) The unit for energy is joules (J).

$\Delta\theta$ = 55 °C – 25 °C = 30 °C
$\Delta E = mc\Delta\theta$
= 0.50 × 320 × 30
= 4800 J

All those symbols are leaving me a bit hot and bothered...

That equation is pretty nasty-looking — make sure you can use it, as it's coming up again on the next page.

Q1 Find the final temperature of 5 kg of water, at an initial temperature of 5 °C, after 50 kJ of energy has been transferred to it. The specific heat capacity of water is 4200 J/kg°C. [3 marks]

Topic 1 — Energy

Investigating Specific Heat Capacity

Time for a practical. 'Woohoo!' I hear you shout. Maybe not, but you do have to know it I'm afraid.

You Could **Investigate** Specific Heat Capacity Like This... **PRACTICAL**

Method

1) Get a block of a solid material with two holes in it.
2) Measure the mass of the block.
3) Wrap it in an insulating layer (e.g. a thick layer of newspaper).
4) Insert the thermometer and heater into the holes and connect up the circuit as shown on the right.
5) Measure the starting temperature of the block.
6) Turn on the power supply and start a stopwatch.
7) Record the potential difference, V, of the power supply and the current, I. They shouldn't change at all.
8) Calculate the power of the heater using $P = VI$ (p.28).
9) After 10 minutes, record the final temperature of the block and turn off the heater.
10) Calculate the change in temperature of the block from your two temperature recordings.

To calculate the specific heat capacity, you need ideas about work done and energy transferred:

1) When you turn on the power, the current in the circuit does work on the heater.
2) Energy is transferred electrically from the power supply to the heater's thermal energy store.
3) The energy transferred to the heater is given by $E = Pt$ (p.8). (P is the power of the heater and t is how long the heater is on for in seconds.)
4) This energy is then transferred to the material's thermal energy store by heating.
5) Assuming all the energy given by the heater is transferred to the block, the value of E calculated in step 3 is equal to the change in thermal energy of the block, ΔE. This means you can use it to find the specific heat capacity of the block, c.
6) Rearrange the equation from page 6 to give you $c = \Delta E \div (m \times \Delta\theta)$, and put in your results.
7) $\Delta\theta$ and m, were measured in the experiment.
8) This example shows how to do the calculation:

> You can repeat this experiment with different materials to see how their specific heat capacities compare.
> For a liquid, place the heater and thermometer into an insulated beaker with a known mass of the liquid.

EXAMPLE

A 1.0 kg block of material is heated using a 10 V power supply.
The starting temperature of the block is 20 °C.
The current through the heater is recorded as 10 A.
After 60 seconds, the final temperature of the block is 26 °C.
Calculate the specific heat capacity of the material of the block.

1) Calculate the power of the heater. $P = V \times I = 10 \times 10 = 100$ W
2) Calculate the energy transferred. $E = P \times t = 100 \times 60 = 6000$ J
3) Find the change in temperature. $\Delta\theta = 26 - 20 = 6$ °C
4) Calculate the specific heat capacity. $c = \Delta E \div (m \times \Delta\theta) = 6000 \div (1.0 \times 6) = 1000$ J/kg°C

I've eaten five sausages — I have a high specific meat capacity...

This is quite a tricky experiment, with lots of steps. Re-read this whole page to get it in your head.

Q1   A student uses an 80 W heater to heat a 2 kg block of metal for 200 s. The temperature of the block increases by 20 °C. Calculate the specific heat capacity of the metal. Assume that all the energy from the heater is transferred to the metal block.   [5 marks]

Power

Punch your fist in the air and repeat after me — 'I HAVE THE POWER'.

Power is the 'Rate of Doing Work' — the Amount of Work Done per Second

1) Power is the rate of energy transfer. You can also say it's the rate of doing work.
2) This just means that power is how fast energy is transferred or how fast work is done.
3) Power is measured in watts.
4) One watt = 1 joule of energy transferred per second.
5) You can calculate power using these equations:

Power (W) — $P = \dfrac{E}{t}$ — Energy transferred (J) / Time (s)

Power (W) — $P = \dfrac{W}{t}$ — Work done (J) / Time (s)

EXAMPLE

a) It takes 11 000 J of work to lift a stuntperson to the top of a building. A motor takes 55 s to make the lift. Calculate the power of the motor.

1) The numbers are in the correct units.
2) Put the numbers into the equation for power in terms of work.

a) $P = W \div t$
= 11 000 ÷ 55
= 200 W

b) A second motor has a power of 300 W. It lifts the stuntperson for 30 s. Calculate the energy transferred by the motor.

1) Rearrange the power equation for energy transferred.
2) Put the numbers in.
3) Remember energy is in joules.

b) $P = E \div t \rightarrow E = P \times t$
= 300 × 30
= 9000 J

A Powerful Machine Transfers a Lot of Energy in a Short Space of Time

- Take two cars that are the same in every way apart from the power of their engines.
- Both cars race the same distance along a straight race track to a finish line.
- The car with the more powerful engine will reach the finish line faster than the other car.
- This is because the car with the more powerful engine transfers more energy in the same amount of time, so it reaches a higher speed.

Watt's power? Power's watts...

You might be tired of hearing this, but energy transferred and work done are the same thing. That's why power can be described using energy or work done, and why those two equations above look so similar.

Q1   A motor transfers 4.8 kJ of energy in 2 minutes. Calculate its power output.   [3 marks]

Reducing Unwanted Energy Transfers

There are a few ways you can reduce the amount of energy running off to a completely useless store.

Energy is Always Wasted in any Energy Transfer

1) When energy is transferred between stores, some energy is transferred to the store you want it in.
2) This energy is usefully transferred.
3) But in any energy transfer, some energy is always dissipated.
4) This means the energy is transferred to useless stores.
5) These useless stores are usually thermal energy stores.
6) This energy is often described as 'wasted' energy.
7) Lubrication and insulation are two ways to reduce unwanted energy transfers...

When you use a mobile phone, energy is transferred from the chemical energy store of the battery.
Some of this energy is usefully transferred.
But some is dissipated to the thermal energy store of the phone.

Lubrication Reduces Frictional Forces

- Friction acts between all objects that rub together.
- This causes some energy in the system to be dissipated.
- Lubricants can be used to reduce the friction between the objects.
- For example, oil in car engines reduces friction between all of the moving parts.
- This reduces the amount of dissipated energy.

Insulation Reduces the Rate of Energy Transfer by Heating

1) If you heat one end of an object, energy is transferred to the thermal energy stores of that part of the object.
2) This energy gradually gets transferred through the rest of the object, so the whole object gets warmer. This is known as conduction.
3) Thermal conductivity is a measure of how quickly energy is transferred by conduction through a material.

> Materials with a high thermal conductivity transfer lots of energy in a short time.
> Materials with a low thermal conductivity are called thermal insulators.

4) Thermal insulators can be used to reduce unwanted transfers by heating, e.g. in the home.
5) Homes can be kept warm by reducing the rate of cooling. How quickly a building cools depends on:

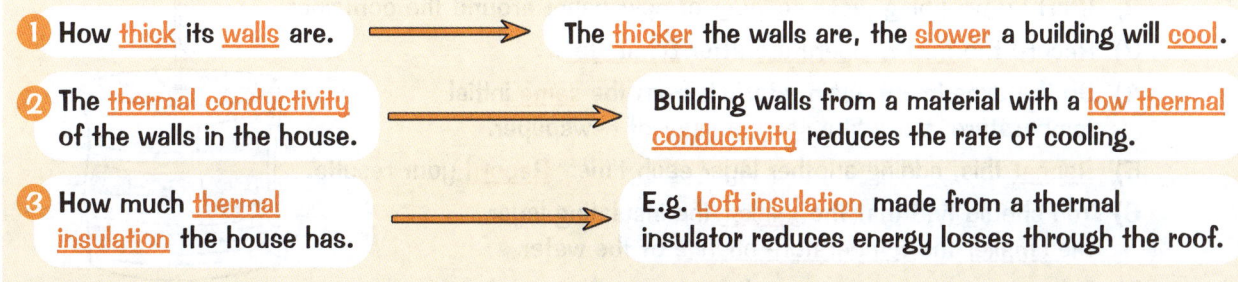

① How thick its walls are. → The thicker the walls are, the slower a building will cool.

② The thermal conductivity of the walls in the house. → Building walls from a material with a low thermal conductivity reduces the rate of cooling.

③ How much thermal insulation the house has. → E.g. Loft insulation made from a thermal insulator reduces energy losses through the roof.

Energy can't be created or destroyed — only talked about a lot...

Remember, when energy is wasted it's not destroyed — it still exists, it just isn't stored usefully anymore.

Q1 A builder is designing a house.
    Give one way the builder could reduce the rate of cooling of the house. [1 mark]

Quick Quiz

Investigating Reducing Energy Transfers

Here's an investigation you can try, to find out how good different materials are at acting as thermal insulators.

Here's One Method for Investigating Thermal Insulation PRACTICAL

You first need to know how much water cools down in a container without any insulation. This is a control experiment (see page 99):

Control experiment

1) Boil water in a kettle and pour 250 ml into a sealable container with a hole in the top (e.g. a beaker with a lid).
2) Seal the container and put a thermometer through the hole. Record the initial temperature of the water.
3) Leave it for 5 minutes. Measure this time using a stopwatch.
4) After this time has passed, measure the final temperature of the water.
5) Pour away the water and let the container cool to room temperature.

You can now measure how much the water cools down when the container is wrapped in different insulating materials.

Testing different materials

1) Repeat the experiment above, but wrap the container in a layer of material (e.g. foil, newspaper).
2) You should use the same volume of water each time and start at the same initial temperature. This makes sure the experiment is a fair test (see page 99).
3) Do this experiment for lots of different materials.
4) Compare the final temperatures for each different material, and the control experiment.

The warmer the water is at the end of the experiment, the better the material works as a thermal insulator. You should find that materials that have lots of air gaps, like bubble wrap and cotton wool, are good thermal insulators. This is because air has a low thermal conductivity (see previous page).

Material Thickness Also Affects Thermal Insulation

You could also test how the thickness of a material affects how good a thermal insulator it is. To test this, you could do a similar experiment but just use one material, like newspaper.

Testing material thickness

1) Fill your beaker with 250 ml of hot water and seal it just like before. Measure the initial temperature.
2) Start by wrapping just one layer of newspaper around the container.
3) Record the final temperature after 5 minutes.
4) Do the experiment again, starting from the same initial temperature, but add a second layer of newspaper.
5) Repeat this, adding another layer each time. Record your results.
6) You should find that the thicker the insulating layer, the smaller the temperature change of the water.
7) This means thicker layers make better insulators.

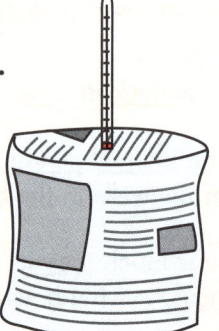

Bundle your brew in newspaper to stop it going cold...

Have a go at writing out all the steps to these experiments to make sure they're in your brain. Then try this question.

Q1 A student is investigating how good some materials are at insulating a beaker of hot water. Suggest one variable the student should keep constant to make the investigation a fair test. [1 mark]

Efficiency

More! More! Tell me more about energy transfers please! Oh go on then, since you insist...

Energy Transfers Are Never 100% Efficient

- You saw on page 9 that some energy is always wasted when energy is transferred.
- The less energy that is wasted, the more efficient the energy transfer is.
- The efficiency of an energy transfer is a measure of the amount of energy that ends up in useful energy stores.
- But as some energy is always wasted, nothing is 100% efficient.

There Are Two Efficiency Equations

The efficiency for any energy transfer can be worked out using this equation:

$$\text{Efficiency} = \frac{\text{Useful output energy transfer}}{\text{Total input energy transfer}}$$

This gives efficiency as a decimal, but you can turn it into a percentage — see below.

EXAMPLE 36 000 J of energy is transferred to a television. It transfers 28 800 J of this energy usefully. Calculate the efficiency of the television. Give your answer as a percentage.

1) Put the numbers you're given into the equation.

   efficiency = useful output energy transfer
   ÷ total input energy transfer
   = 28 800 ÷ 36 000 = 0.8

2) To change a decimal to a percentage, multiply your answer by 100.

   0.8 × 100 = 80, so efficiency = 80%

You might not know the energy input and output of a device.
But you can use its power input and output to calculate its efficiency:

$$\text{Efficiency} = \frac{\text{Useful power output}}{\text{Total power input}}$$

EXAMPLE A blender is 70% efficient. It has a total input power of 600 W. Calculate the useful power output.

1) Change the efficiency from a percentage to a decimal. To do this, divide the percentage by 100.
2) Rearrange the equation for useful power output.
3) Stick in the numbers and find the useful power output.

efficiency = 70% → 70 ÷ 100 = 0.7

useful power output = efficiency × total power input
= 0.7 × 600 = 420 W

Don't waste your energy — turn the TV off while you revise...

Make sure you can use and rearrange the equations for efficiency, then have a go at these questions.

Q1 A motor in a remote-controlled car transfers 300 J of energy into the car's energy stores. 225 J are transferred to the car's kinetic energy stores.
Calculate the efficiency of the motor. [2 marks]

Q2 A machine has a useful power output of 900 W and a total power input of 1200 W.
In a given time, 72 kJ of energy is transferred to the machine.
Calculate the amount of energy usefully transferred by the machine in this time. [4 marks]

Topic 1 — Energy

Quick Quiz

Energy Resources and Their Uses

Energy resources are mostly used to generate electricity or for transport and heating.

Non-Renewable Energy Resources Will Run Out One Day

Non-renewable energy resources are fossil fuels and nuclear fuel.
The three main fossil fuels are:

1) Coal
2) Oil
3) (Natural) Gas

PRO • They are reliable sources of energy.

CONS
• They will all 'run out' one day.
• They damage the environment.

Renewable Energy Resources Will Never Run Out

Renewable energy resources are:

1) The Sun (Solar)
2) Wind
3) Water waves
4) Hydro-electricity
5) Bio-fuel
6) Tides
7) Geothermal

PROS
• They will never run out, since the resource can be 'renewed' as it's used.
• They are less harmful to the environment than fossil fuels.

CONS
• Most still cause some damage to the environment.
• Some are unreliable as they depend on the weather.

Out of office

Energy Resources can be Used for Transport and Heating

TRANSPORT

- Petrol and diesel powered vehicles (including most cars) use fuel created from oil.
- Many vehicles can run on a mix of a bio-fuel and petrol or diesel.
- Some vehicles can even run on pure bio-fuels (p.15).
- Electricity can also be used to power vehicles (e.g. trains and some cars). It can be generated using renewable or non-renewable energy resources.

HEATING

- Natural gas is burnt to heat water in a boiler. This hot water is then pumped into radiators.
- Coal can be burnt in fireplaces.
- The energy generated from burning bio-fuel can be used to heat homes.
- A geothermal heat pump uses geothermal energy resources (p.13) to heat buildings.

Natural gas is the most widely used fuel for heating homes in the UK.

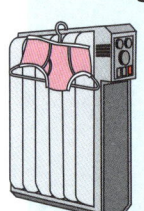

- Solar water heaters work by using the Sun to heat water which is pumped into radiators in the building.
- The electricity generated from renewable or non-renewable resources can also be used for heating. For example, in electric heaters.

I'm pretty sure natural gas is renewable — I make enough of it...

You need to know the difference between the two different types of energy resource, so get cracking.

Q1 Write down whether each of the following is a renewable or non-renewable energy resource.
   a) Tidal power   b) Natural gas   c) Nuclear power   d) Bio-fuel   [4 marks]

12 Topic 1 — Energy

Wind, Solar and Geothermal

Time for the first page on renewable energy resources. You've probably heard about a few of these already.

Wind Power — Lots of Wind Turbines

Wind turbines are put up in open spaces, like on moors or out at sea. When the wind turns the blades, electricity is produced.

PROS
- There's no pollution once they're built.
- There's no permanent (lasting) damage to the landscape. (If you remove the turbines, the area goes back to normal.)

CONS
- The turbines can spoil the view.
- They can be very noisy for people living nearby.
- The turbines will stop if there is little or no wind.
- They also have to be stopped if the wind is too strong. This stops them getting damaged.
- The supply cannot be increased when there is extra demand for electricity.

On average, wind turbines produce electricity 70-85% of the time.

Solar Cells — Electricity Generated Directly from Sunlight

Solar cells generate electricity directly from sunlight.

Solar power is often used in remote places where there's not much choice (e.g. the Australian outback) and to power electric road signs and satellites.

PROS
- There's no pollution once the solar panels have been built.
- They are a very reliable source of energy in sunny countries.
- Once they're made, the energy is free and running costs are almost zero.

CONS
- They only produce energy in the daytime.
- Quite a lot of energy is used to build the solar panels.
- The power output of solar panels cannot be increased with extra demand.

Solar power is still fairly reliable in cloudy places like Britain.

Time to recharge.

Geothermal Power — Energy in Underground Thermal Energy Stores

1) Geothermal power uses energy from the thermal energy stores of hot rocks below the Earth's surface.
2) It can be used to generate electricity or to heat buildings directly.

PROS
- It's a reliable source of energy, because the hot rocks are always hot.
- It does little damage to the environment.

CONS
- There aren't many locations.
- The cost of building a geothermal power plant is usually quite high.

People love the idea of wind power — just not in their backyard...

There are pros and cons to all energy resources. Make sure you know them for solar, wind and geothermal.

Q1 Explain why geothermal power is more reliable than wind power. [2 marks]

Topic 1 — Energy   13

Hydro-electricity, Waves and Tides

Good ol' water. Not only can we drink it, we can also use it to generate electricity.

Hydro-electric Power Uses Falling Water

1) Hydro-electric power usually involves building a big dam across a valley.
2) The valley is usually flooded.
3) Water is allowed to flow out through turbines, which generates electricity.

PROS
- There is no pollution when the power plant is up and running.
- The flow of water can be controlled, so the power plant can respond straight away when there's extra demand (p.29) for electricity.

CONS
- The initial costs to build the power plants are high.
- There's a big impact on the environment from flooding the valley. Plants rot and release greenhouse gases which lead to global warming. Animal and plants also lose their habitats (where they live).

Hydroelectric power is reliable in areas with high rainfall. But it's not suitable in dry climates or in periods of drought.

Wave Power — Lots of Little Wave-Powered Turbines

- Turbines are turned by water waves and electricity is generated.
- The turbines have to be in the sea, and it's usually easiest for them to be by the coast.

PROS
- There is no pollution.
- It could be useful on islands, e.g. where there's a lot of coastline.

CONS
- The turbines can disturb the seabed and habitats of animals.
- The amount of energy they generate is fairly unreliable — the waves tend to die out when the wind drops.
- The turbines are difficult and expensive to maintain.

Tidal Barrages — Using the Sun and Moon's Gravity

1) Tidal barrages are big dams (with turbines in them) built across estuaries (the part of a river that meets the sea).
2) Water passing through the turbines generates electricity.

PROS
- There is no pollution once they're up and running.
- Tides are reliable — they always happen twice a day.

CONS
- The dams can change the habitats of wildlife, e.g. birds and sea creatures.
- There aren't many suitable estuaries.
- The amount of energy changes with the tides — smaller tides don't provide as much energy.

The hydro-electric power you're supplying — it's electrifying...

Learn the differences between all of these water-based resources before having a go at this question.

Q1 Give one negative environmental impact of wave power. [1 mark]

14   Topic 1 — Energy

Bio-fuels and Non-renewables

And the energy resources just keep on coming. It'll be over soon, I promise. Just a few more to go.

Bio-fuels are Made from Plants and Waste

1) Bio-fuels are renewable energy resources created from plant products or animal dung.
2) They can be burnt to produce electricity or used to run cars in the same way as fossil fuels.

PROS
- Crops can be grown all throughout the year.
- Extra bio-fuels can be constantly produced and stored for when they are needed.

Bio-fuels do release carbon dioxide when they are burnt. But the plants used to make the bio-fuels will have absorbed a lot of carbon dioxide when they were growing.

CON
- Areas of forest are often cleared for room to grow bio-fuels. This can lead to lots of plants being destroyed and animals losing their natural habitats.

Non-Renewables are Reliable...

- Fossil fuels and nuclear energy are reliable.
- There's enough of these fuels to meet current demand.
- We always have some in stock so power plants can respond quickly to changes in demand.
- However, these fuels are slowly running out.
- Some fossil fuels may run out within a hundred years if no new ones are found.

...But Create Environmental Problems

GLOBAL WARMING
- Global warming is where greenhouse gases cause the Earth to warm up.
- Coal, oil and gas release CO_2 into the atmosphere when they're burned. All this CO_2 leads to global warming.

ACID RAIN
- Burning coal and oil also releases sulfur dioxide, which causes acid rain.
- Acid rain makes lakes and rivers acidic, which can kill animals and plants. It can also damage trees and soils.

DESTROYING HABITATS
- Coal mining makes a mess of the landscape.
- And it destroys the habitats of local animals and plants.
- Oil spills cause big environmental problems and harm sea creatures.

RADIATION
- Nuclear power is clean but the nuclear waste is very dangerous and difficult to get rid of.
- Nuclear power also carries the risk of a big accident that could release a lot of radiation.
- Radiation can be very dangerous to humans (p.44).

Bio-fuels are great — but don't burn your biology notes just yet...

Make sure you can talk about how bio-fuels and non-renewables affect the environment.

Q1   Give two benefits of using fossil fuels to generate electricity.   [2 marks]

Q2   Give three environmental impacts of using oil as an energy resource.   [3 marks]

Quick Quiz

Trends in Energy Resource Use

Over time, the types of energy resources we use change — like that zebra print leotard in my wardrobe...

Currently We Still Need Non-Renewables

1) Our use of electricity increased a lot in the 20th century.
2) This was because the population and the number of things that used electricity increased.
3) But electricity use in the UK has been decreasing (slowly) since the early 2000s.
4) This is because we're getting better at making appliances more efficient (see p.11) and being more careful with our energy use.
5) At the moment, we still use non-renewables for some of our electricity, transport and heating.

People Want to Use More Renewable Energy Resources

1) We now know that burning fossil fuels is very damaging to the environment (p.15).
2) This makes many people want to use more renewable energy resources as they are better for the environment.
3) Many people also think it's better to move to renewables before non-renewables run out.
4) Pressure from other countries and the public causes governments to set targets for using renewable resources.
5) This puts pressure on energy providers to build new power plants that use renewable resources to make sure they do not lose business and money.

> Car companies have also been affected by the push for increased use of renewables.
> Electric cars and hybrids (cars powered by two fuels, e.g. petrol and electricity) are becoming more popular.

The Use of Renewables is Limited by Lots of Factors

1) There's a lot of scientific evidence supporting renewables.
2) But scientists can only give advice. They don't have the power to make people, companies or governments change their actions (see p.97).
3) Moving to renewables can be limited by money, politics and people:

Some renewables aren't as reliable as fossil fuels because they can't increase their output on demand.

MONEY
- Building new renewable power plants costs money.
- More research is needed to make renewable resources cheaper and more reliable. This takes time and money.
- An electric car is usually more expensive than a petrol car of a similar size.

POLITICS
- The cost of switching to renewable power will have to be paid through energy bills or taxes.
- Some people don't want to or can't afford to pay. There are arguments about whether it's ethical (right or wrong) to make them pay.

PEOPLE
- Many people also don't want to live near to a power plant (like a wind farm or hydro-electric dam).
- And some think it's not ethical to make people put up with new power plants built near to them.

Going green is on-trend this season...

More people want to help the environment and fossil fuels are running out. So the energy resources we use are changing. But for lots of reasons, it's not happening very quickly. Make sure you learn the reasons on this page.

Q1   Give two reasons why we currently do not use more renewable energy resources in the UK.   [2 marks]

Revision Summary Test for Topic 1

I hope your revision resources aren't <u>running out</u> just yet. To <u>test</u> what you've learnt, you can:
- Tackle the <u>revision summary test</u> below, or scan the QR code to do it online.
  The questions are <u>hard</u>, but they'll show you how well you really <u>know your stuff</u>.
- Track your progress <u>online</u> and see which areas need more work.
- Compare your answers with sample answers for the test here: cgpbooks.co.uk/Mass

Energy Stores, Systems and Specific Heat Capacity (p.3-7) ☐

1) What are the eight types of energy store?
2) What are four ways that energy can be transferred?
3) What is a system? What happens when a system changes?
4) Give the conservation of energy principle.
5) Describe the energy transfers that occur when:
   a) a person throws a ball upwards, b) a car slows down using its brakes.
6) What is the formula used to calculate the energy stored in kinetic energy stores?
7) What energy transfer takes place when an object falls (assuming there is no air resistance)?
8) What is the specific heat capacity of a substance?
9) Describe a method you could use to find the specific heat capacity of a solid block of material.

Power and Reducing Unwanted Energy Transfers (p.8-11) ☑

10) What is meant by power? What are the units for power?
11) How can you tell which of two identical buses with different engines is more powerful?
12) What is meant by dissipated energy? Give an example of energy being dissipated.
13) How do lubricants reduce the amount of energy being dissipated?
14) Do materials with a high thermal conductivity transfer energy quickly or slowly?
15) What are three ways you could reduce the rate of cooling of a house?
16) Give a method that could be used to investigate how effective a material is as a thermal insulator.
17) What is the efficiency of an energy transfer?
18) How can efficiency be calculated using energy transfers? How about with power input and output?

Energy Resources, Uses and Trends (p.12-16) ☐

19) Write down four examples of non-renewable energy resources.
20) List four types of renewable energy resources.
21) a) Describe two ways energy resources can be used for transport.
    b) Now describe two ways they can be used for heating.
22) What are the advantages and disadvantages of using wind power?
23) What are three downsides of using solar power?
24) Where does the energy for geothermal power come from?
25) How does flooding a valley for hydroelectric power cause damage to the environment?
    Give one more disadvantage of using hydroelectric power.
26) What are tidal barrages and how do they work?
27) What is one advantage and one disadvantage of using bio-fuels?
28) How does burning coal, oil and gas contribute to global warming?
29) a) What caused electricity use in the UK to increase in the 20th century?
    b) What is causing electricity use in the UK to decrease slowly since the 2000s?
30) Give two ways that money can limit the use of renewable energy resources.

Topic 2 — Electricity

Current and Circuit Symbols

Quick Quiz

No, this page isn't about how to keep up with the latest fashion trends — it's much more exciting than that...

Current Depends on Potential Difference and Resistance

Term	Description	Units
Current	A flow of electrical charge.	Amperes, A
Potential difference	The 'driving force' that pushes charge round.	Volts, V
Resistance	Anything that slows the flow of charge down.	Ohms, Ω

Potential difference is also called voltage or pd.

- Electrical charge will only flow round a complete (closed) loop if there is a source of potential difference.
- The current flowing through a component depends on the potential difference across it and the resistance of the component (p.19):

The greater the resistance, the smaller the current that flows (for a given potential difference).

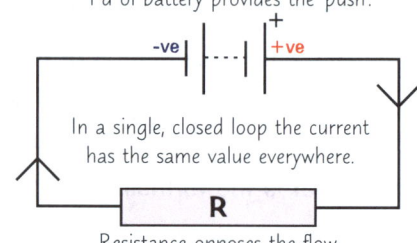

Pd of battery provides the 'push'.
In a single, closed loop the current has the same value everywhere.
Resistance opposes the flow.

Total Charge Through a Circuit Depends on Current and Time

The size of the current tells you how much charge flows past a point every second. This is known as the rate of flow of charge. You can calculate charge flow using this handy formula:

Charge is measured in coulombs, C.

$$\text{Charge flow (C)} = \text{Current (A)} \times \text{Time (s)} \qquad Q = It$$

EXAMPLE A battery charger passes a current of 2 A through a cell over a period of 300 seconds. How much charge is transferred to the cell?

Substitute the values into the equation above. $\quad Q = I \times t = 2 \times 300 = 600$ C

MATHS SKILLS

Circuit Diagrams Use These Symbols

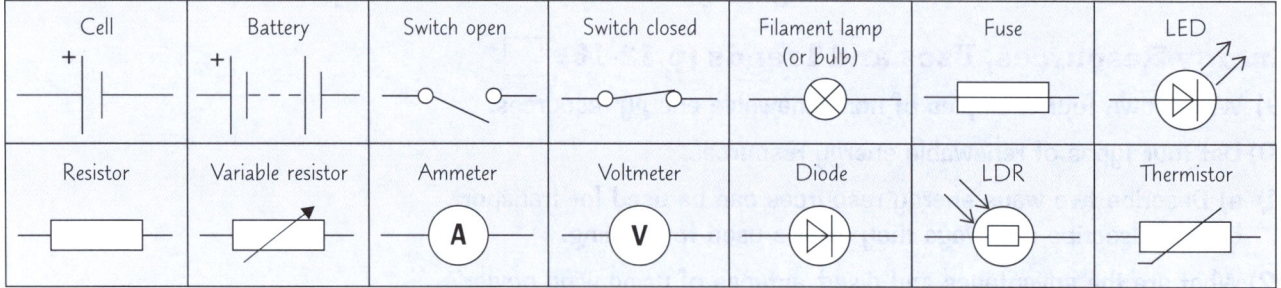

Cell | Battery | Switch open | Switch closed | Filament lamp (or bulb) | Fuse | LED
Resistor | Variable resistor | Ammeter | Voltmeter | Diode | LDR | Thermistor

Follow these rules to draw a circuit diagram:

- Draw all the wires in your circuit as straight lines.
- Make sure that the circuit is closed. This means you can follow a wire from one end of the cell or battery, through any components, to the other end of the cell or battery.

The parts in a circuit e.g. bulbs, resistors, etc. are called 'components'.

I think it's about time you took charge...

Practise drawing all of the circuit symbols above, even if you've seen some of them before. It's no good if you get asked to draw a circuit diagram and you can't tell a resistor from a fuse.

Q1 A laptop charger passes a current of 8 A through a laptop battery. Calculate, in minutes, how long the charger needs to be connected to the battery for 28 800 C of charge to be transferred. [4 marks]

Q1 Video Solution

Resistance and $V = IR$

Quick Quiz

Potential difference, current and resistance are linked by a very important formula.

There's a Formula Linking Potential Difference and Current

Potential difference (V) = Current (A) × Resistance (Ω) $V = IR$

EXAMPLE A 4.0 Ω resistor in a circuit has a potential difference of 6.0 V across it. What is the current through the resistor?

1) Rearrange $V = IR$ for current by dividing both sides by R. $V = IR \rightarrow I = V \div R$

2) Substitute in the values you have to work out the current. $I = V \div R = 6.0 \div 4.0 = 1.5$ A

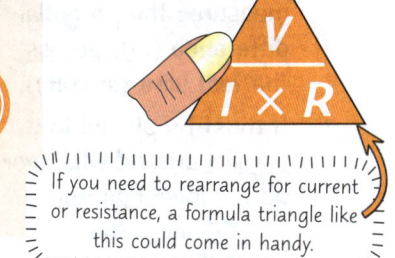
If you need to rearrange for current or resistance, a formula triangle like this could come in handy.

Ohmic Conductors Have a Constant Resistance

1) Wires and resistors are some examples of ohmic conductors.
2) The resistance of an ohmic conductor doesn't change with current.
3) For an ohmic conductor at a fixed temperature:

   The current flowing through it is directly proportional to the potential difference across it.

   You can think about this by looking at the formula $V = IR$. If R is constant, then any change to V must cause a proportional change to I.

4) So if potential difference doubles, the current doubles too. There's more about direct proportionality on page 104.

Some Components Have a Changing Resistance

The resistance of some components DOES change with current, for example:

Diode
- The resistance of a diode depends on the direction of the current.
- A diode will happily let current flow in one direction.
- But it has a very high resistance if the current is reversed.

Filament lamp
- Filament lamps contain a filament (wire).
- The filament is designed to heat up and 'glow' as the current increases.
- Resistance increases with temperature, so the resistance increases with current.

Ohm sweet ohm...

There's loads more coming up on resistance, so make sure you're happy with this page before moving on.

Q1 An appliance is connected to a 230 V source. Calculate the resistance of the appliance if a current of 5.0 A is flowing through it.   [3 marks]

Q1 Video Solution

Investigating Resistance   PRACTICAL

Nothing quite like a physics experiment, eh? Well, here's a simple experiment for investigating resistance.

The Length of a Wire in a Circuit Can Affect Its Resistance

You could use a circuit like this one to see how the length of a wire affects its resistance:

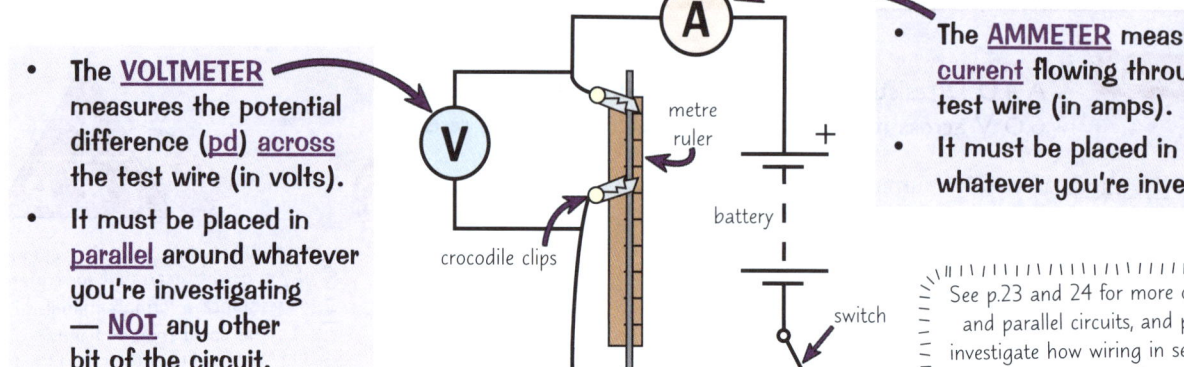

- The VOLTMETER measures the potential difference (pd) across the test wire (in volts).
- It must be placed in parallel around whatever you're investigating — NOT any other bit of the circuit.

- The AMMETER measures the current flowing through the test wire (in amps).
- It must be placed in series with whatever you're investigating.

See p.23 and 24 for more on series and parallel circuits, and p.25 to investigate how wiring in series and parallel circuits can affect resistance.

Method

1) Attach a crocodile clip to the wire level with 0 cm on the ruler.
2) Attach the second crocodile clip to the wire a short distance (e.g. 10 cm) from the first clip.
3) Write down the length of the wire between the clips.
4) Close the switch, then record the current through the wire and the pd across it.
5) Open the switch and move the second crocodile clip along the wire (e.g. by another 10 cm).
6) Repeat steps 3 to 5 for a range of wire lengths.
7) Use your measurements of current and pd to calculate the resistance for each length of wire, using $R = V \div I$ (from $V = IR$).

A thin wire will give you the best results. Make sure it's straight so your length measurements are accurate.

> The wire may heat up during the experiment, which will affect its resistance (p.21). Leave the switch open between readings to let the circuit cool down.

Plot a Graph of your Results

1) Plot a graph of resistance against wire length.
2) Draw a line of best fit through your points.
3) Your graph should be a straight line through the origin (where length and resistance are both zero).
4) This means resistance is directly proportional to length — the longer the wire, the greater the resistance.

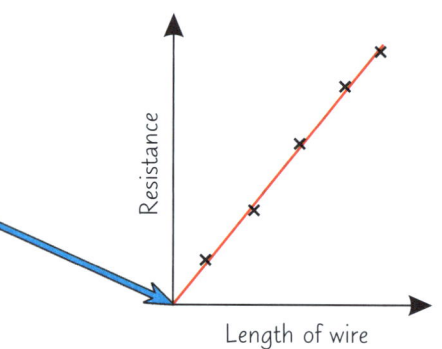

Measure gymnastics — use a vaultmeter...

Opening the switch between readings lets the circuit cool down. This reduces the error in your measurements.

Q1   A student performs an investigation into the effect of wire length on resistance.
Draw a circuit diagram of a circuit the student could use to carry out this investigation.
Use the symbol for a variable resistor to represent the test wire.   [3 marks]

I-V Characteristics

There are three different graphs to learn on this page — you have to know how you get them too.

An I-V Characteristic is a Graph of Current Against Pd

1) An 'I-V characteristic' shows how current (I) through a component changes as pd (V) across it increases.

   Components with straight line I-V characteristics are called linear components (e.g. fixed resistors).
   Components with curved I-V characteristics are non-linear components (e.g. filament lamps or diodes).

2) To find the resistance at any point on the I-V characteristic, first read off the values of I and V at that point. Then use R = V ÷ I (from V = IR on page 19).

You Can Investigate I-V Characteristics   PRACTICAL

You can use this method to plot I-V characteristics of filament lamps or ohmic conductors:

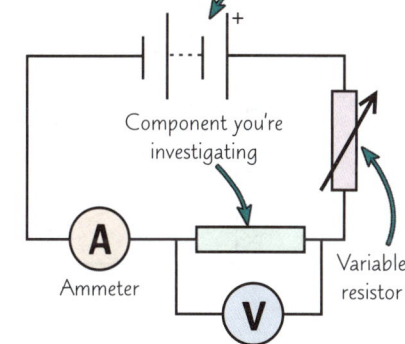

Method

1) Set up the circuit as shown on the right.
2) Begin to vary the variable resistor.
3) Take several sets of readings from the ammeter and voltmeter at the different resistances.
4) Swap over the wires connected to the battery, so the direction of the current is reversed.
5) Use the same method as above to take more readings of pd and current.
6) Plot a graph of current against pd for the component.

The variable resistor is used to change the current in the circuit. This also changes the pd across the component.

- For a diode, you will need to add a protective resistor in series with the component you're testing.
- This protects the diode from too high a current by increasing the overall resistance.
- A milliammeter needs to be used instead of a regular ammeter too.
- This is because the current values you'll be measuring will be very small.

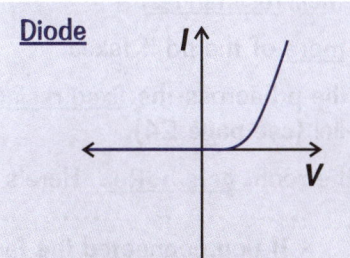

Diode
- Current only flows in one direction.
- Resistance is very high in the reverse direction.
- So the graph starts off flat, then curves up quickly.

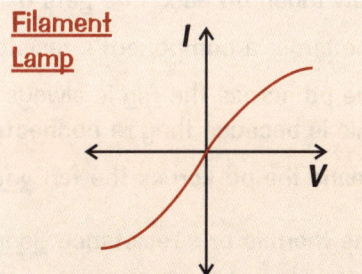

Filament Lamp
- Temperature increases as current increases.
- So resistance increases.
- This makes it harder for current to flow.
- So the graph gets less steep.

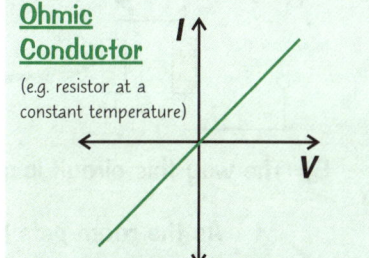

Ohmic Conductor
(e.g. resistor at a constant temperature)
- Current is directly proportional to potential difference.
- So you get a straight line.

In the end you'll have to learn this — resistance is futile...

Draw out those graphs until you're sketching them in your sleep.

Q1 Explain the shape of the filament lamp I-V characteristic above, for the quadrant where I and V are positive.   [3 marks]

Quick Quiz

Circuit Devices

For some components resistance can depend on things like light and temperature, and this can be really handy.

LDR is Short for Light Dependent Resistor

An LDR is a resistor with a resistance that changes depending on the intensity of light.

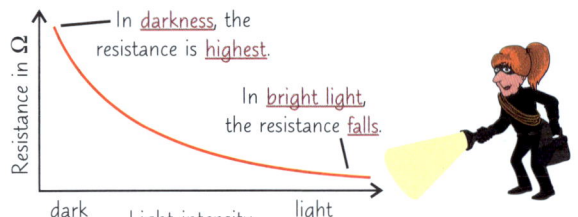

They have lots of applications including automatic night lights, outdoor lighting and burglar detectors.

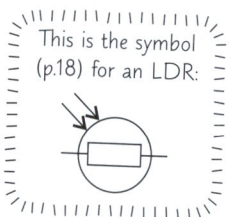

This is the symbol (p.18) for an LDR:

The Resistance of a Thermistor Depends on Temperature

A thermistor is a temperature-dependent resistor.

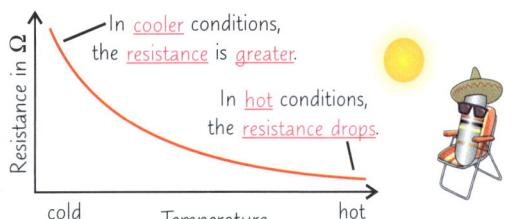

Thermistors make useful temperature detectors, e.g. electronic thermostats. Thermostats turn the heating on when it's cool and off when it's warm.

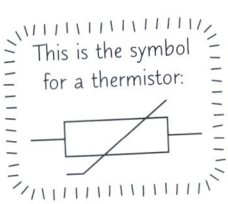

This is the symbol for a thermistor:

You Can Use LDRs and Thermistors in Sensing Circuits

Video

Sensing circuits can be used to turn on or increase the power to components depending on the conditions that they are in. The circuit below is a sensing circuit used to control a fan in a room.

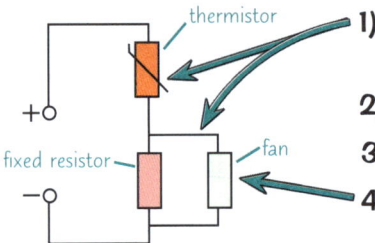

1) The total pd is shared out between the thermistor and the loop with the fixed resistor and the fan (see p.23).
2) How much pd each one gets depends on their resistances.
3) The larger a component's resistance, the more of the pd it takes.
4) The pd across the fan is always equal to the pd across the fixed resistor. This is because they're connected in parallel (see page 24).
5) The way this circuit is set up means the pd across the fan goes up as the room gets hotter. Here's why:

- As the room gets hotter, the thermistor's resistance decreases.
- The thermistor takes a smaller share of the pd from the power supply.
- So the pd across the loop with the fixed resistor and fan rises.
- The greater the pd across a component, the more energy it gets.
- This means the fan goes faster.

If you connected the fan across the thermistor instead, the circuit would do the opposite. The fan would slow down as the room got hotter (not very useful).

LDRs — Light Dependent Rabbits...

When your heating turns on by itself, you can show off and tell everyone how thermistors made it happen.

Q1 An engineer wants to make a circuit containing a bulb that will get brighter when the surroundings get darker. Draw a diagram of a circuit the engineer could make. You can assume the light from the bulb does not affect any of the circuit components. [3 marks]

Q1 Video Solution

Series Circuits

There's a difference between connecting components in series and parallel — first up, series.

Series Circuits Are Just Big Loops

- In series circuits, the components are all connected in a line between the ends of the power supply.
- Only voltmeters break this rule. They're always connected in parallel (p.24), but they don't count as part of the series circuit.
- If you remove one component, the circuit is broken. So all the components stop working.
- This is generally not very handy, and in practice very few things are connected in series.
- Series circuits can be useful though, especially for measuring quantities and testing components (e.g. the test circuit on p.21).
- You can use these rules to analyse and design series circuits:

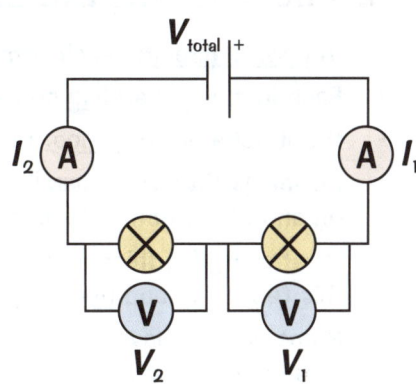

Potential difference	• The total pd of the supply is shared between all components. • If you add up the potential difference across each component, you get the potential difference of the power supply.	$V_{total} = V_1 + V_2 + ...$
Current	• The same current flows through all components. • The size of the current is determined by the total pd of the cells and the total resistance of the circuit: i.e. $I = V \div R$.	$I_1 = I_2 = ...$
Resistance	• The total resistance of the circuit is the sum of the resistances of all the components.	$R_{total} = R_1 + R_2 + ...$

1) This is because adding a resistor in series means the resistors have to share the total pd.
2) So the pd across each resistor is lower, meaning the current through each resistor is lower ($V = IR$).
3) In a series circuit, the current is the same everywhere.
4) So the total current in the circuit is reduced when a resistor is added.
5) This means the total resistance of the circuit has gone up.

The bigger a component's resistance, the bigger its share of the total pd.

EXAMPLE For the circuit diagram below, calculate the current passing through the circuit.

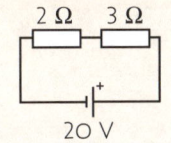

1) First find the total resistance by adding together the resistance of the two resistors. $R_{total} = 2 + 3 = 5\ \Omega$
2) Then rearrange $V = IR$ for I. $V = IR \rightarrow I = V \div R$
3) Substitute in the values you have. $I = V \div R = 20 \div 5 = 4$ A

Cell Potential Differences Add Up in Series Circuits

- There is a bigger pd when more cells are in series, if they're all connected the same way.
- For example, when two cells with a potential difference of 1.5 V are connected in series they supply 3 V between them.

Series circuits — they're no laughing matter...

Get those rules straightened out in your head, then have a quick go at this question to test yourself.

Q1   A battery is connected in series with a 4 Ω resistor, a 5 Ω resistor and a 6 Ω resistor. A current of 0.6 A flows through the circuit. Calculate the potential difference of the battery.   [3 marks]

Parallel Circuits

Parallel circuits are much more sensible than series circuits, so they're much more common in real life.

Parallel Circuits Are All About Independence

- In parallel circuits, each component is on its own loop (or branch).
- Each loop is separately connected to the power supply.
- If you take out one loop, the things in the other loops will still work.
- So things that are in parallel can be switched on and off without affecting one another.
- Most everyday things are connected like this (e.g. cars and household electrics).
- Some circuits have a mix of components wired in series and in parallel.
- You can use these rules to analyse and design parallel circuits:

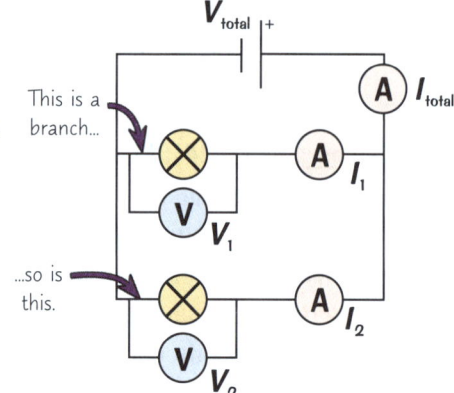

Ammeters are always connected in series, but they don't count as part of the circuit.

Potential difference	• All components get the full source pd. So, the pd is the same across all components.	$V_1 = V_2 = ...$
Current	• The total current in a circuit is equal to the sum of all the currents through the separate branches. • The total current going into a junction (where current splits or rejoins) has to equal the total current leaving.	$I_{total} = I_1 + I_2 + ...$
Resistance	• The total resistance is less than the resistance of any of the individual resistors.	$R_{total} < R_1$ or R_2 or...

If two identical components are in parallel, the same current will flow through each of them.

EXAMPLE
Find the pd measured by V_1 and the current measured by A_1. The resistors are identical.

1) The resistors are in parallel, so the pd across each resistor is the same as the cell pd.
2) The total current into the first junction is the same as the total current out of it.

Cell pd = 6 V
V_1 = 6 V

In: 2 A   Out: 1 A + A_1
So A_1 = 2 − 1 = 1 A

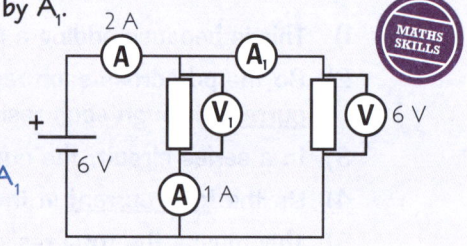

Adding a Resistor in Parallel Reduces the Total Resistance

1) In parallel, all resistors have the same potential difference across them as the power supply.
2) This means the 'pushing force' making the current flow is still the same, however many resistors you add.
3) But by adding another loop, the current has one more direction to go in.
4) This doesn't change the current through the existing branches. You're just adding on the current that flows through the new branch.
5) This means that the total current that flows around the circuit increases.
6) So the total resistance of the circuit is lower (as $R = V \div I$).

The currant is shared between branches.

A current shared (between identical components) is a current halved...

Parallel circuits are a bit more complicated but they crop up a lot, so get learning them.

Q1 A circuit contains three resistors, each connected in parallel with a cell. Explain what happens to the total current and resistance in the circuit when one resistor is removed. [4 marks]

PRACTICAL

Investigating Circuits

Quick Quiz

You saw on page 20 how the length of the wire used in a circuit affects its resistance. Now it's time to do an experiment to see how adding resistors in series or in parallel can affect the resistance of the whole circuit.

You Can Investigate Adding Resistors in Series...

This way of investigating resistance in series circuits calls for at least four identical resistors.

Method

1) Build the circuit shown on the right using one of the resistors.
2) Write down the potential difference of the battery (V).
3) Measure the current (I) through the circuit using the ammeter.
4) Calculate the resistance of the circuit using $R = V \div I$.
5) Add another resistor, in series with the first.
6) Again, measure the current through the circuit and use this and the potential difference of the battery to calculate the overall resistance of the circuit.
7) Repeat steps 5 and 6 until you've added all of your resistors.
8) Plot a graph of the total resistance of the circuit against the number of resistors (see below).

... or in Parallel

You can investigate the effect of adding resistors in parallel with a very similar method to the one above.

- Start with the same initial circuit.
- The only difference is that in step 5 (and every time you repeat it), you should add the resistor in PARALLEL with the first.

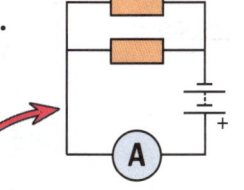

If you want to compare your results for series and parallel circuits, use the same equipment for each experiment. This will make it a fair test.

Your Results Should Match the Resistance Rules

You should find that your results from the two bits of the investigation show that:

Adding a resistor in SERIES...	Adding a resistor in PARALLEL...
...decreases the total current.	...increases the total current.
...increases the total resistance.	...decreases the total resistance.

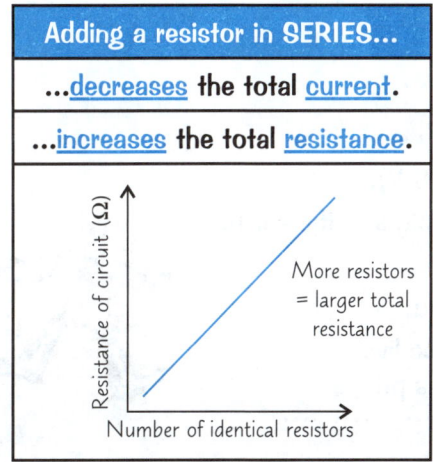
More resistors = larger total resistance

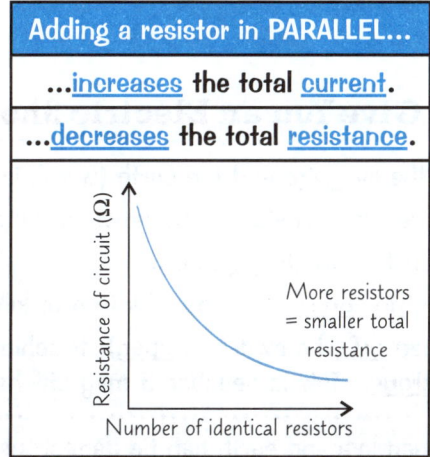
More resistors = smaller total resistance

These results agree with what you learnt about resistance in series and parallel circuits on pages 23 and 24.

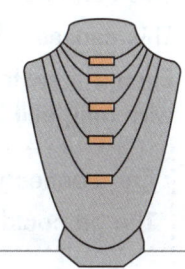

I can't resist a good practical...

Make sure you're completely happy building circuits from diagrams — this experiment is good practice.

Q1   A student is investigating how the resistance of a circuit changes as identical resistors are added in parallel. She plans to plot a graph of the total resistance of the circuit against the number of resistors in the circuit. Sketch the graph that you expect her to get.   [2 marks]

Quick Quiz

Electricity in the Home

Unless you're cool like me, you may not think about electrical plugs much. But you will by the end of this page...

Mains Supply is ac, Battery Supply is dc

There are two types of electricity supplies — alternating current (ac) and direct current (dc).

Alternating current (ac)
- In ac supplies, the current is constantly changing direction.
- Alternating currents are produced by alternating voltages.
- The UK mains supply (the electricity in your home) is an ac supply at around 230 V.
- The frequency of the ac mains supply is 50 Hz (hertz).

Direct current (dc)
- Direct current always flows in the same direction.
- It's created by a direct voltage.
- Cells and batteries supply direct current (dc).

Most Cables Have Three Separate Wires

- Most electrical appliances are connected to the mains supply by three-core cables.
- They have three wires covered with plastic insulation inside them.
- They are coloured so that it is easy to tell the different wires apart.

LIVE WIRE — brown.
1) The live wire provides the alternating potential difference from the mains supply.
2) It is at about 230 V.

NEUTRAL WIRE — blue.
1) The neutral wire completes the circuit — when the appliance is operating normally, current flows through the live and neutral wires.
2) It is around 0 V.

EARTH WIRE — green and yellow.
1) The earth wire is a safety wire.
2) It stops the appliance becoming live.
3) It doesn't usually carry a current — unless there's a fault.
4) It's at 0 V.

The Live Wire Can Give You an Electric Shock

1) There is a pd between the live wire and the earth (which is at 0 V).
2) If you touch the live wire, you provide a link between the supply and the earth.
3) This can cause a current to flow through you.
4) This causes a large electric shock which could injure or kill you.
5) Even if a switch is turned off (the switch is open), touching the live wire may still be dangerous. This is because it may still have a pd.

> Any connection between live and earth can be dangerous.
> The pd could cause a huge current to flow, which could result in a fire.

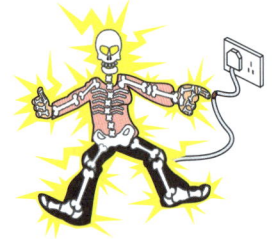

Why are earth wires green and yellow — when mud is brown..?

Electricity is very useful, but it can also be very dangerous. Make sure you know the risks.

Q1 State the potential difference of: a) the live wire b) the neutral wire c) the earth wire. [3 marks]

Power of Electrical Appliances

Quick Quiz

ALL HAIL THE MIGHTY APPLIANCE, TO WHOM ENERGY IS AS PUTTY IN THEIR MIGHTY METAL HANDS...

Energy is Transferred from Cells and Other Sources

1) When a charge moves around a circuit, work is done against the resistance of the circuit.
2) When work is done by a charge, energy is transferred electrically.
3) Electrical appliances transfer energy to components in the circuit when a current flows.

Remember, whenever work is done, energy is transferred. See page 4.

Kettles transfer energy electrically from the mains ac supply to the thermal energy store of the heating element inside the kettle.

Energy is transferred electrically from the battery of a handheld fan to the kinetic energy store of the fan's motor.

Remember, no appliance transfers all of its energy to useful stores (p.9).

Energy Transferred Depends on the Power and Time

- The total energy transferred by an appliance depends on how long the appliance is on for and its power.
- The power of an appliance is the energy that it transfers per second.
- So the more energy it transfers in a given time, the higher its power.
- The amount of energy transferred by electrical work is given by:

> Energy transferred (J) = Power (W) × Time (s) $E = Pt$

This equation should be familiar from page 8.

EXAMPLE   A 500 W microwave is used for 1 minute. How much energy does it transfer?

1) Convert the time into seconds. $t = 1 \times 60 = 60$ s
2) Substitute the numbers into $E = Pt$ to find the energy transferred. $E = Pt = 500 \times 60 = 30\,000$ J

MATHS SKILLS

A Power Rating is the Maximum Safe Power an Appliance Can Run At

1) Appliances are often given a power rating. This is the maximum power that they work at.
2) The power rating tells you the maximum amount of energy transferred between stores per second when the appliance is used.
3) An appliance with a higher power rating will cost more to run for a given time, as it uses more energy.

> An 850 W microwave will transfer more energy between stores during 5 minutes than the 600 W microwave in the example above. This means it will cost more to use it for 5 minutes. But a higher power rating means an appliance transfers energy faster, so it might not need to be on for as long.

My power rating is SUPER STRONG cos I work out...

Get that equation for power stuck into your brain. Then become a powerful physicist by practising it.

Q1 An appliance transfers 6000 J of energy in 30 seconds. Calculate its power. [3 marks]

Q2 Calculate the difference in the amount of energy transferred by a 250 W TV and a 375 W TV when they are both used for two hours. [4 marks]

Q2 Video Solution

More on Energy Transfers and Power

Get the kettle back on — we're not done yet. There are more power equations for you to get your head around.

Potential Difference is Energy Transferred per Charge Passed

- As a charge moves around a circuit, energy is transferred to or from it.
- The energy transferred by a component depends on the potential difference across it and the charge flowing through it.
- The formula is real simple:

> Energy transferred (J) = Charge flow (C) × Potential difference (V) $E = QV$

EXAMPLE

An electric toothbrush contains a 3.0 V battery.
140 C of charge passes through the toothbrush as it is used.
Calculate the energy transferred.

Just plug the numbers straight in: $E = QV = 140 \times 3.0 = 420$ J

Power Also Depends on Current and Potential Difference

1) You saw on the previous page that power is energy transferred in a given time.
2) The power of an appliance can also be found using:

> Power (W) = Potential difference (V) × Current (A) $P = VI$

3) Or if you don't know the potential difference, you can find the power using:

> Power (W) = Current² (A²) × Resistance (Ω) $P = I^2R$

EXAMPLE   A motor with a power of 1250 W has a resistance of 50 Ω.
Calculate the current flowing through the motor.

1) First rearrange the formula $P = I^2R$ to get I on its own.
   - Divide both sides by R. $P = I^2R \rightarrow P \div R = I^2$
   - Flip things around so I is on the left. $I^2 = P \div R$
   - Find the square root of both sides. $I = \sqrt{P \div R}$
2) Now just plug in the numbers. $I = \sqrt{1250 \div 50} = \sqrt{25} = 5$ A

Your calculator should have a '√' (square root) button to help with these calculations.

You have the power — now use your potential...

It's just some equations... I mean, how bad could it be? *[A few questions later]* AAAAAAAAAAAAAAAAAAA

Q1   Calculate the energy transferred from a 200 V source as 10 000 C of charge passes.   [2 marks]

Q2   An appliance is connected to a 12 V source. A current of 4.0 A flows through it.
Calculate the power of the appliance.   [2 marks]

Q3   An appliance has a power of 2300 W and has a current of 10.0 A flowing through it.
Calculate the resistance of the appliance.   [3 marks]

The National Grid

Whoever you pay for your electricity, it's the National Grid that gets it to you.

Electricity is Distributed via the National Grid

- The National Grid is a giant system of cables and transformers that covers Great Britain.
- It transfers electrical power from power stations to consumers (anyone who is using electricity) across Great Britain.

Electricity Production has to Meet Demand

1) Throughout the day, the amount of electricity used (the demand) changes.
2) Power stations have to produce enough electricity for everyone to have it when they need it.
3) Power stations often run at well below their maximum power output, so that they can increase their power if needed.
4) This means that the National Grid can cope with a high demand, even if one power station shuts down without warning.

> More electricity is used when people get up in the morning, come home from school or work and when it starts to get dark or cold outside.

The National Grid Uses a High Pd and a Low Current

To transmit the huge amount of power needed, you need either a high current or a high pd. This is because $P = VI$ (from the previous page).

High current
- A high current means the wires heat up more.
- Lots of energy is lost to the thermal energy store of the surroundings.
- This is inefficient, so the National Grid does not use a high current to transmit power.

High pd
- Instead, the National Grid transfers energy at a very high pd.
- For a given power, the higher the pd, the lower the current.
- This minimises the energy lost to heating the wires.
- This is a much cheaper, more efficient way of transferring electricity.

A higher power means more energy transferred in a given time.

Potential Difference is Changed by a Transformer

To get the voltage up for efficient transmission, the National Grid uses transformers.

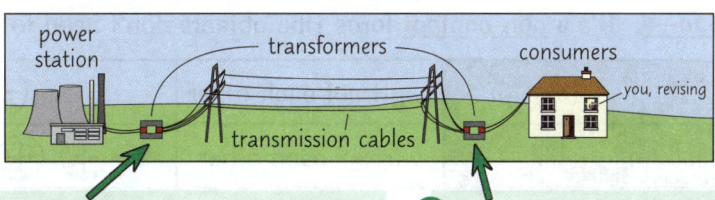

1
- A step-up transformer increases the pd from the power station to the transmission cables.
- This means power is transmitted to homes efficiently.
- As pd is increased, current is decreased.

2
- A step-down transformer brings the pd back down before electricity gets to homes.
- This makes the pd safe for consumers.
- As pd is decreased, current is increased.

Transformers — NOT robots in disguise...

Transformers can be a little tricky, but it's important that you can explain why they're used in the National Grid.

Q1   What is the National Grid?   [1 mark]

Static Electricity

Attraction... Sparks... Rubbing together... No, it's not a dating show — it's static electricity.

Build-up of Static is Caused by Friction

1) Electrons are negatively charged.
2) Rubbing certain insulating materials together causes some electrons to be transferred from one material to the other.
3) This gives the materials static charge.
4) The material that gains electrons gets a negative static charge.
5) The material that loses the electrons gets an equal positive static charge.
6) Which way the electrons are transferred depends on the two materials involved.

> Positive static charge is only ever caused by ELECTRONS moving away. Positive charges DO NOT MOVE.

The classic examples are polythene and acetate rods being rubbed with a cloth duster.

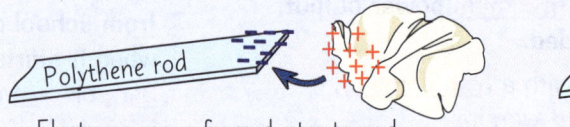

Electrons move from duster to rod.

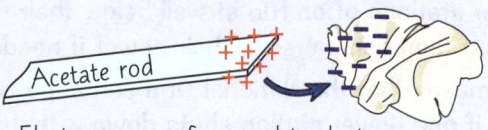

Electrons move from rod to duster.

Too Much Static Causes Sparks

1) When electric charge builds up on an object, the potential difference between the object and the earth increases. The earth is at 0 V.
2) The bigger the charge, the bigger the potential difference.
3) If this potential difference gets large enough, electrons can jump across the gap between the charged object and the earth. This is called a spark.

> Electrons can also jump to any conductor that is connected to the earth. This is why you can get static shocks when getting out of a car. A charge builds up on the car's frame. When you touch the car, a charge travels through you giving you a shock.

For more on how sparks actually jump across gaps, see the next page.

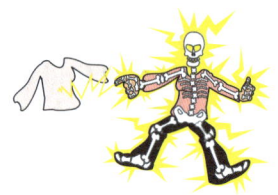

Like Charges Repel, Opposite Charges Attract

1) When two electrically charged objects are brought close together they exert a force on each other.
2) This is electrostatic force. It's a non-contact force (the objects don't need to touch, p.48).

Objects with opposite types of charge...	...attract each other	⊕→ ←⊖
Objects with the same type of charge...	...repel each other	←⊕ ⊕→ ←⊖ ⊖→

3) The further apart the objects are, the weaker the force between them.
4) These forces will cause the objects to move if they are able to do so. One way to see this is to suspend a rod with a known charge from a piece of string, so it is free to move:
   - Placing an object with the same charge nearby will cause the rod to move away from the object.
   - If an object with opposite charge is used, the rod will move towards the object.

Stay away from electrons — they're a negative influence...

Electrons jumping about the place and giving us all shocks, the cheeky so-and-sos.

Q1 Describe what happens when you get a static shock after touching a charged car. [1 mark]

Electric Fields

Electric fields — not just an exciting setting for a once-in-a-lifetime game of Extreme Croquet...

Electric Charges Create an Electric Field

1) Any object with an electric charge has its own electric field.
2) The electric field is strongest close to the charged object.
3) The further away from the object you get, the weaker the field is.
4) You can show an electric field around an object by drawing field lines.
5) For example, here are the field lines for two isolated, charged spheres:

Isolated means it's not interacting with anything.

The electric field lines are always at a right angle to the surface.

They have arrows on them that always point from positive to negative.

The closer together the lines are, the stronger the field is.

As you get further away from the charge, the lines get more spread out.

So the field gets weaker further away from the charge.

Charged Objects in an Electric Field Feel a Force

- If you put two charged objects near to each other, they both experience a force.
- This is because their electric fields are interacting with each other.
- This force causes the attraction or repulsion you saw on the previous page. For example:

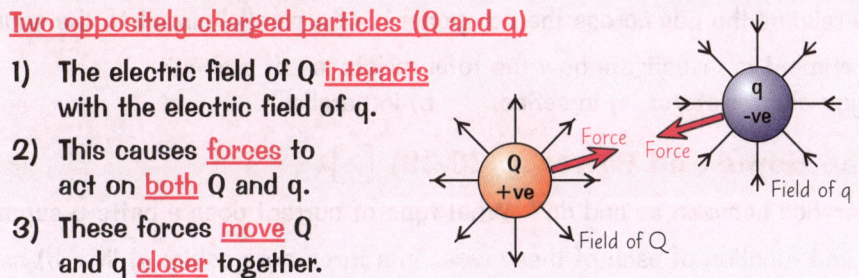

Two oppositely charged particles (Q and q)
1) The electric field of Q interacts with the electric field of q.
2) This causes forces to act on both Q and q.
3) These forces move Q and q closer together.

- The stronger the electric fields, the stronger the forces on the objects.
- If the objects move closer together, the fields get stronger, so the forces between them are stronger.

Of course... it all makes sense.

Sparking Can Be Explained By Electric Fields

1 The high pd causes a strong electric field between the charged object and the earthed object.

2 The strong electric field causes electrons to be removed from air particles.

3 The air particles become charged. So the air becomes a conductor. This means a current can flow through the air. This is the spark.

You're one bright spark if you've managed to finish this topic...

And we've saved the toughest 'til last. Don't worry if it takes a while to get to grips with electric fields — it's a pretty tricky topic. Re-read the page a few times to really get your head around it.

Q1 Draw the field lines surrounding an isolated, positively charged sphere. [2 marks]

Revision Summary Test for Topic 2

Well done for powering through that section. To keep the spark of knowledge alive, you can:
- Tackle the revision summary test below, or scan the QR code to do it online.
  The questions are hard, but they'll show you how well you really know your stuff.
- Track your progress online and see which areas need more work.
- Compare your answers with sample answers for the test here: cgpbooks.co.uk/Mass

Circuit Basics, Resistance and *I-V* Characteristics (p.18-22)

1) What is meant by current, potential difference and resistance in a circuit? What are their units?
2) How does an increase in resistance affect the current that flows in a circuit (for a given pd)?
3) What is the equation that links current, charge and time? What are the units for each term?
4) What is an ohmic conductor?
5) a) Explain how you could investigate how the length of a wire affects its resistance.
   b) What would you expect the results of this experiment to show?
6) What is an *I-V* characteristic?
7) a) Describe how you could use a standard test circuit to find the *I-V* characteristic for a resistor.
   b) How would the circuit need to change for you to investigate the *I-V* characteristic of a diode?
8) a) Draw the circuit symbols for an LDR and a thermistor.
   b) How does the resistance of an LDR and a thermistor change with the conditions that they are in?
9) Explain one way a thermistor could be used as part of a sensing circuit.

Series and Parallel Circuits (p.23-25)

10) What is a series circuit? Describe how current behaves in a series circuit.
11) What is a parallel circuit? Describe how current behaves in a parallel circuit.
12) What is the rule relating the pds across the components of a parallel circuit to the source pd?
13) Describe an experiment to investigate how the total resistance of a circuit changes when you add resistors: a) in series, b) in parallel.

Electricity in the Home and Power (p.26-29)

14) What is the difference between ac and dc? What type of current does a battery supply?
15) Give the colour and function of each of these wires in a three-core cable: a) live, b) neutral, c) earth.
16) Explain why touching a live wire could be dangerous even if a plug socket is turned off.
17) Describe the main energy transfer involved in using a kettle.
18) What is the power rating of an appliance? Why might a consumer pick one with a lower power rating?
19) What is the equation that relates energy transferred in a circuit to potential difference?
20) Give one way that the National Grid is set up to deal with surges in demand for electricity.
21) How are step-up and step-down transformers used in the National Grid?

Static Electricity and Electric Fields (p.30-31)

22) How does the rubbing of materials cause static electricity to build up?
23) Explain how you can use a charged rod to show how electrostatic attraction and repulsion works.
24) What type of object produces an electric field?
25) How does the strength of an electric field change as you move closer to the object?
26) In which direction do the arrows on electric field lines point?
27) What happens when a charged object is placed in the electric field of another charged object? How does this change as the objects are moved further apart?
28) Using the concept of electric fields, explain why a build-up of static electricity can cause a spark.

Topic 3 — Particle Model of Matter

The Particle Model and Density

Everything is made up of small particles — even this lovely revision guide you're holding right now...

There are Three States of Matter

The three states of matter are solid (e.g. ice), liquid (e.g. water) and gas (e.g. water vapour). The particle model explains the differences between the states of matter:

1) The particles of a certain substance are always the same, no matter what state it is in.
2) So a single particle of ice is exactly the same as a single particle of water.
3) But the particles have different amounts of energy in different states.
4) And the forces between particles are different in each state.
5) All this means that particles are arranged (laid out) differently in different states:

	Arrangement	Energy
Solid	Strong forces hold the particles close together. They are held in a fixed, regular pattern.	Not much energy — they can only vibrate (jiggle about) around their fixed points.
Liquid	Slightly weaker forces hold the particles close together in an irregular pattern. They can move past each other.	More energy than in solids — they move in random directions at low speeds.
Gas	There are almost no forces between the particles. They aren't held close together and they constantly move.	More energy than liquids — they move in random directions at a range of high speeds.

The Particle Model can also Explain Density

- Density is a measure of how much mass there is in a certain space.
- You can work out density using the equation:

$$\text{Density (kg/m}^3\text{)} = \frac{\text{mass (kg)}}{\text{volume (m}^3\text{)}} \quad \text{or:} \quad \rho = \frac{m}{V}$$

The symbol for density is a Greek letter rho (ρ).

EXAMPLE

A block of aluminium with volume 0.0020 m³ has a mass of 5.4 kg. Calculate the density of aluminium.

Put the values of mass and volume into the density equation.

density = mass ÷ volume
= 5.4 ÷ 0.0020 = 2700 kg/m³

- The density of an object depends on what it's made of and how its particles are arranged.
- The denser a material, the more tightly packed its particles are.
- So solids are generally denser than liquids. And liquids are generally denser than gases.

My brain must be dense — there's a lot tightly packed in there...

Get your head around the particle model before moving on to the rest of the topic.

Q1 Describe the arrangement of particles in a substance when it is:
a) a liquid   b) a solid. [2 marks]

Q2 An inflated football has an internal volume of 0.0048 m³. The density of the air in the football is 2.5 kg/m³. Calculate the mass of air in the football in kilograms. [3 marks]

Investigating Density **PRACTICAL**

There are lots of different ways to find the densities of real objects — here are some methods you could use.

You Need to be Able to Measure the Density of Different Solids

To find the density of a regularly-shaped object (e.g. a cuboid)

1) Use a balance to measure its mass (see p.107).
2) Measure its length, width and height with a ruler.
3) Then calculate its volume using the formula for that shape.
4) Use density = mass ÷ volume (p.33) to find the density.

The volume of a cuboid is equal to length × width × height.

To find the density of an irregularly-shaped object (e.g. an awards statue)

1) Use a balance to measure its mass.
2) Fill a eureka can (a can with a spout in its side) with water.
3) Place a measuring cylinder (p.108) under the spout.
4) Lower your object into the water. This will push some of the water out through the spout.
5) Measure the volume of water that has collected in the measuring cylinder. This is equal to the volume of the object.
6) Use the formula from p.33 to find the object's density.

Eureka cans are also known as displacement cans.

EXAMPLE A dinosaur toy is lowered into a full eureka can. A measuring cylinder placed under the spout collects 250 ml of water from the eureka can. The toy's mass is 350 g. Calculate the average density of the toy in kg/m³.

1) Convert the units for mass to kg.   350 g = 0.35 kg
2) Convert the units for volume to m³.   250 ml = 250 cm³ = 0.00025 m³
3) Calculate the density in kg/m³.
   density = mass ÷ volume
   = 0.35 ÷ 0.00025
   = 1400 kg/m³

Make sure you're happy with conversions. You should know that 1 ml = 1 cm³ and that 1 cm³ = 0.000001 m³. There's lots more about conversions on p.103.

Measuring the Density of a Liquid is a Bit Different

To find the density of a liquid

1) Place an empty measuring cylinder on a balance and zero the balance (p.107).
2) Pour 50 ml of the liquid into the measuring cylinder.
3) Record the liquid's mass that is shown on the mass balance.
4) Use the formula from p.33 to find the density (the volume is 50 cm³, or 0.00005 m³).

Who can measure volume — the eureka can can, oh the eureka can can...

That must be a huge eureka can to fit an entire stegosaurus inside it. Anyway, give this question a go:

Q1 A 0.019 kg gemstone is placed into a full eureka can, causing 7.0 cm³ of water to be pushed out the spout into a measuring cylinder. Calculate the density of the gemstone in g/cm³. [3 marks]

Topic 3 — Particle Model of Matter

Internal Energy and Changes of State

Quick Quiz

The changes of state we're talking about here are to do with particles, not with flying from New York to Texas...

Internal Energy is the Energy Stored by the Particles Making Up a System

The particles in a system (p.3) can store energy in their:
- Kinetic energy stores — because the particles move or vibrate.
- Potential energy stores — because of the positions of the particles.

> The INTERNAL ENERGY of a system is the TOTAL ENERGY that its particles have in their KINETIC and POTENTIAL energy stores.

Heating Increases Internal Energy

1) Heating a system transfers energy to its particles.
2) This increases the system's internal energy.
3) This leads to a change in temperature or a change of state:

Change in temperature
- How much the temperature changes depends on the mass of the system, its specific heat capacity (p.6) and how much energy is transferred to it.
- You can see this from the equation $\Delta E = mc\Delta\theta$.

Change of state
- There's a change of state if a solid or liquid is heated enough.
- Energy goes into breaking the bonds between the particles, increasing the energy in the potential energy stores of the particles.

Mass Doesn't Change When There's a Change of State

1) A change of state can happen because of cooling, as well as heating. The changes of state are:

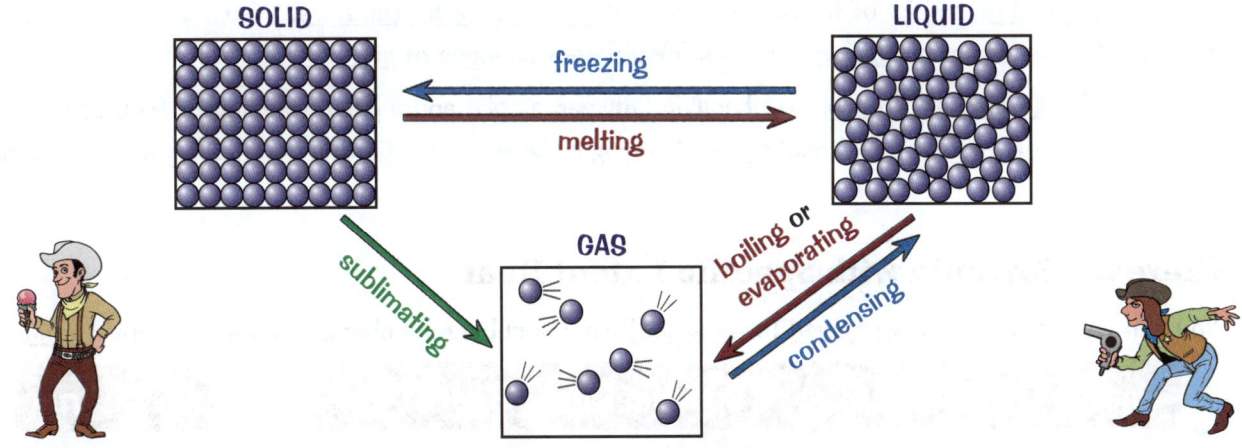

2) A change of state is a physical change (not a chemical change).
3) This means you don't end up with a new substance — the particles are just arranged in a different way.
4) If you reverse a change of state, the material will get back all the properties it had before the change.
5) The number of particles stays the same when the state changes.
6) This means the mass is conserved (it doesn't change).

Breaking Bonds — Blofeld never quite manages it...

Have a look back over your specific heat capacity notes (see p.6). You'll need them soon, I promise.

Q1 Name the following changes of state:
  a) solid to liquid   b) liquid to gas   c) gas to liquid   [3 marks]

Specific Latent Heat

Specific latent heat sounds like specific heat capacity but it's very different. It's all to do with changing state.

Latent Heat is the Energy Transferred When There's a Change of State

HEATING
- When you boil or melt a substance, energy is transferred to the particles by heating.
- This increases the internal energy, which is all used for breaking bonds between particles.
- The temperature stays the same.

COOLING
- When a substance condenses or freezes, bonds form between particles, which releases energy.
- This decreases the internal energy, but the temperature stays the same during the change of state.

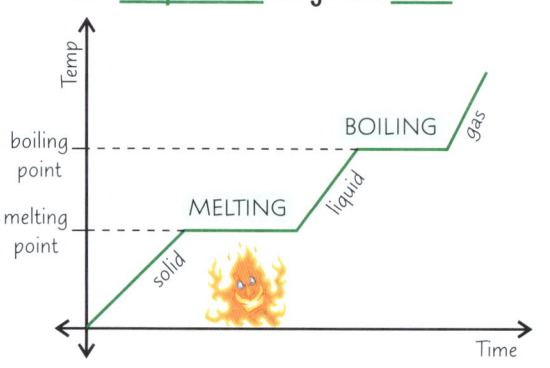

The flat spots on both graphs show that the temperature doesn't change during a change of state.

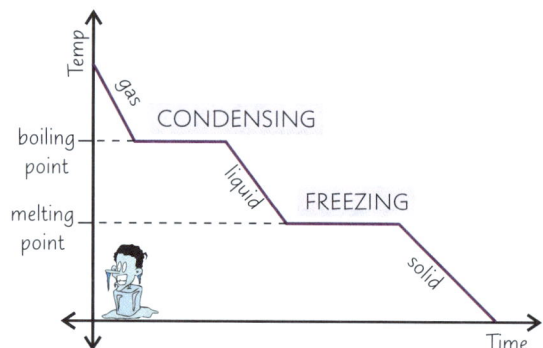

Specific Latent Heat is the Energy Needed for a 1 kg Mass to Change State

- The energy transferred during a change of state is called latent heat.
- For heating, latent heat is the energy gained to cause a change of state.
- For cooling, it is the energy released by a change of state.
- The specific latent heat of a material is the amount of energy needed to change the state of 1 kg of the material without changing its temperature.
- Specific latent heat has different names for different changes of state:

    Specific latent heat of fusion — changing between a solid and a liquid (melting or freezing).
    Specific latent heat of vaporisation — changing between a liquid and a gas (boiling or condensing).

Don't get this confused with specific heat capacity (p.6) which is to do with changes in temperature, not changes of state.

There's a Formula with Specific Latent Heat

You can work out the energy gained (or released) when a substance changes state using this formula:

Energy (J) = Mass (kg) × Specific Latent Heat (J/kg)   or: $E = mL$

EXAMPLE   The specific latent heat of vaporisation for water (boiling) is 2 260 000 J/kg. How much energy is needed to completely boil 1.50 kg of water once it has reached its boiling point?
1) Just plug the numbers into the formula. $E = mL = 1.50 \times 2\,260\,000$
2) The units are joules because it's energy. $= 3\,390\,000$ J

My specific latent heat of revision* is 500 J/kg...

There's a lot on this page. Re-read it and then have a go at this question to practise what you've learnt.

Q1   The SLH of fusion for a particular substance is 120 000 J/kg. How much energy is needed to melt 250 g of the substance when it is already at its melting temperature?   [2 marks]

*the amount of energy required to turn 1 kg of revision notes into exam success

Particle Motion and Pressure in Gases

Gas particles move pretty randomly. But the temperature, pressure and volume of gases are all related.

Gas Particles Bump into Things and Create Pressure

1) Particles in a gas are always moving in random directions.
2) They collide with (bump into) each other and the walls of the container they're in.
3) When they hit something, they apply a force to it.
4) The pressure is the net (total) force of all the particles over a given area of container wall.
5) This net force acts outwards, at right angles to the walls of the container.

See page 55 for more on pressure.

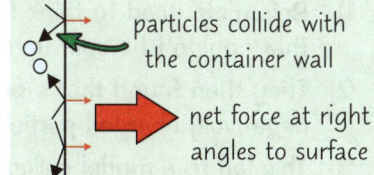

particles collide with the container wall

net force at right angles to surface

Increasing the Temperature of a Gas Increases its Pressure

1) The temperature of a gas depends on the average energy in the kinetic energy stores of the gas particles:

   Hotter gas ⟶ Higher average kinetic energy of particles ⟶ Particles move faster on average

2) Faster particles hit the sides of the container more often and with more force. This increases the overall force on the container.
3) So increasing the temperature of a gas increases its pressure.
4) This only works if the space the gas takes up (the volume) doesn't change.

Pressure and Volume are Connected

- If the temperature and mass of a gas are constant, its volume and pressure are linked by this equation:

  $pV = \text{constant}$ p = pressure, in pascals (Pa)
  V = volume (m^3)

- When volume goes up, pressure goes down (and when volume goes down, pressure goes up).
- This happens because making the volume bigger means that the gas particles get more spread out.
- At a constant temperature, this means they hit the container walls less often, so the pressure decreases.

EXAMPLE 4.0 m^3 of a gas is at a pressure of 675 Pa. Its volume is changed while its temperature is kept constant. The new pressure is 250 Pa. What is the new volume of the gas?

1) Find the value of pV when p = 675 Pa. $pV = 675 \times 4.0 = 2700$
2) Rearrange pV = constant for V. $pV = \text{constant} \to V = \text{constant} \div p$
3) Substitute in values for when p = 250 Pa. $V = 2700 \div 250 = 10.8\ m^3 = 11\ m^3$ (to 2 s.f.)

A Change in Pressure can Cause a Change in Volume

- A container of gas that is sitting in air feels two different pressures from gases:

  1) The pressure from the air outside pushes on the walls with an inward force.
  2) The gas pressure from inside pushes on the walls with an outward force.

- If there is a change in either pressure, there is a change in the overall force that the container walls feel.
- Some containers can easily change their size, like a balloon.
- A change in the net force on a container like this will cause the container to expand (grow) or shrink.
- If the pressure inside the container is greater, it expands. If the pressure outside is greater, it shrinks.

Help — the pressure of exams is getting to me...

Remember, the faster particles are moving or the closer together they are, the higher the pressure.

Q1 3.5 m^3 of a gas is at a pressure of 520 Pa. It is compressed to a volume of 1.0 m^3 at a constant temperature. What is the new pressure of the gas? [3 marks]

Topic 4 — Atomic Structure

Developing the Model of the Atom

Quick Quiz

Hold on to your hat — we're going on a journey through time, to see how models of the atom were born...

Ideas About What Atoms Look Like Have Changed Over Time

1) Scientists used to think that atoms were solid spheres that couldn't be split up any further.
2) They then found that atoms contain even smaller, negatively charged particles — electrons.
3) This led to a model called the 'plum pudding model' being created.
4) The plum pudding model described the atom as a ball of positive charge with electrons scattered in this ball.

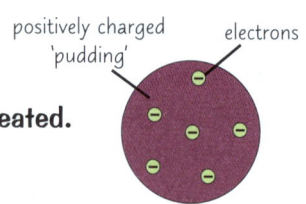

positively delicious pudding

Experiments Proved the Plum Pudding Model was Wrong...

1) Later, scientists did an experiment where they fired positively charged alpha particles at a very thin sheet of gold.
2) From the plum pudding model, they expected most particles to pass straight through the gold sheet, or only slightly change direction.
3) The actual results of this alpha scattering experiment were different:

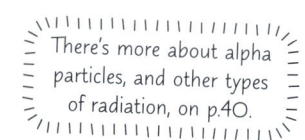
There's more about alpha particles, and other types of radiation, on p.40.

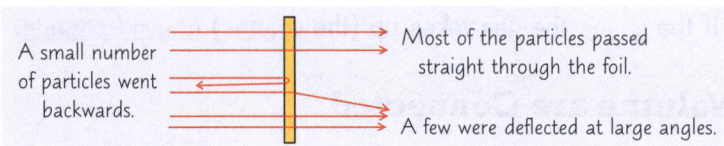

4) This meant the plum pudding model couldn't be right. So scientists came up with the nuclear model.
5) Here's what they observed in the experiment, and how they used it to come up with the nuclear model:

Most alpha particles passed straight through the foil. → Most of the atom is empty space.

A tiny number of particles went backwards. This suggests they bounced off something very small. → Most of the mass is concentrated in a tiny nucleus at the centre of the atom.

Some of the positive alpha particles were deflected at a large angle, and like charges repel (see p.30). → The nucleus is positively charged.

...Then Bohr Proposed a Different Nuclear Model

- Niels Bohr developed the nuclear model of the atom further.
- He suggested that electrons orbit (go round) the nucleus in energy levels.
- Each energy level is at a fixed distance from the nucleus.
- Bohr's theory was supported by many calculations. Experiments later provided more support for Bohr's theory.

Results from more experiments showed that the nucleus can be divided into smaller, positively charged particles. These particles were named protons.
Experiments by James Chadwick showed that the nucleus also contained neutral particles — neutrons. This happened about 20 years after scientists agreed that atoms have nuclei.

I guess I'll shelve my jam roly-poly model for a rainy day...

This is science in action folks — as new evidence came along, the model of the atom was changed and updated.

Q1   Describe the 'plum pudding' model of the atom.   [1 mark]

The Structure of the Atom

Protons, neutrons, electrons, energy levels — the atom really has it all. There's a simple model that's a great way to visualise what is going on in the tiny world of the atom...

You Need to Know About this Modern Model of the Atom

There are a few different models of the atom used by scientists today — this is the one you need to know about. It's a nuclear model, meaning there's a nucleus in the centre surrounded by electrons:

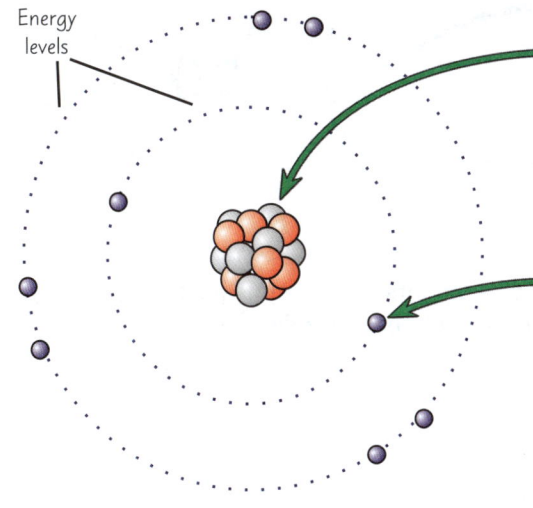

Energy levels

- The nucleus is tiny, but it makes up most of the mass of the atom.
- The nucleus is made up of protons and neutrons.
- Protons are positively charged and neutrons have no charge. So the nucleus has an overall positive charge.

Electrons have a negative charge. They orbit the nucleus at different distances, known as energy levels.

Protons	positively charged	relative charge +1
Neutrons	neutral	relative charge 0
Electrons	negatively charged	relative charge –1

- Atoms have no overall charge. The number of protons = number of electrons.
- Atoms are very small. The radius of an atom is about 1×10^{-10} m (or 0.000 000 000 1 m — see page 104 for more on standard form).
- The radius of the nucleus is over 10 000 times smaller than the radius of the atom.

Electrons can Move Between Energy Levels

1) The further an energy level is from the nucleus, the more energy an electron in that energy level has.
2) Electrons can move between energy levels by absorbing (taking in) or releasing electromagnetic (EM) radiation (p.75).

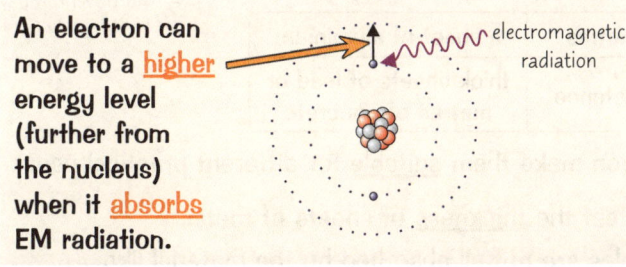

An electron can move to a higher energy level (further from the nucleus) when it absorbs EM radiation.

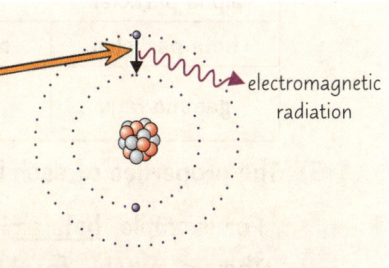

An electron can move to a lower energy level (closer to the nucleus) by releasing EM radiation.

3) If an electron in an outer energy level absorbs electromagnetic radiation, it can leave the atom.
4) If an atom loses one or more electrons it turns into a positively charged ion.

This model doesn't have anything on my toy trains...

So protons and neutrons are in the nucleus, and electrons orbit the nucleus in energy levels. Good to know...

Q1 a) What particles make up the nucleus? [2 marks]
b) State the typical radius of an atom and describe how this compares to the size of its nucleus. [2 marks]

Isotopes and Nuclear Radiation

Isotopes and ionisation. They sound similar, but they're not, so read this page carefully.

Isotopes are Different Forms of the Same Element

- All atoms of a given element have the same number of protons. The number of protons in an atom is called its atomic number.
- The mass number of an atom is: the number of protons + the number of neutrons.
- You can show this information about an atom like this:
- Atoms of an element with the same number of protons but a different number of neutrons are called isotopes.
- Isotopes of an element have the same atomic number, but a different mass number. E.g. $^{18}_{8}O$ is an isotope of oxygen.

The atomic number also tells you the charge of the nucleus.

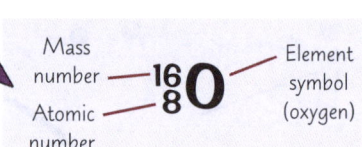

Some Isotopes are Unstable

- Unstable (radioactive) isotopes tend to decay into other elements. They emit (give out) radiation from their nuclei to try to become more stable. This process is called radioactive decay.
- The radiation emitted by radioactive isotopes is called nuclear radiation.
- There are four different types of nuclear radiation:

Nuclei means more than one nucleus.

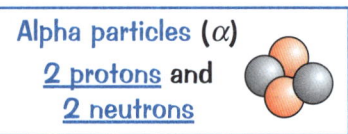

Alpha particles (α)
2 protons and 2 neutrons

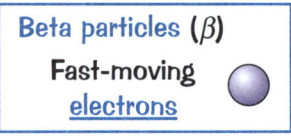

Beta particles (β)
Fast-moving electrons

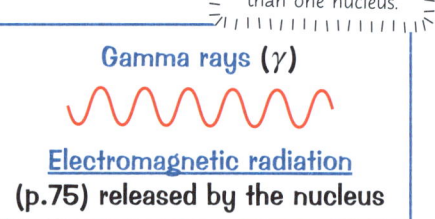

Gamma rays (γ)
Electromagnetic radiation (p.75) released by the nucleus

Neutrons (n) can also be released when atoms decay.

You Need to Know the Properties of Ionising Nuclear Radiation

1) Ionising radiation is radiation that can knock electrons off atoms and turn them into positive ions.
2) The ionising power of radiation is how easily it can do this.
3) Alpha particles, beta particles and gamma rays are all types of ionising radiation.
4) They all have different properties:

Type of radiation	Ionising power	Range in air	Stopped by
alpha particles	strong	a few centimetres	a sheet of paper
beta particles	moderate	a few metres	a sheet of aluminium
gamma rays	weak	a long distance	thick sheets of lead or metres of concrete

'Range in air' is the distance the radiation can travel through air.

5) The properties of each kind of ionising radiation make them suitable for different practical uses:

- For example, beta emitters can be used to test the thickness of sheets of metal.
- They're suitable for this because beta particles are not all absorbed by the material like alpha radiation would be. But they won't all penetrate all the way through like gamma rays.
- The amount of beta radiation passing through the sheet will be lower the thicker the metal is.

See page 45 for more uses of ionising radiation.

Ionising radiation — good for getting creases out of clothes...

Knowing different kinds of radiation and what can absorb them can bag you a few easy marks in an exam.

Q1 In order to sterilise medical equipment, radiation is directed at the equipment while it is sealed in packaging. Explain whether alpha radiation would be suitable for this use. [2 marks]

Nuclear Equations

Nuclear equations show radioactive decay. They look quite scary but this should help you get the hang of them.

Mass Numbers and Atomic Numbers Have to Balance

1) Nuclear equations are a way of showing radioactive decay (p.40). They're normally written like this:

> Nucleus before decay → nucleus after decay + radiation emitted

2) You need to remember this golden rule:

> The total atomic and mass numbers on both sides of the arrow must be equal.

Alpha Decay Decreases the Charge and Mass of the Nucleus

- Alpha decay is when an alpha particle is emitted from a radioactive nucleus.
- When a nucleus undergoes alpha decay, its atomic number goes down by 2 and its mass number goes down by 4.
- The charge of the nucleus decreases when it gives out an alpha particle.
- An alpha particle is the same as a helium nucleus, so it can be written in a nuclear equation as $^{4}_{2}He$.

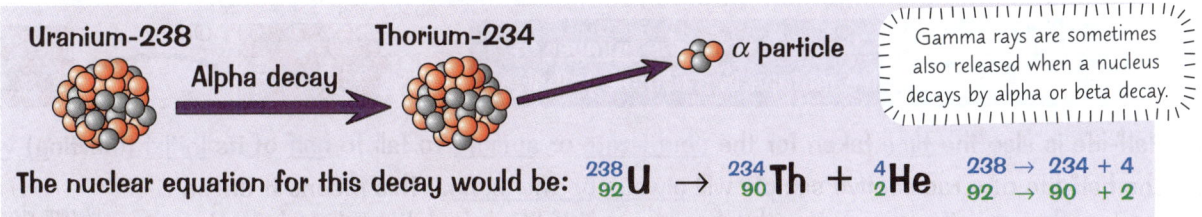

Gamma rays are sometimes also released when a nucleus decays by alpha or beta decay.

The nuclear equation for this decay would be: $^{238}_{92}U \rightarrow {}^{234}_{90}Th + {}^{4}_{2}He$ 238 → 234 + 4
    92 → 90 + 2

Beta Decay Increases the Charge of the Nucleus

- Beta decay is when a beta particle is emitted from a radioactive nucleus.
- During beta decay, a neutron in the nucleus turns into a proton.
- The nucleus has one more proton, so its atomic number goes up by 1.
- It also means the positive charge of the nucleus increases.
- A beta particle has an atomic number of –1, so the atomic numbers balance on each side of the equation.
- Protons and neutrons have the same mass, so the mass of the nucleus doesn't change.
- A beta particle is an electron. It is written as $^{0}_{-1}e$ in nuclear equations.

In both alpha and beta emissions, a new element will be formed, as the number of protons (atomic number) changes.

The nuclear equation for this decay would be: $^{14}_{6}C \rightarrow {}^{14}_{7}N + {}^{0}_{-1}e$ 14 → 14 + 0
    6 → 7 − 1

Gamma Rays Don't Change the Charge or Mass of the Nucleus

1) Gamma rays are a way of getting rid of extra energy from a nucleus.
2) When they are emitted, they don't change the mass or charge of the atom and nucleus.

Don't beta round the bush — learn nuclear equations now...

Nuclear equations need practice to really get your head around. Why not try these questions on for size?

Q1 What type of radiation is given off in this decay? $^{8}_{3}Li \rightarrow {}^{8}_{4}Be$ + radiation. [1 mark]

Q2 Write the nuclear equation for $^{219}_{86}Rn$ decaying to polonium (Po) by emitting an alpha particle. [3 marks]

Half-life

How quickly unstable isotopes decay is measured using activity and half-life — two very important terms.

Radioactivity is Something That You Can Measure

- Radioactive substances give out radiation from the nuclei of their atoms.
- It's important to know the difference between these ways of measuring radioactivity:

COUNT-RATE	The number of radiation counts measured by a detector (e.g. by a Geiger-Muller tube and counter) per second.
ACTIVITY	The rate at which a source decays. It is measured in becquerels (Bq). 1 becquerel is equal to 1 decay per second.

The count-rate can be measured in counts per second (cps).

Radioactivity is a Totally Random Process

1) You can't predict exactly which nucleus in a radioactive sample will decay next, or when any one of them will decay.
2) But you can predict how long it will take for half of the nuclei to decay. This is known as the half-life:

> The half-life is the time taken for the number of nuclei of a radioactive isotope in a sample to halve.

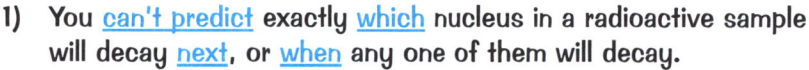

One half-life

3) Half-life is also the time taken for the count-rate or activity to fall to half of its initial (starting) value.
4) The half-life of a radioactive sample will always be the same. This means it doesn't matter what activity you start with when doing half-life calculations (see below).

Different elements, and different isotopes of the same element, can have different half-lives.

You Need to be Able to Calculate Half-Lives

EXAMPLE The activity of a radioactive source over time is shown on the graph on the right. Use the graph to find the half-life of the source.

1) The initial activity when time = 0 s is 800 Bq.
2) Use the graph to find the time when the activity has halved to 400 Bq. Here, it is at $t = 2$ s.
3) So, the time for the activity to halve was 2 s.

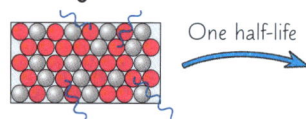

EXAMPLE The activity of a radioactive isotope was measured. Initially it was 64 Bq. 12 seconds later it had fallen to 16 Bq. Calculate the half-life of the sample.

1) First, find how many half-lives it takes for the activity to fall from 64 Bq to 16 Bq.   After one half-life, the activity will be 64 ÷ 2 = 32 Bq
   After two half-lives, the activity will be 32 ÷ 2 = 16 Bq
2) So you know 12 seconds is equal to two half-lives. Divide 12 by 2 to find the time for one half-life.   Time for one half-life = 12 ÷ 2 = 6 s

The half-life of a box of chocolates is about five minutes...

Half-life is really important in radioactivity. Make sure you know what it is and how to calculate it.

Q1   What is meant by the activity of a radioactive substance? [1 mark]

Q2   The initial count-rate of a sample is 168 counts per second (cps). After 60 minutes, the count-rate of the sample is 21 cps. Calculate the half-life of the sample. [3 marks]

42   Topic 4 — Atomic Structure

Background Radiation and Radiation Dose

Quick Quiz

Forget love — radiation is all around. Don't panic too much though, it's usually a pretty small amount.

Background Radiation Comes from Many Sources

1) Background radiation is radiation that's around us all the time.
2) It usually exists at very low levels, so it's not very dangerous.
3) It comes from:

- Naturally occurring unstable isotopes (e.g. in air, food and building materials)
- Rocks underneath our feet
- Radiation from space (cosmic rays)
- Radiation from human activity (e.g. fallout from nuclear explosions or nuclear waste)

Coloured bits indicate more radiation from rocks.

Background Radiation Needs to be Subtracted from the Count-Rate

1) When measuring the count-rate of a radioactive source, you need to measure and subtract the background radiation from your results.
2) Doing this makes sure you're only recording the radiation emitted by the source.

EXAMPLE

A scientist is measuring the count-rate of a radioactive source. She measures a value of 520 counts per minute. The background count-rate is 65 counts per minute. Calculate the true count-rate of the radioactive source.

Subtract the background count-rate from the measured count-rate.

true count-rate = value measured − background count-rate
= 520 − 65 = 455 counts per minute

MATHS SKILLS

Radiation Dose Measures Your Risk of Harm from Radiation

- Radiation dose is measured in sieverts (Sv) (see page 78).
- The dose from background radiation is small, so millisieverts are often used.
- 1 Sv = 1000 mSv (for more on units, see page 103).
- Your radiation dose (e.g. from background radiation) varies depending on where you live and if you have a job that involves radiation.

For example, someone working with ionising radiation in a hospital will have a higher radiation dose than someone who works in a bank.

Radiation Dose Depends on Half-Life

Radioactive sources with short and long half-lives can both be dangerous, but in different ways.

SHORT HALF-LIFE → Activity falls quickly → Dose is high at the start because there's high amounts of radiation, but activity drops to safe levels quickly.

LONG HALF-LIFE → Activity falls slowly → Small radiation dose, but for a long time — dangerous for nearby areas which are constantly exposed.

Background radiation — the ugly wallpaper of the universe...

Background radiation is always there, so you need to remember to account for it in any count-rate measurements.

Q1 Give three sources of background radiation. [3 marks]

Irradiation and Contamination

Contamination in physics isn't like when your mum sneaks a Brussels sprout onto your dinner plate...

Exposure to Radiation is called Irradiation

1) Objects near a radioactive source can be irradiated by it. This simply means that objects are exposed to the radiation.
2) The further you are from a source, the less radiation will reach you.
3) If you are far enough away from a source, or the radiation is being blocked by something, the radiation can't reach you. This means you won't be irradiated by it.
4) Irradiating something does not make it radioactive (and won't turn you into a superhero).
5) To help stop irradiation happening, you should:

- Store radioactive sources in lead-lined boxes when they're not being used.
- Stand behind barriers that will absorb radiation when using sources.
- Keep the source as far away from you as possible, e.g. hold it at arm's length.

If ionising radiation enters living cells, it can cause cancer or kill cells off completely (see next page).

Contamination is Radioactive Particles Getting onto Objects

1) If unwanted radioactive atoms get onto or into an object, the object is contaminated.
2) These contaminating atoms might then decay and release radiation which could harm you.
3) Contamination is especially dangerous because radioactive material could get inside your body.
4) Gloves and tongs should be used when handling radioactive sources. This can stop radioactive material getting stuck to your skin or under your nails.
5) People whose jobs involve radioactive materials often wear protective suits and face masks to help stop them breathing in radioactive dust and gas.

How Dangerous Irradiation and Contamination are Depends on the Source

Irradiation or contamination can cause different amounts of harm based on the radiation type.

	Alpha sources	Beta sources	Gamma sources
IRRADIATION	Least dangerous of the sources as they can't penetrate (go through) the skin and are stopped by a small air gap.	Dangerous as both sources can penetrate the body and damage delicate organs.	*High levels of irradiation from all sources are dangerous.*
CONTAMINATION (inside of the body)	Most dangerous of the sources as they do all of their damage in a very localised area and have the highest ionising power.	Less damaging as radiation is absorbed over a wider area and is less ionising.	Least dangerous, as they mostly pass straight out of the body and are the least ionising.

Outside of the body, alpha sources are the least dangerous to be contaminated by — they can't get through the skin. It only becomes dangerous if the alpha source get inside the body.

It's important that research about radiation is published and checked by peer review (see p.96). Research can help improve how we protect ourselves when using radioactive sources.

Top tip number 364 — if something is radioactive, don't lick it...

Make sure you can describe how to prevent irradiation and contamination, and why it's so important that you do.

Q1 Explain why a gamma source is more dangerous to be irradiated by than an alpha source. [2 marks]

Topic 4 — Atomic Structure

Uses and Risk

Radiation can be pretty useful. Using radiation is all about reducing the risks whilst still keeping the benefits.

There are Risks to Using Radiation

Radiation can enter living cells and ionise atoms and molecules within them.
This can cause damage to the body.

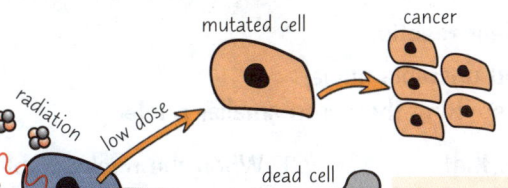

Lower doses tend to cause minor damage without killing the cells. This can lead to mutant cells which divide uncontrollably. This is cancer.

Higher doses tend to kill cells, causing radiation sickness if a lot of cells all get killed at once.

Medical Tracers Often Use Gamma Sources

1) Medical tracers are certain radioactive isotopes that can be injected into the body or swallowed.
2) The tracers then move around or collect in certain areas of the body.
3) Their progress is tracked using a radiation detector. This is useful to see if certain areas of the body are working normally.
4) The isotopes used should have a short half-life so the radioactivity inside the patient quickly disappears.
5) Gamma radiation is typically used because it can easily pass through the body without causing much damage (since its ionising power is low, but its penetration is high).

Radiation detector

Gamma rays emitted by the tracer

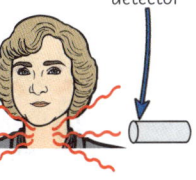

Alpha sources would never be used as tracers. Alpha particles are very ionising and can't pass through the body.

Radiotherapy — Treating Cancer with Radiation

- Since high doses of ionising radiation will kill all living cells, it can be used to treat cancers.
- Just the right amount of gamma rays are directed carefully at the cancer cells to kill them.
- However, damage is still done to some normal cells, which can make the patient feel ill after treatment.
- Radiation-emitting implants (usually beta emitters) can also be put next to or inside tumours.

You Have to Weigh Up the Risks and Benefits

There are risks and benefits to using tracers and radiotherapy that people must consider.

	Tracers	Radiotherapy
Risk	There is a very small risk of getting cancer.	Makes patients feel very ill. Can lead to some future risks, e.g. slightly increasing the chance of getting another type of cancer.
Benefit	Can be used to diagnose life-threatening conditions.	If it is successful, it will get rid of cancer entirely.

People decide whether to use radiation based on perceived risk (how risky they think something is). It is not the same as the actual risk, and it depends on the person (see p.98 for more on risks).

Revision sickness — well yes, it does all get a bit tiring...

Using any kind of radiation has risks, but the benefits are often good enough that the risks are considered worth it.

Q1 Describe how gamma emitters are used as medical tracers. [3 marks]

Fission and Fusion

Splitting up or squishing together atoms releases lots of useful energy. But the results can be explosive.

Nuclear Fission — Splitting a Large, Unstable Nucleus

- Nuclear fission is a type of nuclear reaction.
- It releases energy from large and unstable nuclei (e.g. uranium or plutonium) by splitting them into smaller nuclei.

1) Spontaneous fission (fission that happens on its own) rarely happens. Usually, the nucleus has to absorb a neutron before it will split.

2) When the nucleus splits it forms two new, lighter elements. These new elements are about the same size.

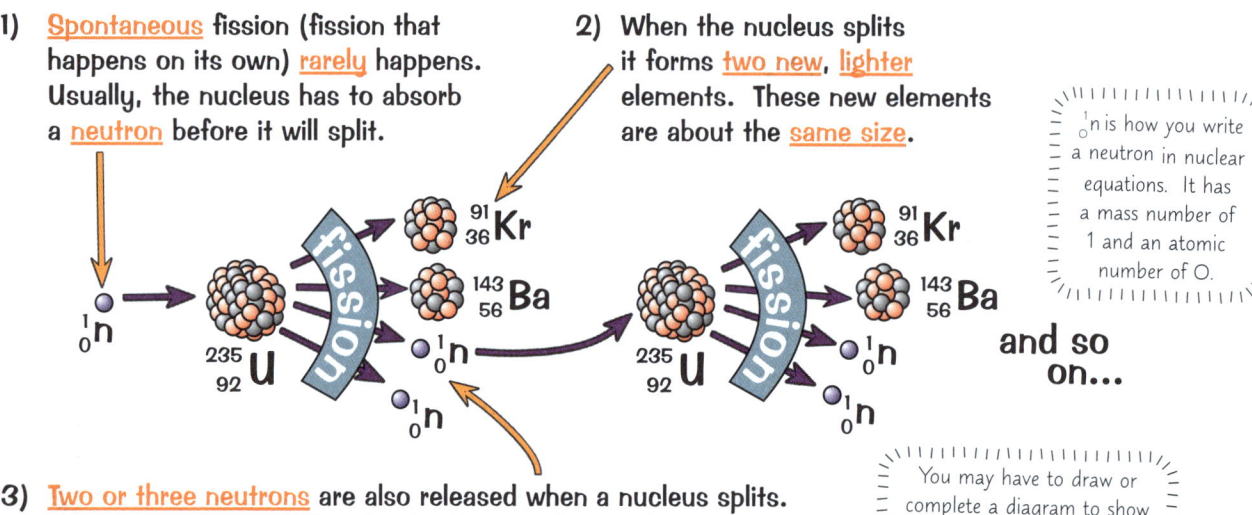

$_0^1 n$ is how you write a neutron in nuclear equations. It has a mass number of 1 and an atomic number of 0.

and so on...

You may have to draw or complete a diagram to show a chain reaction in the exam.

3) Two or three neutrons are also released when a nucleus splits. These neutrons could be absorbed by another nucleus, causing more fission to occur. This is a chain reaction.

- The new nuclei formed and the neutrons released will have some energy in their kinetic energy stores.
- Any leftover energy is carried away by gamma rays.
- All of the energy released can be used in nuclear reactors.

> - The amount of energy produced in a nuclear reactor is controlled using control rods.
> - These limit how quickly the chain reaction can occur, by absorbing neutrons.
> - Uncontrolled chain reactions quickly lead to lots of energy being released in an explosion. This is how nuclear weapons work.

Nuclear Fusion — Joining Small Nuclei

Nuclear fusion is the opposite of nuclear fission.
1) In nuclear fusion, two light nuclei collide at high speeds.
2) They then join (fuse) together to create a larger, heavier nucleus.
3) At the beginning of the reaction, there are two separate light nuclei. The total mass of these nuclei combined is slightly more than the mass of the larger nucleus produced at the end of the reaction.
4) This is because some of the mass of the lighter nuclei is turned into energy (don't panic, you don't need to know how) and released.

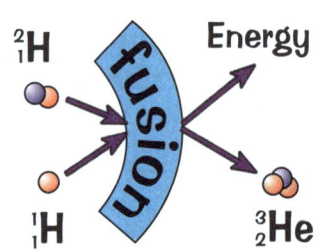

Two types of hydrogen nuclei fusing to produce a helium nucleus.

Pity they can't release energy by confusion...*

You don't need to know the complicated processes behind fission and fusion, but you need to know the key steps.

Q1   A neutron is absorbed by a large, unstable nucleus and causes a nuclear fission reaction.
      Give the products produced when the unstable nucleus is split.   [3 marks]

*There'd be plenty of physics books to use as fuel.

Revision Summary Test for Topics 3 & 4

Particles and atoms may be small, but you need to know a lot about them. Try testing yourself:
- Tackle one of the revision summary tests below, or scan the QR code to do it online. The questions are hard, but they'll show you how well you really know your stuff.
- Track your progress online and see which areas need more work.
- Compare your answers with sample answers for the tests here: cgpbooks.co.uk/Mass

Topic 3

Density of Materials (p.33-34)

1) Describe the energy and movement of particles for each of the three states of matter.
2) What is meant by the "density" of a material? What is the formula for density?
3) How could you find the density of: a) a regular solid object, b) an irregular solid object?

Internal Energy, Changes of State and Pressure in Gases (p.35-37)

4) What is the internal energy of a system?
5) Give the names of three changes of state. What does each one mean?
6) What is specific latent heat? What about specific latent heat of vaporisation?
7) Describe how a gas in a sealed container exerts a pressure on the walls of the container.
8) Explain how a higher temperature increases the pressure of a gas with a constant mass and volume.
9) What happens to the volume of a gas at a constant temperature, when its pressure goes up?
10) Describe the two different pressures from gases experienced by a helium balloon in the air.

Topic 4

The Atomic Model, Nuclear Decay and Half-life (p.38-42)

1) Give three key observations from the alpha scattering experiment.
2) Describe Bohr's nuclear model. What particle did Chadwick discover in the atom 20 years later?
3) What happens to an electron in an atom when it: a) absorbs EM radiation, b) emits EM radiation?
4) What do the following terms mean: a) atomic number, b) mass number, c) isotopes?
5) What is radioactive decay? Describe four things that may be emitted during decay.
6) Give the ionising power and range in air of: a) alpha radiation, b) beta radiation, c) gamma radiation.
7) How do the mass numbers and atomic numbers of nuclei change during:
    a) alpha decay, b) beta decay, c) gamma decay?
8) What is the count-rate of a source? And what about the activity of a source?
9) What is the half-life of a source? How can you find the half-life from an activity-time graph?

Dangers and Uses of Radiation (p.43-46)

10) How can you account for background radiation when measuring the activity of a radioactive source?
11) What does radiation dose tell you? How does the half-life of a source affect a person's radiation dose?
12) Define irradiation and contamination. Give an example of how you can protect against each of them.
13) Compare the hazards of alpha, beta and gamma sources when someone is:
    a) irradiated by them, b) contaminated by them inside the body.
14) Give one benefit and one risk of using radiation: a) as a medical tracer, b) to treat cancer.
15) What happens in nuclear fission? Explain how chain reactions are controlled in nuclear reactors.
16) Describe what happens in nuclear fusion. What can happen to some of the mass in this process?

Topic 5a — Forces, Moments and Pressure

Contact and Non-Contact Forces

When you're talking about the forces acting on an object, it's not enough to just talk about the size of each force. You need to know their direction too — force is a vector, with a size and a direction.

Force is a Vector Quantity

Physical quantities can be vector or scalar:

	Definition	Examples
Vector quantity	Has magnitude (size) and direction.	Force, velocity, displacement, acceleration.
Scalar quantity	Only has magnitude.	Speed, distance, mass, temperature, time.

- Vectors are usually represented by an arrow.
- The length of the arrow shows the magnitude (size) of the quantity.
- The direction of the arrow shows the direction of the quantity.

Forces Can be Contact or Non-Contact

1) A force is a push or a pull that acts on an object.
2) Forces are measured in newtons (N).
3) Forces are caused by objects interacting with each other.
4) All forces are either contact or non-contact forces:

	Definition	Examples
Contact force	A force that acts when two objects touch.	Friction, air resistance, tension in ropes, normal contact force.
Non-contact force	A force that can act without objects touching.	Magnetic force, gravitational force, electrostatic force.

I should have chosen a non-contact sport...

When one object exerts a contact force on another object, the other object pushes back. This is the normal contact force.

5) When two objects interact, a force is produced on both objects. The forces on the two objects are equal in size but act in opposite directions.
6) These two forces are called an interaction pair.

- The gravitational attraction between the Earth and the Sun is an example of an interaction pair.
- A gravitational force acts on the Earth attracting it to the Sun.
- At the same time, a force acts on the Sun attracting it towards the Earth.
- These forces are the same size but act in opposite directions.

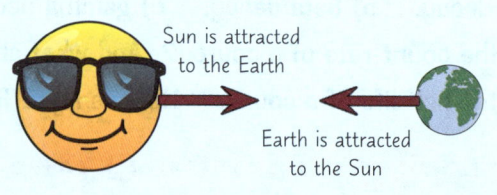

Sun is attracted to the Earth

Earth is attracted to the Sun

My life's feeling pretty scalar — I've no idea where I'm headed...

This stuff is vital to understand if you want to make it through the rest of this topic. Better get your head down.

Q1 Name two examples of: a) a scalar quantity   b) a vector quantity   [4 marks]

Q2 A tennis ball is dropped from a height. Name one contact force and one non-contact force that act on the ball as it falls.   [2 marks]

Weight, Mass and Gravity

Mass and weight are NOT the same... Read on to find out why. You know you want to.

Mass is Measured in kg

- Mass is just the amount of matter (stuff) in an object.
- It's measured in kilograms, kg.

Scientists sometimes think of all the mass in an object as being at one single point in the object. This point is called the centre of mass.

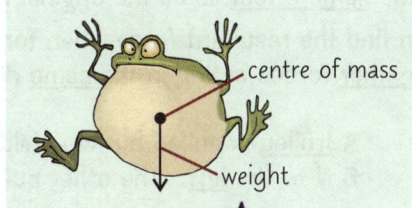

Weight is Measured in Newtons

1) Weight is the force acting on an object due to gravity.
2) You can think of this force as acting from an object's centre of mass.
3) Close to Earth, this force is caused by the gravitational field around the Earth.

- The weight of an object depends on its mass and the strength of the gravitational field it's in.
- Gravitational field strength changes depending on where you are.
- So the weight of an object depends on its location. This is unlike the mass of an object, which is always the same.

The further you are from Earth's surface, the weaker the gravitational field is. And the gravitational field strength on the surface of the Moon is much weaker than it is on the surface of the Earth.

4) Weight is measured in newtons, N.
5) It can be measured with a calibrated spring balance (or newtonmeter).

Mass and Weight are Directly Proportional

- You can calculate the weight of an object if you know its mass (m) and the strength of the gravitational field that it is in (g):

Weight (N) = Mass (kg) × Gravitational Field Strength (N/kg) $W = mg$

- For Earth, g is around 9.8 N/kg. For the Moon it's around 1.6 N/kg. Don't worry, you'll always be given a value of g to use in the exam.
- Mass and weight are directly proportional (see p.104) when in a constant gravitational field — if you increase the mass, the weight increases at the same rate.
- You can write this, using the direct proportionality symbol, as $W \propto m$.

EXAMPLE
A motorcycle weighs 2450 N on Earth. Calculate the mass of the motorcycle. (g = 9.8 N/kg)

1) First, rearrange $W = mg$ to find mass. $W = mg \rightarrow m = W \div g$
2) Then, put in the numbers to calculate the mass. $m = 2450 \div 9.8 = 250$ kg

---

I don't think you quite understand the gravity of this situation...

Remember that weight is a force due to gravity and mass is just how much stuff there is.

Q1 Calculate the weight in newtons of a 5 kg mass:
   a) on Earth ($g \approx 9.8$ N/kg)   b) on the Moon ($g \approx 1.6$ N/kg)   [4 marks]

Resultant Forces and Work Done

I'm sure you're no stranger to doing work, but in physics it's all to do with transferring energy.

A Resultant Force is the Overall Force on a Point or Object

1) If a number of forces act at a single point, you can replace them with a single force.
2) This single force is called the resultant force.
3) It has the same effect as all the original forces added together.
4) You can find the resultant force when forces are acting in a straight line. Add together forces acting in the same direction and take away any going in the opposite direction.

A trolley is pulled by two children. One child pulls the trolley with a force of 5 N to the left. The other pulls the trolley with a force of 10 N to the right.

So the resultant force, F, is:
$F = 10\ N - 5\ N$
$= \underline{5\ N\ to\ the\ right}$.

If a Resultant Force Moves an Object, Work is Done

When a force moves an object through a distance, ENERGY IS TRANSFERRED and WORK IS DONE on the object.

1) To start an object moving, a force must act on it.
2) The force does 'work' to accelerate (p.58) the object.
3) This causes energy to be transferred to the object.
4) The force usually does work against frictional forces too.
5) Doing work against frictional forces causes energy to be transferred to the thermal energy store of the object.
6) This causes the temperature of the object to increase.

'Work done' and 'energy transferred' are the same thing. You need to be able to describe how energy is transferred when work is done. Look back at p.4 for more on this.

- When you push something along a rough surface (like a carpet) you are doing work against frictional forces.
- Some energy is transferred to the kinetic energy store of the object because it starts moving.
- Some is also transferred to the object's thermal energy stores due to the work done against friction.
- This causes the overall temperature of the object to increase.

7) You can find out how much work has been done using:

$$W = Fs$$

Work done (J) — Force (N) — Distance (moved along the line of action of the force) (m)

The line of action of the force is the direction of the force.

8) One joule of work is done when a force of one newton causes an object to move a distance of one metre.
9) You need to be able to convert joules to newton-metres: $1\ J = 1\ Nm$

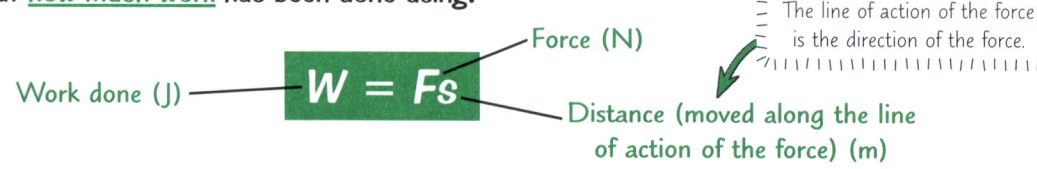

Force yourself to do some work and learn this page...

Remember, when you use a force to move an object, you do work. And if you do work, energy is transferred.

Q1   A force of 20 N pushes an object 20 cm. Calculate the work done on the object. [3 marks]

Forces and Elasticity

You can use forces to <u>stretch things</u> and <u>compress things</u> too. The fun never ends...

Stretching, Compressing or Bending Transfers Energy

- When you apply forces to an object you may change its shape by <u>stretching</u>, <u>compressing</u> or <u>bending</u> it.
- To change the shape of an object (<u>deform</u> it), you need <u>more than one</u> force acting on the object. <u>One</u> force would just make the object <u>move</u>.
- There are two types of <u>deformation</u>:

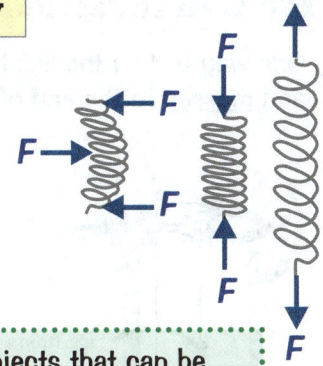

Elastic deformation	The object <u>returns</u> to its <u>original shape</u> and <u>length</u> after the forces have been removed.
Inelastic deformation	The object <u>doesn't return</u> to its <u>original shape</u> and <u>length</u> after the forces have been removed.

Objects that can be elastically deformed are called <u>elastic objects</u> (e.g. a spring).

- <u>Work is done</u> when a force deforms an object. This causes energy to be transferred to the <u>elastic potential energy</u> store of the object.

Extension is Directly Proportional to Force...

If a spring is fixed at the top and has a mass attached to the bottom, it <u>stretches</u>:

1) The <u>extension</u> of the spring is the <u>difference in length</u> between the stretched and unstretched spring.
2) Up to a <u>given force</u> (from the weight of the hanging mass), the extension is <u>directly proportional</u> to the force.
3) The formula that shows this relationship is:

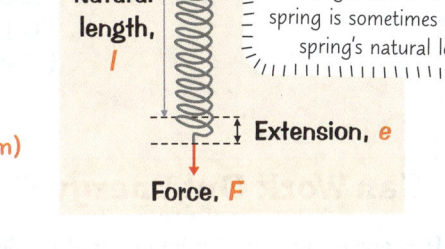

$F = ke$

- Force (N)
- Spring constant (N/m)
- Extension (m)

The length of the unstretched spring is sometimes called the spring's natural length.

4) The value of the <u>spring constant</u> depends on the <u>object</u> that you are stretching.

The equation also works for <u>compression</u> (where e is the <u>difference</u> between the <u>natural</u> and <u>compressed</u> lengths).

...but this Stops Working when the Force is Too Great

You can plot a <u>graph</u> of the force applied to a spring and the extension caused by the force.

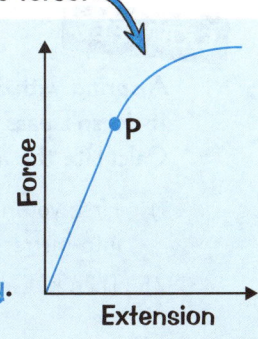

- When the graph is a <u>straight line</u>, there is a <u>linear relationship</u> between force and extension.
- This shows force and extension are <u>directly proportional</u>.
- The <u>gradient</u> of the <u>straight line</u> is equal to k, the <u>spring constant</u>.
- When the line begins to <u>bend</u>, the relationship is now <u>non-linear</u>. Force and extension are <u>no longer</u> directly proportional.
- Point P on the graph (when the line starts to bend) is the <u>limit of proportionality</u>. <u>Past</u> this point, the equation $F = ke$ is <u>no longer</u> true.

I could make a joke, but I don't want to stretch myself...

Make sure you don't skip any bits of this page — it's all rather important. Have a crack at this question.

Q1 A spring is fixed at one end and a force of 1 N is applied to the other end, causing it to stretch. The spring extends by 2 cm. Calculate the spring constant of the spring. [4 marks]

Quick Quiz

Investigating Springs

You can do an easy experiment to see exactly how adding masses to a spring causes it to stretch.

You Can Investigate the Link Between Force and Extension — PRACTICAL

One way to test the link between force and extension is to add masses to the end of a spring and record its extension.

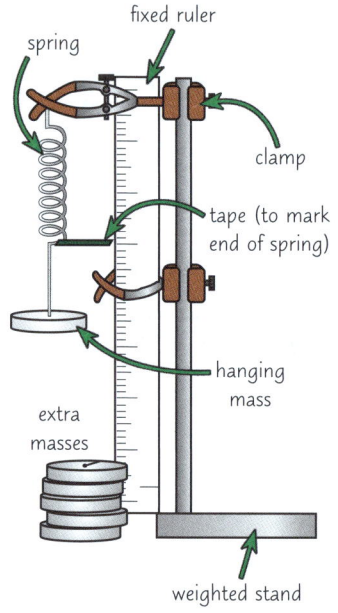

1) Set up the apparatus as shown in the diagram, but with no masses hanging from the spring to start with.
2) Measure the exact mass of each of the masses using a mass balance.
3) Calculate the weight of each mass (the force applied) using $W = mg$ (p.49).
4) Measure the original (natural) length of the spring.
5) Add a mass to the spring and allow it to come to rest.
6) Record the force and measure the new length of the spring.
7) Find the extension: 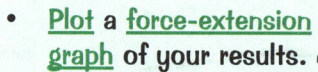 extension = new length − original length
8) Repeat steps 5 to 7 until you've added all the masses.

- Plot a force-extension graph of your results.
- You should make sure you have at least 5 measurements before the limit of proportionality (where the line starts to curve).

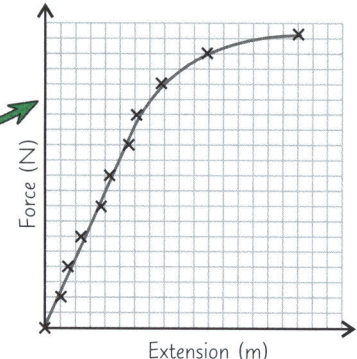

You Can Work Out Energy Stored for Linear Relationships

1) If a spring is not stretched past its limit of proportionality, the work done in stretching the spring can be found using:
2) For an elastic deformation, this formula can be used to calculate the energy stored in a spring's elastic potential energy store.
3) It's also the energy transferred to the spring as it's deformed (or the energy transferred by the spring as it returns to its original shape).

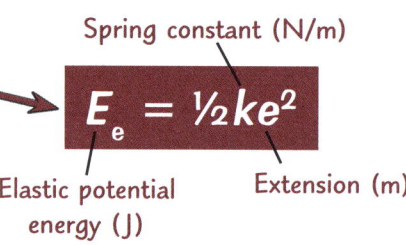

$$E_e = \tfrac{1}{2}ke^2$$

Elastic potential energy (J), Spring constant (N/m), Extension (m)

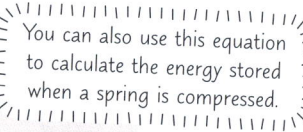
You can also use this equation to calculate the energy stored when a spring is compressed.

EXAMPLE

A spring with a spring constant of 500 N/m extends elastically by 10 cm. It doesn't pass its limit of proportionality. Calculate the amount of energy stored in its elastic potential energy store.

1) First, you need to convert the spring's extension into metres. 100 cm = 1 m, so divide by 100: 10 cm = 10 ÷ 100 = 0.1 m
2) Then put in the numbers you've been given. $E_e = \tfrac{1}{2}ke^2 = 0.5 \times 500 \times 0.1^2 = 2.5$ J

Time to spring into action and learn all this...

Make sure you know how to carry out the experiment above — you might be asked about it in your exam.

Q1 A spring with a spring constant of 25 N/m extends elastically by 4.0 cm.
    Calculate the amount of energy stored in its elastic potential energy store.   [3 marks]

Topic 5a — Forces, Moments and Pressure

Moments

Quick Quiz

A <u>force</u> can cause an object to <u>turn</u> around a <u>point</u>. Like the <u>axle</u> of a wheel or the <u>hinge</u> of a door.

A Moment is the Turning Effect of a Force

1) A force can cause an object to <u>rotate</u>.
2) The <u>turning effect</u> of a force is called its <u>moment</u>.
3) The <u>size</u> of the <u>moment</u> of a force depends on the <u>size of the force</u> and the <u>perpendicular distance</u> from the pivot.
4) The force applied to an object has a '<u>line of action</u>' — this is just the <u>direction</u> the force acts.
5) So in the diagram on the right and on the exam, the distance you use for calculating a moment is just the <u>distance</u> between the point where the <u>force</u> acts and the <u>pivot</u>. This is the perpendicular distance.

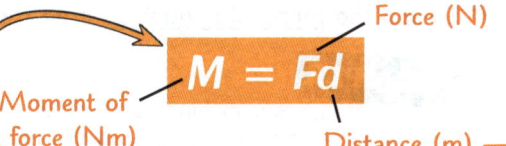

$M = Fd$

Moment of a force (Nm)
Force (N)
Distance (m) — perpendicular distance from the pivot to the line of action of the force

6) One example of a moment is using a <u>spanner</u> to <u>turn</u> a <u>nut</u>:
   - A <u>force</u> is applied (from your hand and arm) to the <u>end</u> of the handle on the spanner.
   - This force causes a <u>moment</u> on the nut.
   - The nut acts as a <u>pivot</u> — the point of turning.
   - If you applied a force at a <u>shorter distance</u> (e.g. <u>halfway</u> down the handle), you would find it <u>harder</u> to turn the spanner. This is because a <u>smaller distance</u> from the pivot produces a <u>smaller moment</u>.
   - You would also find it more <u>difficult</u> if you applied <u>less force</u> (e.g. if you didn't <u>push</u> as hard on the handle). A <u>bigger</u> force means a <u>bigger</u> turning effect.

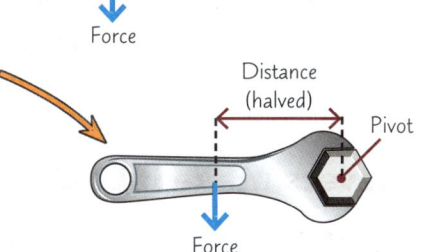

Line of action is vertically downwards — Distance — Pivot — Force

Distance (halved) — Pivot — Force

EXAMPLE

A force of 20 N is applied to a gate at a perpendicular distance of 1.5 m from its hinge. What is the size of the moment of the force on the gate?

Put the values for <u>force</u> and <u>distance</u> into the equation: $M = Fd = 20 \times 1.5 = 30$ Nm

MATHS SKILLS

An Object Doesn't Turn When it's Balanced

no more clocks!

- An object is <u>balanced</u> when the moment in <u>one direction</u> about a pivot is <u>equal</u> to the moment in the <u>other direction</u> about the same pivot.
- If an object is <u>balanced</u>, then:

Total anticlockwise moment = Total clockwise moment

- If two people sit on <u>either end</u> of a seesaw and it <u>doesn't move</u>, the seesaw is <u>balanced</u>.
- One person causes a moment in a <u>clockwise</u> direction.
- The other person causes a moment in an <u>anticlockwise</u> direction.
- These moments are <u>equal</u>, so the seesaw <u>doesn't turn</u>.

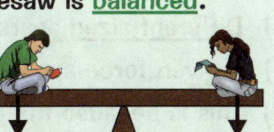

Physics revision — it couldn't be over a moment too soon...

Push a door near the doorknob and it'll open a lot easier than if you push it near its hinge. That's moments.

Q1   A force is applied to a door handle at a perpendicular distance of 6.0 cm from the pivot. This produces a moment of 1.44 Nm. Calculate the size of the force that was applied.   [4 marks]

Q1 Video Solution

More on Moments

Once you can calculate moments, you can work out if things are balanced. Useful thing, physics.

You Need to Be Able to Work Out Moments on a Balanced Object

- You can use the idea of balanced moments to calculate things you don't know.
- Using the moments equation from the previous page, you can find an unknown force or distance.

EXAMPLE

A 4 m long steel beam weighs 1000 N. The weight acts from the centre of the beam. The beam rests on a pivot at one end. There is a rope attached at the other end and the upwards force due to the tension in the rope balances the beam. Calculate the size of the force in the rope.

1) Find the total clockwise moment (due to the weight of the beam).

   $M = Fd = 1000 \times 2 = 2000$ Nm

2) Find the total anticlockwise moment (due to the tension in the rope).

   $d = 2 + 2 = 4$, so $M = Fd = T \times 4$

3) For the beam to balance, the total clockwise moment (from step 1) must equal the total anticlockwise moment (from step 2).

4) Rearrange for T.

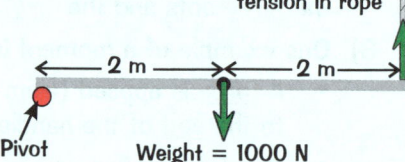

$2000 = T \times 4$

$T = 2000 \div 4 = 500$ N

Levers Make it Easier for us to Do Work

- Levers increase the distance between the pivot and where the force is applied.
- Remember $M = Fd$. So for a bigger distance, you need less force to get the same moment.
- If you have to apply less force, it makes it easier to do work (p.50).
- So levers make it easier to do things like lift a load or turn a nut.

Example — a wheelbarrow has handles that act as levers

1) The wheelbarrow has a pivot at the wheel.
2) The weight of the load applies a moment about this pivot.
3) To lift the load, you need to apply a moment just larger than this moment.
4) Lifting from the handle makes it easier to lift the load.
5) This is because less force is needed to provide a large enough moment to lift the load.

Gears Transmit Rotational Effects

1) Gears are circular discs with 'teeth' around their edges.
2) Their teeth fit together so that turning one gear causes another one to turn, in the opposite direction.
3) They can transmit (carry across) the rotational effect (moment) of a force from one place to another.
4) Different sized gears affect the size of the moment of the force.
5) A given force applied to a larger gear will cause a bigger moment.
6) This is because the distance to the pivot (shown by the blue arrows) is greater.
7) When this moment is transmitted to a smaller gear, it will turn faster than the larger gear.

Don't get in a spin — gear up for more about forces...

Moments can be used in lots of different situations, so get your head around them sooner rather than later.

Q1 Your brother weighs 300 N and sits 2 m from the pivot of a seesaw. If you weigh 600 N, what distance from the pivot, on the other side of the seesaw, should you sit to balance it? [3 marks]

54   Topic 5a — Forces, Moments and Pressure

Fluid Pressure and Atmospheric Pressure

Hopefully reading this page will make you feel a little less pressured about your physics exam.

Pressure is the Force per Unit Area

1) A fluid is a substance that can 'flow' because the particles in it are able to move around.
2) This means that liquids and gases are fluids.
3) As the particles move around, they collide with (hit) surfaces and other particles.
4) When the particles collide with an object, they apply a force to it.
5) Pressure is the force per unit area, so the particles apply a pressure (p.37).
6) The pressure of a fluid means a force is applied normal (at a right angle) to any surface the fluid touches.
7) You can calculate the pressure at the surface of a fluid by using:

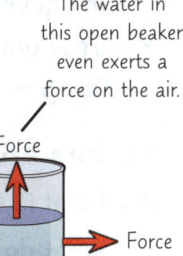

The water in this open beaker even exerts a force on the air.

$$p = \frac{F}{A}$$

Pressure in pascals (Pa) — Force normal to a surface (N) — Area of that surface (m²)

EXAMPLE

A fluid is in a container with a surface area of 0.50 m². The fluid pressure on the walls of the container is 9.2 kPa. Calculate the force normal to the surface of the container.

1) Convert the units for pressure into Pa. (1 kPa = 1000 Pa, so multiply by 1000.)
   9.2 kPa = 9.2 × 1000 = 9200 Pa
2) Rearrange $p = F \div A$ for F.
   $p = F \div A \rightarrow F = p \times A$
3) Put in the numbers to calculate the force.
   $F = 9200 \times 0.50 = 4600$ N

Atmospheric Pressure Decreases with Height

1) The atmosphere is a layer of air that goes all around the Earth.
2) This layer is thin compared to the size of the Earth.
3) There is a pressure created by the atmosphere as air molecules collide with surfaces.
4) This is called atmospheric pressure.
5) As the altitude (the height above the surface of the Earth) increases, atmospheric pressure decreases.
6) This is because the atmosphere gets less dense (the air molecules become more spaced out).
7) This means there are fewer collisions of air particles with a surface at that height — the pressure decreases.
8) The number of air molecules above a surface also decreases the higher up you go.
9) This means the weight of the air above a surface decreases the higher up you go, so this also causes the pressure to decrease.

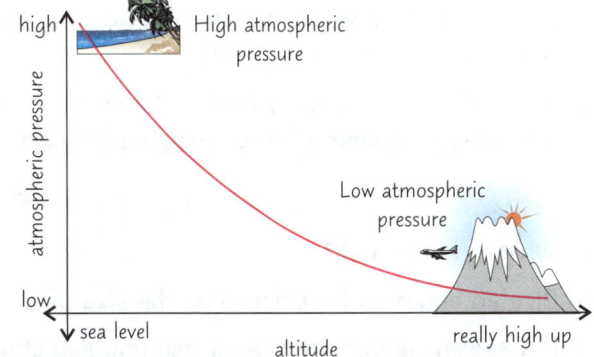

Next time you're feeling pressured, go on a hike...

Pressure = force ÷ area doesn't just apply to fluids. It's true anywhere that a force is acting on an area.

Q1 The fluid pressure of a gas in a container is 120 000 Pa. The total force normal to the surfaces of the container is 220 000 N. Calculate the surface area of the container. [3 marks]

Revision Summary Test for Topic 5a

There's not a moment to waste — if you want to become a force to be reckoned with, you can:
- Tackle the revision summary test below, or scan the QR code to do it online. The questions are hard, but they'll show you how well you really know your stuff.
- Track your progress online and see which areas need more work.
- Compare your answers with sample answers for the test here: www.cgpbooks.co.uk/Mass

Forces and Work Done (p.48-50)

1) What is the difference between a vector and a scalar quantity? Give four examples of each.
2) What do the length and direction of an arrow used to represent a vector tell you?
3) What is a force?
4) What is the difference between a contact and a non-contact force? Give three examples of each.
5) Give two differences between mass and weight.
6) Define the centre of mass of an object in terms of weight.
7) What is the formula for calculating the weight of an object from its mass?
8) What is a resultant force?
9) Two forces are acting on an object in a straight line. How do you calculate the resultant force when the forces are acting: a) in the same direction, b) in opposite directions?
10) Why does the temperature of an object increase when it is pushed along a rough surface?
11) What is the formula for the work done by a force when it moves an object?
12) How many joules of work is 1 Nm equal to?

Elasticity and Springs (p.51-52)

13) What is the difference between elastic and inelastic deformation?
14) Give the equation that links force, extension and the spring constant of an object.
15) What is the limit of proportionality? Where is it on a graph of force against extension?
16) Describe an experiment you could do to investigate the relationship between the force applied to a spring and how much it extends by.
17) What quantity does each letter represent in the formula $E_e = ½ke^2$? Give the units for each quantity.
18) True or false? The formula $E_e = ½ke^2$ can be used to calculate the energy transferred to a spring as it's elastically deformed.

Moments and Fluid Pressure (p. 53-55)

19) What is a moment?
20) Give an equation for calculating the size of the moment of a force.
21) If a seesaw is balanced, what can you say about the moments acting on it?
22) Describe how a lever can increase the moment of a force.
23) True or false? A larger gear will produce a smaller moment for a given force.
24) In what direction does the force from the pressure of a fluid act on the walls of its container?
25) What is the formula for the pressure exerted at the surface of a fluid? Give the units of pressure.
26) How does the size of the atmosphere compare to the size of the Earth?
27) Give two reasons why atmospheric pressure decreases with height above the Earth.

Topic 5b — Forces and Motion

Distance, Displacement, Speed and Velocity

Time for a quick recap on distance and speed. You'll probably race through this page. On your marks...

Distance and Displacement are Both How Far You've Travelled

- Distance is just how far an object has moved.
- Distance is a scalar quantity (p.48), so it doesn't involve direction.
- Displacement is a vector quantity.
- It measures the distance and direction in a straight line from an object's starting point to its finishing point.
- The direction could be in relation to a point, e.g. towards the school.

> If you walk 5 m north, then 5 m south, your displacement is 0 m but the distance travelled is 10 m.

Speed is a Scalar, Velocity is a Vector

> SPEED is just how fast you're going (e.g. 30 mph or 20 m/s).
> VELOCITY is speed in a given direction, e.g. 30 mph north or 20 m/s to the right.

1) To measure the speed of an object that's moving with a constant speed, you can time how long it takes the object to travel a certain distance. Make sure you use the correct equipment (see p.107).
2) You can then calculate the object's speed using this formula:

> distance travelled (m) = speed (m/s) × time (s)

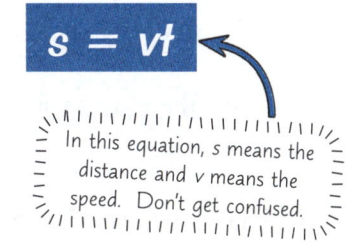

$s = vt$

In this equation, s means the distance and v means the speed. Don't get confused.

3) Objects rarely travel at a constant speed.
4) When you walk, run or travel in a car, your speed tends to vary.
5) In these cases, the formula above gives the average (mean) speed during that time.

You Need to Know Some Typical Everyday Speeds

- Lots of things affect the speed something travels at, but you need to remember these typical speeds:

	Walking	Running	Cycling	Car	Train	Plane
Typical speed	1.5 m/s	3 m/s	6 m/s	25 m/s	30 m/s	250 m/s

- The speed at which a person can walk, run or cycle depends on things like:
  - their fitness
  - their age
  - the distance they've travelled
  - the terrain (what type of ground they are on)

- The speeds of sound and wind also vary.
- A typical speed for sound in air is 330 m/s.

Ah, speed equals distance over time — that old chestnut...

Remember those typical speeds of objects — you might need to use them to make estimates.

Q1 A sprinter runs 200 m in 25 s. Calculate his speed. [3 marks]

Acceleration

Wait, we're getting faster now? Keep calm — it's a marathon, not a sprint...

Acceleration is How Quickly You're Speeding Up

1) Acceleration is the change in velocity in a certain amount of time.
2) You can find the average acceleration of an object using this formula:

$$a = \frac{\Delta v}{t}$$

Acceleration (m/s²) — Change in velocity (m/s) — Time taken (s)

3) Deceleration (when something slows down) is just negative acceleration.

You Need to be Able to Estimate Accelerations

You might have to estimate the acceleration of an object. To do this, you need the typical speeds from the previous page.

An estimate is just a guess using rough numbers for things.

EXAMPLE A woman gets onto a bike and accelerates to a typical speed from stationary in 10 seconds. Estimate the acceleration of the bicycle.

1) First, give a sensible speed for the bicycle to be travelling at.

The typical speed of a bike is about 6 m/s. The bicycle accelerates in 10 s.

2) Put these numbers into the acceleration equation.

$a = \Delta v \div t$
$= 6 \div 10 = 0.6$ m/s²

3) The ~ symbol just means it's an approximate answer.

So the acceleration is ~0.6 m/s²

Uniform Acceleration Just Means a Constant Acceleration

- You can use this equation for uniform acceleration:

$$v^2 - u^2 = 2as$$

Final velocity (m/s) — Initial velocity (m/s) — Acceleration (m/s²) — Distance (m)

Be careful — both the velocities in this equation are squared.

Initial velocity is just the starting velocity of the object.

EXAMPLE A van travelling at 23 m/s starts decelerating uniformly at 2.0 m/s² as it heads towards a built-up area 112 m away. What will its speed be when it reaches the built-up area?

1) First, rearrange the equation so v^2 is on one side. $v^2 = u^2 + 2as$
2) Now put the numbers in — remember a is negative because it's a deceleration. $v^2 = 23^2 + (2 \times -2.0 \times 112)$
   $= 81$
3) Finally, square root the whole thing. $v = \sqrt{81} = 9$ m/s

- Acceleration due to gravity (g) is uniform for objects falling freely.
- It's roughly equal to 9.8 m/s² near the Earth's surface.

Uniform problems — get a clip-on tie or use the equation above...

You might not be told what equation to use in the exam, so make sure you can spot when to use the one for uniform acceleration. Make a list of the information you're given to help you see what to do.

Q1 A ball is dropped from a height, h, above the ground. The speed of the ball just before it hits the ground is 7.0 m/s. Calculate the height the ball is dropped from. (acceleration due to gravity ≈ 9.8 m/s²)   [3 marks]

Distance-Time Graphs

Quick Quiz

You need to be able to draw and describe distance-time graphs. And no, it's not enough to just say it's a wiggly line that looks a bit like a ski slope. Examiners can be so picky...

You Can Show Journeys on Distance-Time Graphs

1) If an object moves in a straight line, the distance it travels can be plotted on a distance-time graph.
2) You may be asked to draw a distance-time graph for a journey.
3) Or you might have to describe the journey of an object if you're shown it on a distance-time graph:

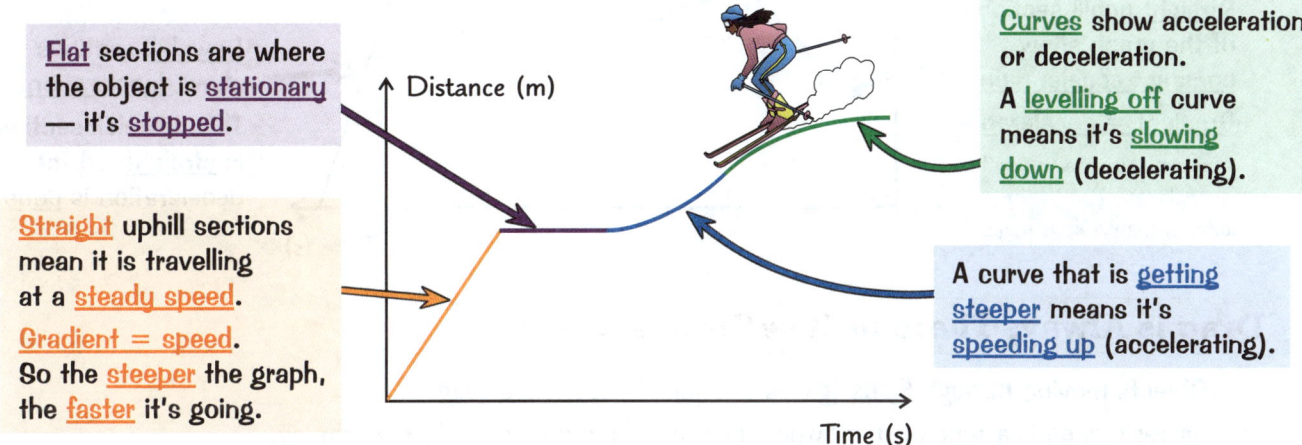

- Flat sections are where the object is stationary — it's stopped.
- Straight uphill sections mean it is travelling at a steady speed. Gradient = speed. So the steeper the graph, the faster it's going.
- Curves show acceleration or deceleration. A levelling off curve means it's slowing down (decelerating).
- A curve that is getting steeper means it's speeding up (accelerating).

You Can Calculate Speed From a Distance-Time Graph

The gradient of a distance-time graph tells you the speed of the object.

EXAMPLE The distance-time graph for a car travelling at a steady speed is shown below. Calculate the speed of the car using the graph.

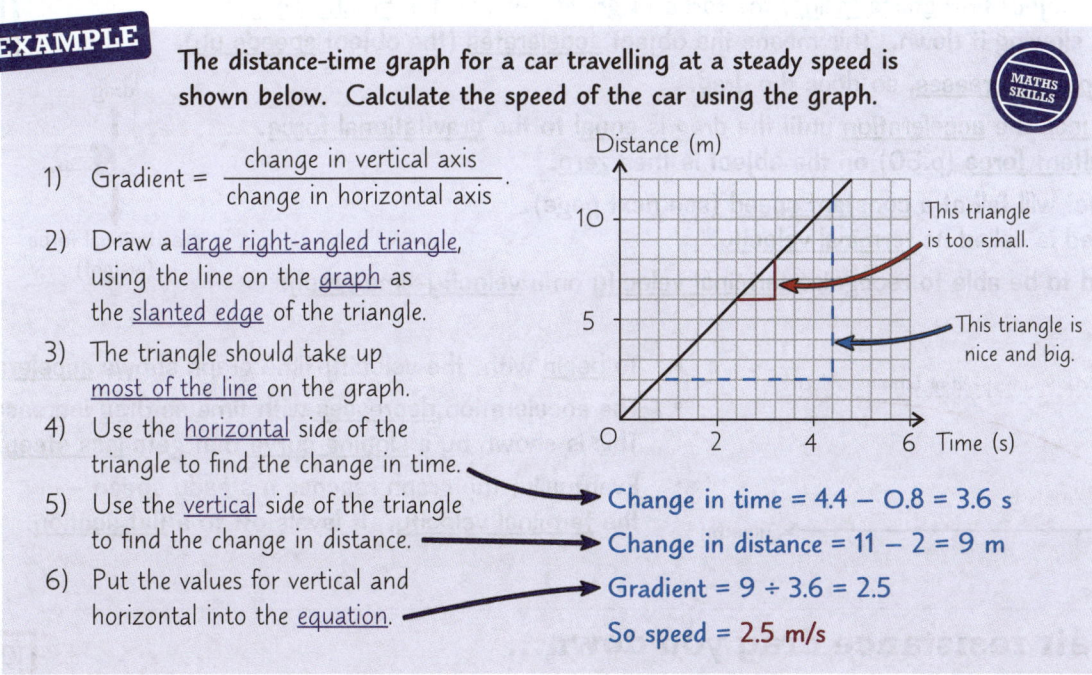

1) Gradient = $\dfrac{\text{change in vertical axis}}{\text{change in horizontal axis}}$.
2) Draw a large right-angled triangle, using the line on the graph as the slanted edge of the triangle.
3) The triangle should take up most of the line on the graph.
4) Use the horizontal side of the triangle to find the change in time.
5) Use the vertical side of the triangle to find the change in distance.
6) Put the values for vertical and horizontal into the equation.

Change in time = 4.4 − 0.8 = 3.6 s
Change in distance = 11 − 2 = 9 m
Gradient = 9 ÷ 3.6 = 2.5
So speed = 2.5 m/s

Understanding motion graphs can be a real uphill struggle...

Make sure you know how to use distance-time graphs to find an object's speed.

Q1   Sketch the distance-time graph for an object that accelerates, then travels at a steady speed, and then comes to a stop. [3 marks]

Q1 Video Solution

Velocity-Time Graphs and Terminal Velocity

This page is on velocity-time graphs and terminal velocity. Just when you thought it couldn't get more exciting.

Journeys Can be Shown on a Velocity-Time Graph

How an object's velocity changes as it travels can be plotted on a velocity-time graph.
You might have to draw a velocity-time graph for a journey, or describe a journey from a graph:

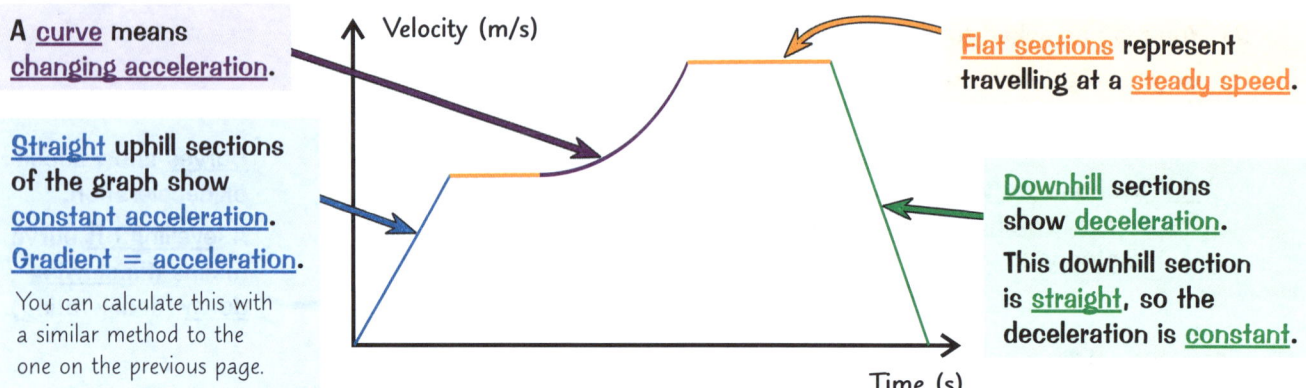

A curve means changing acceleration.

Straight uphill sections of the graph show constant acceleration.
Gradient = acceleration.
You can calculate this with a similar method to the one on the previous page.

Flat sections represent travelling at a steady speed.

Downhill sections show deceleration. This downhill section is straight, so the deceleration is constant.

Drag is Always There to Slow Things Down

- Objects moving through fluids (gases or liquids) experience drag.
- Air resistance is a type of drag, which acts on objects moving through the air.
- Drag acts in the opposite direction to the movement of the object, so it slows the object down.
- The faster an object is moving, the more drag it experiences.

Objects Falling Through Fluids Reach a Terminal Velocity

1) When an object first starts falling, the force of gravity (weight) is much larger than the drag slowing it down. This means the object accelerates (the object speeds up).
2) As the speed increases, so does the drag.
3) This reduces the acceleration until the drag is equal to the gravitational force. The resultant force (p.50) on the object is then zero.
4) The object will fall at a constant speed (see next page). This speed is called its terminal velocity.
5) You need to be able to recognise terminal velocity on a velocity-time graph:

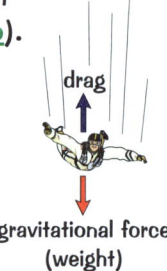

gravitational force (weight)

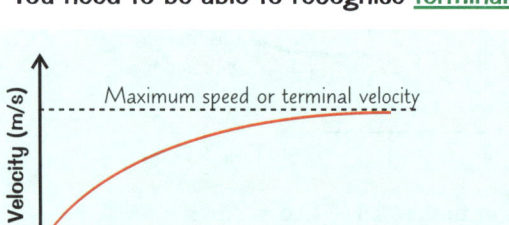

- To begin with, the velocity-time graph shows acceleration.
- The acceleration decreases with time as drag increases. This is shown by a sloping curve that gets less steep.
- Eventually, the graph reaches a steady speed — the terminal velocity. It levels off to a flat section.

Don't let air resistance drag you down...

Make sure you know what a velocity-time graph is telling you about the acceleration of an object.

Q1 Sketch a velocity-time graph for an object that travels at a constant speed, then accelerates at a constant rate, then moves at a constant speed (that is different to the initial speed). [3 marks]

Q2 A stationary car starts accelerating increasingly for 10 s until it reaches a speed of 20 m/s. It travels at this speed for 20 s until the driver sees a hazard and brakes. He decelerates uniformly, coming to a stop 4 s after braking. Draw the velocity-time graph for this journey. [3 marks]

60 Topic 5b — Forces and Motion

Newton's First and Second Laws

In the 1660s, a chap called Isaac Newton worked out his dead useful Laws of Motion. Here are the first two.

Newton's First Law — a Resultant Force is Needed to Change Motion

If the resultant force on a stationary object is zero, the object will remain stationary.
If the resultant force on a moving object is zero, it'll carry on moving at the same velocity.

See p.50 for a reminder on resultant forces.

- So, when a bus (or anything else) is stationary or moving at a constant velocity (same speed and direction) then either:
  a) there are no resistive or driving forces acting on it, or
  b) the resistive and driving forces acting on it must be balanced.

- The velocity will only change if there's a non-zero resultant force.
- A non-zero resultant force produces a change in motion in the direction of the force.
- This change in motion can take five different forms: starting, stopping, speeding up, slowing down and changing direction.

Newton's Second Law — Acceleration is Proportional to Resultant Force

1) The larger the resultant force acting on an object, the more the object accelerates.
2) The force acting on an object and the acceleration are directly proportional. You can write this as $F \propto a$.
3) Acceleration is also inversely proportional to the mass of the object.
4) So an object with a larger mass will accelerate less than one with a smaller mass, for a given force.
5) There's a formula that describes Newton's Second Law:

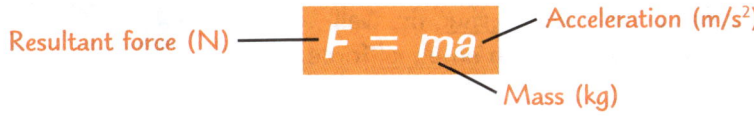

Resultant force (N) — $F = ma$ — Acceleration (m/s^2)
Mass (kg)

6) You can use Newton's Second Law to get an idea of the forces involved in everyday transport.
7) Large forces are needed to produce large accelerations.

EXAMPLE Estimate the resultant force on a car as it accelerates from rest to a typical speed.

1) Estimate the speed of the car (see p.57) and the time taken to reach that speed.

   A typical speed of a car is ~25 m/s. It takes ~10 s to reach this.

2) Use the speed and time taken to estimate the acceleration of the car.

   So $a = \Delta v \div t$
   $= 25 \div 10 = 2.5$ m/s^2

   Remember, the ~ sign means approximately.

3) Estimate the mass of the car.

   Mass of a car is ~1000 kg.

4) Put these numbers into Newton's 2nd Law.

   $F = ma = 1000 \times 2.5 = 2500$ N
   So the resultant force is ~2500 N

Accelerate your learning — force yourself to revise...

It'll be useful to get your head around both these laws, before moving on to Newton's third and final law.

Q1 Find the force needed for a 70 kg man on a 10 kg bike to accelerate at 0.25 m/s^2. [2 marks]

Newton's Third Law

Newton's Third Law might seem simple on the surface, but it can get confusing quite quickly. Make sure you really understand what's going on with it — especially if an object is in equilibrium.

Newton's Third Law Involves Equal and Opposite Forces

When two objects interact, the forces they exert on each other are equal and opposite.

1) If you push something, say a shopping trolley, the trolley will push back against you, just as hard.
2) And as soon as you stop pushing, so does the trolley. Kinda clever really.
3) The slightly tricky thing to get your head round is this — if the forces are always equal, how does anything ever go anywhere?
4) The important thing to remember is that the two forces are acting on different objects.

Example 1 — A pair of skaters

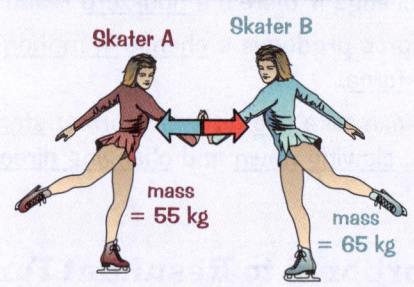

- Skater A pushes on skater B.
- Skater A feels an equal and opposite force from skater B's hand.
- Both skaters feel the same sized force, in opposite directions.
- This causes them to accelerate away from each other.
- Skater A will be accelerated more than skater B, because she has a smaller mass.
- Remember $a = F \div m$.

Example 2 — A man pushing a wall

- This is Newton's Third Law for an equilibrium situation.
- As the man pushes the wall, there is a normal contact force (p.48) acting back on him. These two forces are the same size.
- As the man applies a force and pushes the wall, the wall 'pushes back' on him with an equal force.

Be Careful When Objects are in Equilibrium

Not every pair of forces that are 'equal and opposite' is an example of Newton's Third Law...

Example 3 — A book resting on a table

1) The book is in equilibrium because the resultant force on the book is zero.
2) The weight of the book pulls it down.
3) The normal contact force from the table pushes it up.
4) But this is NOT Newton's Third Law because:
   - The forces are different types.
   - The forces are both acting on the book.

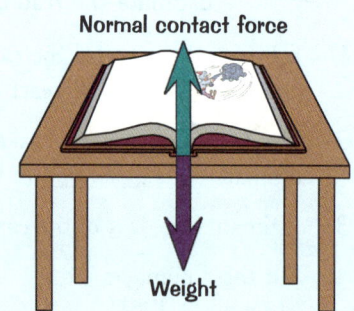

Newton's fourth law — revision must be done with tea...

Thankfully, Newton only came up with three laws that you have to learn, although his third law can be quite tricky. Take your time, look at each object one by one, and work out all the forces acting on it.

Q1 A car moves at a constant velocity along a road, so that it is in equilibrium. Give an example of a pair of forces that demonstrate Newton's Third Law in this situation. [1 mark]

PRACTICAL — **Investigating Motion**

Quick Quiz

Read on for some snazzy methods you could use to investigate Newton's Second Law in the lab...

You can Investigate how Mass and Force Affect Acceleration

- This method uses light gates (there's more about how light gates work on page 109).
- The mass, *m*, that you'll be accelerating is the total mass of the trolley, hook and the added masses.
- You can measure *m* using a mass balance.
- The force, *F*, causing the acceleration is the weight of the hook and the masses on the hook (not the trolley).
- To find *F*, first measure the mass of the hook and any masses on the hook. Then multiply this by *g* (as $W = mg$, see page 49).
- This is how you find the acceleration, *a*:

Method

1) Set up the apparatus like in the diagram above — the trolley is connected to a piece of string that goes over a pulley and is connected on the other side to the hook.
2) Mark a starting line on the table the trolley is on. This is so that the trolley always travels the same distance to the light gate.
3) Place the trolley on the starting line.
4) Hold the trolley so the string is tight and not touching the table. Then release it.
5) Record the acceleration measured by the light gate as the trolley passes through it.

Instead of using light gates, you can do a similar experiment with a stopwatch and chalk lines marked on the table.

Add Masses to Change the Mass, Transfer Masses to Change the Force

Investigating Mass

To investigate the effect of mass on acceleration, change the mass but keep the force the same.

1) The force is the weight of the hook and any masses on the hook. So don't add masses to the hook, or you'll change the force.
2) Add masses to the trolley one at a time to increase the total mass being accelerated.
3) Record the acceleration, *a*, for each total mass, *m*.
4) You should find that as the mass goes up, the acceleration goes down.
5) This agrees with Newton's Second Law — mass and acceleration are inversely proportional.

Investigating Force

This time, you need to change the force without changing the total mass of the trolley, hook and masses.

1) Start with all the extra masses loaded onto the trolley.
2) Move the masses from the trolley to the hook one at a time. This will keep the total mass the same but increase the force.
3) Measure the acceleration for each new force.
4) You should find that as the force goes up, the acceleration goes up.
5) This agrees with Newton's Second Law — force and acceleration are directly proportional.

My acceleration increases with nearby cake...

Learn the ins and outs of that experiment — you could be asked about any part of it, or to describe the whole thing.

Q1   In the experiment above, describe the force that accelerates the trolley.   [1 mark]

Stopping Distance and Thinking Distance

This page is all about cars, but unfortunately it's not as fun as it sounds... It's even better — it's about safety...

Stopping Distance is the Total Distance it Takes for a Vehicle to Stop

1) In an emergency, a driver may perform an emergency stop.
2) During an emergency stop, the maximum force is applied by the brakes. This is so the vehicle stops in the shortest possible distance.
3) This distance is the vehicle's stopping distance. It is found by:

| Stopping Distance | | Thinking Distance | + | Braking Distance |

> The heavier a vehicle is, or the faster it's travelling, the longer its stopping distance will be. There's more about this on page 66.

Thinking Distance	How far the car travels during the driver's reaction time. The reaction time is the time between the driver seeing a hazard and applying the brakes.
Braking Distance	The distance taken to stop under the braking force (once the brakes are applied).

Stopping Distances Affect Safety

- The longer it takes to perform an emergency stop, the higher the risk of crashing into whatever's in front. So the shorter a vehicle's stopping distance, the safer it is.
- This means anything that affects either the driver's thinking distance or the car's braking distance will affect safety.
- You need to be able to describe how different factors can affect the safety of a journey.
- For example, how driving if you're tired is unsafe. There's more on this below and on the next page.

Thinking Distance is Determined by the Driver's Reactions

Thinking distance is affected by:

Speed
1) The faster you're going, the further you'll travel in the time you take to react.
2) This increases your thinking (and so stopping) distance.
3) Roads that have a higher risk of hazards have a lower speed limit to reduce stopping distances.
4) Driving above the speed limit is unsafe.

Reaction Time
1) Driving while tired, or under the influence of drugs or alcohol, is unsafe as it makes you slower to react.
2) This increases your reaction time, which increases your thinking distance.
3) This means your stopping distance is longer, so you're more likely to crash.

Distractions can also affect reaction time, or your ability to react. For example, a driver is likely to take longer to spot a hazard if they are on their phone. This can be very dangerous.

Now, where's that brake pedal again?...

If you want to stop fast — think fast, then breakfast (mmmm)...

Before moving on, make sure you can explain the factors that affect a person's thinking distance.

Q1 Give one factor that affects thinking distance. [1 mark]

64 Topic 5b — Forces and Motion

Braking Distance

You need to know what energy changes occur when the drivers applies the brakes.

Braking Distance Depends on a Few Different Factors

SPEED	For a given braking force, the faster the vehicle travels, the longer it takes to stop.
WEATHER OR ROAD SURFACE	Water, ice, oil or leaves on the road all reduce grip. If there is less grip between a vehicle's tyres and the road, it can cause the vehicle to skid. Skidding increases the braking distance of a car.
CONDITION OF TYRES	Bald tyres (ones that don't have any tread left) cannot get rid of water in wet conditions. This leads to them skidding on top of the water.
CONDITION OF BRAKES	If brakes are worn, they won't be able to apply as much force. So it takes longer to stop a vehicle travelling at a given speed (see below).

Icy conditions increase the chance of skidding. This increases braking distance, which increases the stopping distance. So more room should be left between cars to be safe.

Braking Relies on Friction Between the Brakes and Wheels

- When the brake pedal is pushed, brake pads are pressed onto the wheels.
- The contact with the brake pads causes friction, which causes work to be done (p.50).
- Remember, when work is done, energy is transferred (p.4).
- Energy is transferred from the vehicle's kinetic energy store to the thermal energy stores of the brakes.
- The brakes increase in temperature.

1) To stop a vehicle, the brakes must transfer all of the energy from the kinetic store, so:

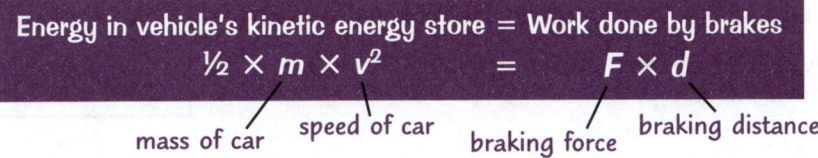

Energy in vehicle's kinetic energy store = Work done by brakes

$$\tfrac{1}{2} \times m \times v^2 = F \times d$$

(mass of car, speed of car, braking force, braking distance)

Very large decelerations can be dangerous because they may cause brakes to overheat. This means the brakes won't work as well. Very large decelerations may also cause the vehicle to skid.

2) The faster a vehicle is going, the more energy it has in its kinetic energy store. So more work needs to be done to stop it.
3) This means that as the speed of a vehicle increases, the force needed to make it stop within a certain distance also increases.
4) A larger braking force means a larger deceleration.

Replace bald tyres — or get them a hat...

If you ever find yourself in charge of a vehicle, hopefully you'll remember this page and it'll help you to be safer on the roads. Even if you don't ever plan on driving, this page is still important for your exams.

Q1 A car with a mass of 1000 kg is travelling in a straight line at a speed of 10 m/s. The driver spots a hazard and applies the brakes. The car is 50 m from the hazard when the brakes are applied. Calculate the minimum braking force required for the car to stop before the hazard. [5 marks]

More on Stopping Distances

So now you know what affects stopping distances, let's have a look at the facts and figures.

Leave Enough Space to Stop

1) The figures below for typical stopping distances are from the Highway Code:

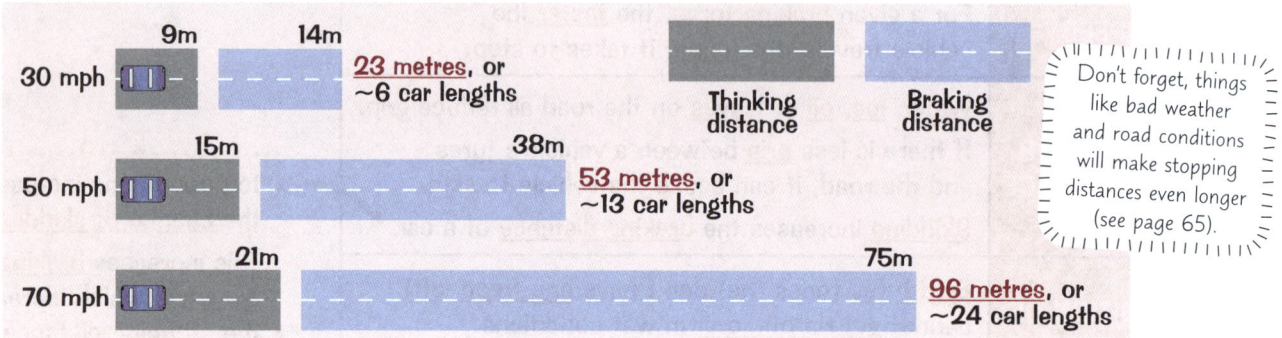

Don't forget, things like bad weather and road conditions will make stopping distances even longer (see page 65).

2) To avoid an accident, drivers need to leave enough space between their car and the one in front.
3) 'Enough space' means at least the stopping distance for whatever speed they're going at.

Speed Affects Braking Distance More Than Thinking Distance

THINKING DISTANCE increases at the same rate as the speed of a car.
If the speed doubles, the thinking distance also doubles. So far so good...

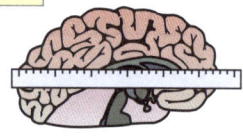

BRAKING DISTANCE is a bit more tricky. It increases faster and faster the more you speed up...
- If the speed (v) doubles, the kinetic energy ($\frac{1}{2}mv^2$) increases by a factor of (is multiplied by) 4.
- This is because v is squared in the kinetic energy equation ($2^2 = 4$).
- Kinetic energy is equal to the work done to stop the car, so work done also increases by a factor of 4.
- So for a constant braking force, if the speed doubles, the braking distance must increase by a factor of 4. This is because braking distance is a term in the work done equation (see previous page).

STOPPING DISTANCE is the thinking and braking distances added together.
The graph of stopping distance against speed for a car looks like this:
You need to be able to read values from graphs like these — they will all look similar to this one.

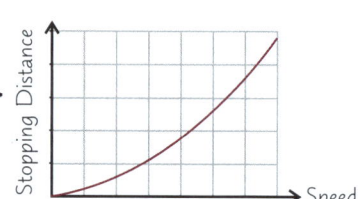

EXAMPLE
A graph of stopping distance against speed for two vehicles, A and B, is shown below.
Compare the stopping distance for both vehicles at a speed of 40 mph.

1) Read off the graph to find the stopping distance for each vehicle at 40 mph.
2) Find the difference between these two values.

Vehicle A stopping distance = 34 m
Vehicle B stopping distance = 41 m

41 − 34 = 7 m

So the stopping distance for vehicle B is 7 m longer than for vehicle A.

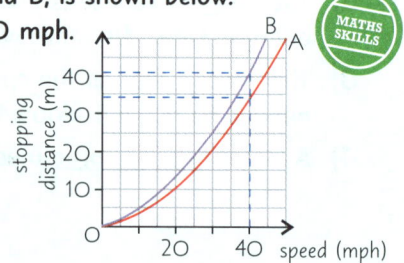

If you live life in the fast lane — leave plenty of space in front...

Make sure you're comfortable finding information from graphs of stopping distance against speed.

Q1 A driver performs an emergency stop. His thinking distance and braking distance are both 6 m. Estimate his total stopping distance if he had been travelling three times as quickly. [4 marks]

Topic 5b — Forces and Motion

Reaction Times

Go long! You need fast <u>reaction times</u> to avoid getting hit in the face when playing catch.

Reaction Time is How Long a Person Takes to React to an Event

1) <u>Everyone's</u> reaction time is <u>different</u>.
2) A <u>typical</u> reaction time is between <u>0.2</u> and <u>0.9 s</u>.
3) You can do <u>simple experiments</u> to investigate your reaction time — more on these below.

You can Measure Reaction Times with the Ruler Drop Test

- Reaction times are <u>so short</u> — you've got no chance measuring one with a <u>stopwatch</u>.
- One way of measuring reaction times is to use a <u>computer-based test</u>, e.g. <u>clicking a mouse</u> when the screen changes colour. Another way is the <u>ruler drop test</u>:

Method — Ruler Drop Test

1) Sit with your arm resting on the edge of a <u>table</u>.
2) Get someone else to hold a ruler so it <u>hangs between</u> your thumb and forefinger, lined up with <u>zero</u>.
3) You may need a <u>third person</u> to be at <u>eye level</u> with the <u>ruler</u> to check it's lined up.

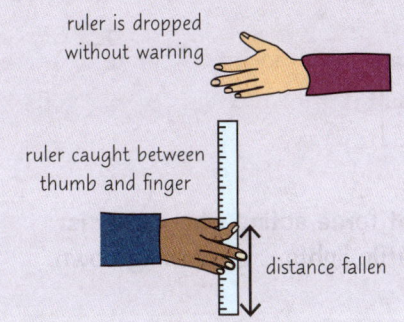

4) Without giving any warning, the person holding the ruler should <u>drop it</u>.
5) Close your thumb and finger to try to <u>catch the ruler as quickly as possible</u>.
6) The measurement on the ruler at the point where it is caught is <u>how far</u> the ruler dropped in the time it took you to react.
7) The <u>longer</u> the <u>distance</u>, the <u>longer</u> the <u>reaction time</u>.

It's <u>hard</u> to do this experiment <u>accurately</u>, but you can do a few things to <u>improve</u> your <u>results</u>:

- Do a lot of <u>repeats</u> and calculate an <u>average</u> reaction time.
- Add a <u>blob of modelling clay</u> to the bottom to help the ruler to fall straight down.
- Make it a <u>fair test</u> — use the <u>same ruler</u> for each repeat, and have the <u>same person</u> dropping it.

- You can calculate <u>how long</u> the ruler falls for (the <u>reaction time</u>) because <u>acceleration due to gravity</u> is <u>constant</u>.
- Use the formula $v^2 - u^2 = 2as$ (p.58) to find the <u>velocity</u> when the ruler is caught.
- Then use the equation $a = \Delta v \div t$ (p.58) to find the <u>time taken</u> for the ruler to drop.

Test a friend's reaction time by throwing this book at them...

Not really. Instead re-read this page and make sure you can describe the experiment. Much more fun.

Q1 Mark's reaction time is tested using the ruler drop test. He is tested in the early afternoon and at night. In the afternoon, he catches the ruler after it has fallen a distance of 16.2 cm. At night, he catches the ruler after it has fallen 18.5 cm.
   a) Did Mark have a faster reaction time in the early afternoon or at night? Explain your answer. [2 marks]
   b) Explain why Mark's thinking distance may be longer when driving at night. [2 marks]

Revision Summary Test for Topic 5b

Nearly at the finish line — don't let all those lovely facts race away from you, now. Go on and:
- Tackle the revision summary test below, or scan the QR code to do it online. The questions are hard, but they'll show you how well you really know your stuff.
- Track your progress online and see which areas need more work.
- Compare your answers with sample answers for the test here: www.cgpbooks.co.uk/Mass

Displacement, Velocity and Acceleration (p.57-58)

1) What does 'displacement' mean? How is it different from distance travelled?
2) Write a definition of velocity.
3) What is the formula for working out speed in terms of distance travelled and time? If the object's speed isn't constant, what does this formula give you?
4) What are typical speeds in m/s for: a) a person walking, b) a person running, c) a car, d) a train?
5) Define acceleration in terms of velocity and time. Write down the formula.
6) For what type of acceleration can you use the equation $v^2 - u^2 = 2as$?
7) What does it mean if the acceleration of an object is negative?

Motion Graphs and Terminal Velocity (p.59-60)

8) What does an upwards curve mean on a distance-time graph? What about a flat section?
9) What does the gradient represent for: a) a distance-time graph, b) a velocity-time graph?
10) What is air resistance? What direction does it act in?
11) What is terminal velocity?
12) Explain why an object reaches terminal velocity as it falls through air.

Newton's Laws and Investigating Motion (p.61-63)

13) What is Newton's First Law of motion?
14) Use Newton's First Law to decide whether or not there's a resultant force acting when a car is: a) travelling in a straight line at a steady speed, b) stopped at traffic lights, c) slowing down.
15) Write down Newton's Second Law of motion as a formula.
16) Two balls of different masses are fired from a slingshot. If the same force is applied each time, explain why the lighter ball will accelerate faster than the heavier ball.
17) A book is sitting at rest on a table. Give two reasons why the weight of the book and the normal reaction force of the table on the book are not a Newton's Third Law pair.
18) Describe an experimental set-up to test Newton's Second Law using a light gate and data logger.

Stopping Distances and Reaction Times (p.64-67)

19) Define thinking distance and braking distance.
20) How can you calculate stopping distance from thinking distance and braking distance?
21) Explain how thinking distance is affected by: a) higher speeds, b) a longer reaction time.
22) What are four factors that could increase the braking distance of a car?
23) What are two dangers of large decelerations whilst driving?
24) Use formulas for kinetic energy ($E_k = \frac{1}{2}mv^2$) and work done ($W = Fs$) to explain how the braking distance of a car changes as its speed doubles.
25) a) Briefly describe the method for the Ruler Drop Test to investigate reaction time.
    b) List two things you could do to improve the accuracy of results from this experiment.
    c) How could you make sure this experiment is a fair test?

Topic 6a — Wave Basics and EM Waves

Transverse and Longitudinal Waves

Waves <u>transfer energy</u> from one place to another <u>without</u> transferring any <u>matter</u> (stuff).

Waves Transfer Energy in the Direction they are Travelling

1) When a wave <u>travels through</u> a medium (e.g. water or air), the particles of the <u>medium</u> vibrate.
2) The particles <u>transfer energy</u> between each other as they vibrate (see p.3).
3) <u>BUT</u> overall, the particles stay in the <u>same place</u> — <u>only energy</u> is transferred.

- For example, if you drop a twig into calm water, <u>ripples</u> spread out. The ripples <u>don't</u> carry the <u>water</u> (or the twig) away with them though.
- And if you strum a <u>guitar string</u>, the sound waves don't carry the <u>air</u> away from the guitar. If they did, you'd feel a <u>wind</u> whenever there was a sound.

Waves can be Transverse or Longitudinal

Transverse waves

The vibrations are <u>perpendicular</u> (at right angles) to the <u>direction</u> of energy transfer. Examples are:
1) All <u>electromagnetic waves</u>, e.g. light (p.75).
2) <u>Ripples</u> on the surface of <u>water</u> (see p.71).
3) A wave on a <u>string</u>.

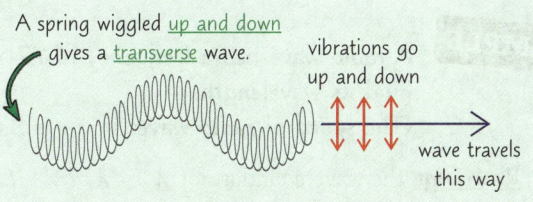
A spring wiggled <u>up and down</u> gives a <u>transverse</u> wave. vibrations go up and down. wave travels this way

Longitudinal waves

The vibrations are in the <u>same direction</u> as the energy transfer. They have <u>compressions</u> (where the particles squish together) and <u>rarefactions</u> (where they spread out). A <u>sound wave</u> is an example of a longitudinal wave.

If you <u>push</u> the end of a spring you get a <u>longitudinal</u> wave. vibrations in the same direction as wave travels. compressions, rarefactions

You Need to Know These Words to Describe Waves

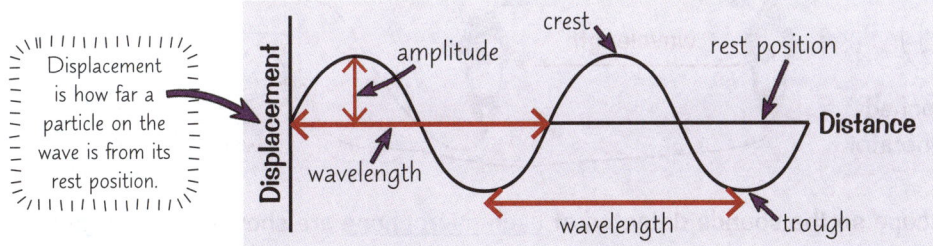

Displacement is how far a particle on the wave is from its rest position. amplitude, crest, rest position, wavelength, trough, Distance, Displacement

AMPLITUDE	<u>Maximum displacement</u> of a point on the wave from its <u>undisturbed (rest) position</u>.
WAVELENGTH	Distance between <u>one point</u> on a wave and the <u>same point</u> on the next wave. E.g. the distance between the trough of one wave and the trough of the wave next to it.
FREQUENCY	<u>Number</u> of complete waves passing a certain point <u>per second</u>. Frequency is measured in <u>hertz</u> (Hz). 1 Hz is <u>1 wave per second</u>.
PERIOD	<u>Time</u> taken for one <u>complete wave</u> to pass a certain point.

So, that's the wave basics...

Make sure you've got all this clear in your head, otherwise the rest of the topic will just be a blur of nonsense.

Q1 Give two examples of transverse waves. [2 marks]

Frequency, Period and Wave Speed

You need to know how to calculate and measure the speed of a wave.

You can find the Period of a Wave from its Frequency

Period (s) — $T = \dfrac{1}{f}$ — Frequency (Hz)

EXAMPLE

Calculate the period of a wave with a frequency of 2 Hz.
$T = 1 \div f = 1 \div 2 = 0.5$ s

Wave Speed = Frequency × Wavelength

Wave speed is how fast energy is being transferred through the medium (or the speed the wave is moving at). The wave equation applies to all waves:

Wave speed (m/s) = Frequency (Hz) × Wavelength (m) $v = f\lambda$

EXAMPLE

A radio wave has a frequency of 1.2×10^7 Hz. Find its wavelength. (The speed of radio waves in air is 3.0×10^8 m/s.)

1) Rearrange the wave equation for λ. $\lambda = v \div f$
2) Put in the values you've been given. Watch out — the values are in standard form (p.104).
   $\lambda = (3.0 \times 10^8) \div (1.2 \times 10^7)$
   $= 25$ m

> When a sound wave moves into a different medium, the wave speed changes. But the frequency doesn't change. So if the wave speed changes (e.g. increases), the wavelength must change in the same way (increase).

You can Use an Oscilloscope to Measure the Speed of Sound

1) Connect two microphones to an oscilloscope (a device which shows waves on a screen).
2) Connect a signal generator to a speaker, so you can generate sound waves at a set frequency.

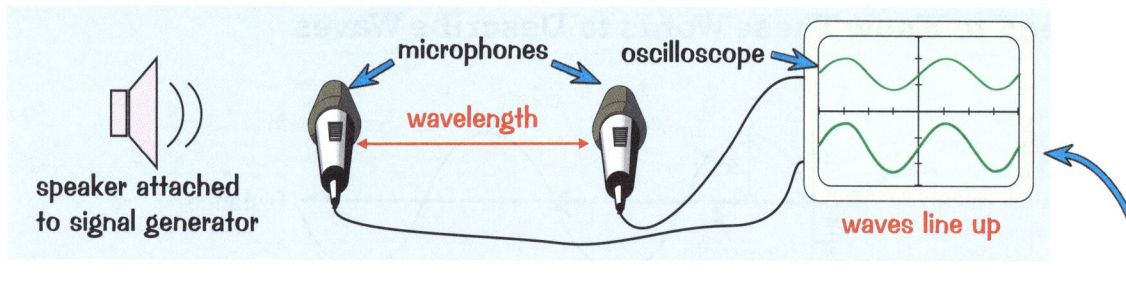

3) Set up the oscilloscope so the sounds detected at each microphone are shown as separate waves.
4) Start with both microphones next to the speaker. The waves on the oscilloscope should line up.
5) Slowly move one microphone away. Stop when the two waves line up again on the display.
6) This means the microphones are now exactly one wavelength apart.
7) Measure the distance between the microphones to find the wavelength (λ).
8) Use the formula $v = f\lambda$ to find the speed (v) of the sound waves passing through the air.
9) The frequency (f) is whatever you set the signal generator to.
10) The speed of sound in air is around 330 m/s, so check your results roughly agree with this.

Looks like the perfect set-up for a karaoke duet...

Make sure you understand each step of that method above — you could be tested on it in the exams.

Q1   A wave has a speed of 0.15 m/s and a wavelength of 7.5 cm. Calculate its frequency.   [4 marks]

PRACTICAL

Investigating Waves

Quick Quiz

Next up are a couple more ways you could measure wave speed. Just look at those fancy bits of equipment...

You can Measure the Speed of Water Ripples Using a Ripple Tank

Method

1) Attach a signal generator to the dipper of a ripple tank. Turn on the signal generator to create waves.
2) The frequency of the water waves will just be the set frequency of the signal generator.
3) Dim the lights and use a lamp to create shadows of the ripples on a screen below the tank. Place a metre ruler beside the shadows.
4) The distance between each shadow line is equal to one wavelength.
5) To get a more accurate value for wavelength, measure the distance between shadow lines that are 10 wavelengths apart. Divide this distance by 10 to find the average wavelength.

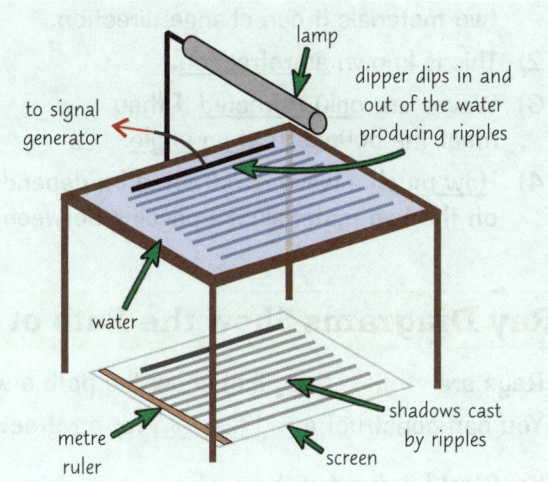

- Use $v = f\lambda$ to calculate the wave speed of the waves.
- This set-up is suitable for investigating water waves, because it lets you measure the wavelength without disturbing the waves.

When setting up this experiment, you should position the lamp so the shadows cast are as close to the size of the water waves as possible.

You can Measure Waves on a Vibrating String

Method

1) Set up the equipment shown on the right.
2) Turn on the signal generator and the string will start to vibrate at the frequency set on the signal generator.
3) Adjust the frequency of the signal generator until there's a clear wave on the string.
4) To measure the wavelength of the wave accurately:
   - Count how many wavelengths are on the string. Each vibrating loop is half a wavelength.
   - Measure the length of the whole vibrating string.
   - Divide by the number of wavelengths to give the length of one wavelength.

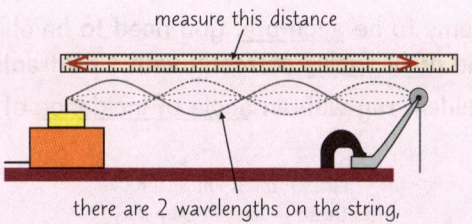
there are 2 wavelengths on the string, so divide the distance by 2

Don't worry if you have an odd number of loops. E.g. if there are 3 loops, there are one-and-a-half wavelengths on the string. Divide the length of the string by 1.5.

- The frequency of the wave is just whatever the signal generator is set to.
- You can find the speed of the wave using $v = f\lambda$.
- This set-up is suitable for investigating waves on a string because it's easy to see and measure the wavelength (and frequency).

Surf's up, it's time to, like, totally measure some waves...

We use sound waves, ripples and waves on strings as they're easy to make and there are ways of 'seeing' them.

Q1   Describe a suitable experiment to measure the wavelength of ripples on the surface of water.   [3 marks]

Refraction

Grab a glass of water and put a straw in it. The straw looks like it's <u>bending</u>. But it's not magic, it's refraction.

Refraction — Waves Changing Direction

1) When a wave crosses a <u>boundary</u> between two materials it can change direction.
2) This is known as <u>refraction</u>.
3) Waves are <u>only refracted</u> if they meet the boundary <u>at an angle</u>.
4) <u>How much</u> a wave is refracted by depends on the two materials it's passing between.

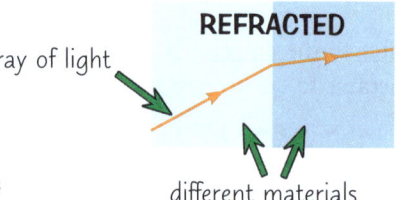
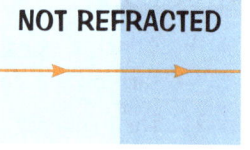

Ray Diagrams Show the Path of a Wave

Rays are <u>straight lines</u> that show the path a wave travels along. You can construct a <u>ray diagram</u> for a refracted light ray:

① Start by drawing the <u>boundary</u> between your two materials.

② Then draw a dotted line at <u>right angles</u> to the boundary. This line is the '<u>normal</u>' to the boundary.

'Normal' just means 'at right angles'.

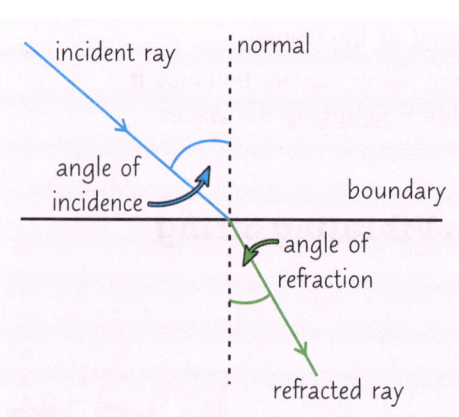

You should always use a ruler to draw rays.

③ Next you should draw the <u>incident ray</u>. The incident ray meets the <u>boundary</u> at the <u>normal</u>.

Use a <u>protractor</u> to draw the incident ray (see below).

The angle of incidence is the angle between the <u>incident ray</u> and the <u>normal</u>.

④ Now draw the <u>refracted ray</u> on the other side of the boundary.

⑤ The <u>angle of refraction</u> is the angle between the <u>refracted ray</u> and the <u>normal</u>.

You Need to be Able to Use a Protractor Properly

For your ray diagrams to be <u>accurate</u>, you need to be able to <u>measure angles</u> and <u>draw angles</u> correctly with a protractor.

E.g. to draw an incident ray with an <u>angle of incidence</u> of <u>50°</u>:

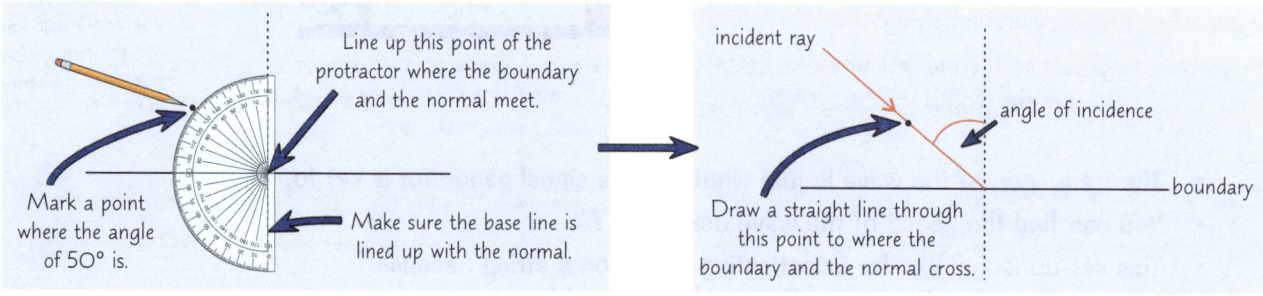

Lights, camera, refraction...

Refraction is a common behaviour of waves, so make sure you really understand it before moving on.

Q1   Draw a ray diagram for a ray of light meeting a boundary at an angle of incidence of 55°, and crossing into a second material with an angle of refraction of 35°.   [3 marks]

Topic 6a — Wave Basics and EM Waves

Reflection

If you're anything like me, you'll have spent hours gazing into a mirror in wonder. Here's why...

All Waves Can be Absorbed, Transmitted or Reflected

You've seen that waves can refract when crossing a boundary between two different materials (see the previous page). Here are all the things that can happen to waves at a boundary:

Absorption	Transmission	Reflection
Energy is transferred to the material's energy stores (like in a microwave oven, page 76).	The waves carry on travelling through the new material. This often leads to refraction.	The waves bounce back off the boundary — more on this below.

You Can Draw a Simple Ray Diagram for Reflection

There's one simple rule to learn for all reflected waves:

Remember, a ray shows the path a wave travels along (see previous page).

Angle of incidence = Angle of reflection

The normal is perpendicular (at right angles) to the surface at the point of incidence (the point where the wave hits the boundary).

The angle of incidence is the angle between the incoming ray (wave) and the normal.

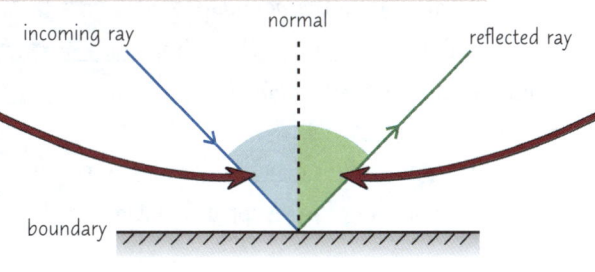

The angle of reflection is the angle between the reflected ray (wave) and the normal.

Reflection can be Specular or Diffuse

The way waves are reflected depends on the boundary. (There's an investigation on this on the next page.)

Specular reflection

This happens when a wave is reflected in a single direction by a smooth surface.

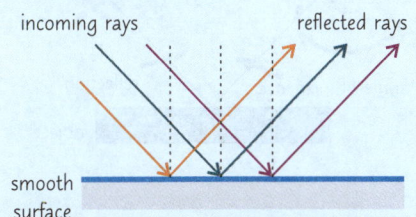

For example, when light rays reflect off a mirror you get a nice clear reflection.

Diffuse reflection

This happens when a wave is reflected by a rough surface (e.g. a piece of paper). The reflected rays are scattered in lots of different directions.

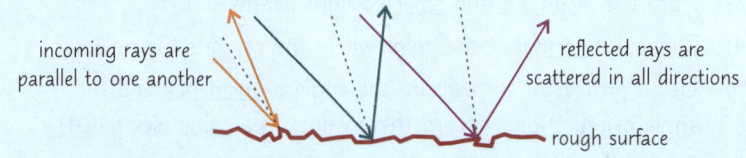

- This happens because the normal is different for each incoming ray, which means that the angle of incidence is different for each ray. The angle of incidence still equals the angle of reflection.
- When light is reflected by a rough surface, the surface appears matt (not shiny) and you don't get a clear reflection of objects.

My reflection is absolutely spectacular...

Remember, the angle of incidence is always equal to the angle of reflection of a wave.

Q1   A light ray is incident on a mirror at an angle of 30°.
Draw a ray diagram to show its reflection. [3 marks]

Quick Quiz

Investigating Light — PRACTICAL

Hurrah — it's time to whip out your ray box and get some reflection and refraction going on...

You Need to Do Both of These Experiments in a Dim Room

Both of these experiments use a ray box to produce thin rays of light.
So it's best to do them in a dim room so you can clearly see and measure the light rays.

You Can Use Transparent Materials to Investigate Refraction

Here's a method you could use to investigate how light refracts when it passes from air into different materials:

Method

1) Place a transparent rectangular block on a piece of paper and draw around it.
2) Use a ray box to shine a ray of light at the middle of one side of the block.
3) Trace the incident ray and mark where the light ray emerges on the other side of the block with a cross.
4) Remove the block. Join up the incident ray and the cross with a straight line — this is the refracted ray.
5) Draw a normal through the point where the light ray entered the block, making sure it's at 90° to the boundary.
6) Use a protractor to measure the angle of incidence (*I*) and the angle of refraction (*R*).
7) Repeat this experiment using rectangular blocks made from different materials. Each block should be placed in the same position.
8) Keep the ray box where it is so the angle of incidence is the same every time.
9) You should find that the angle of refraction changes for different materials.

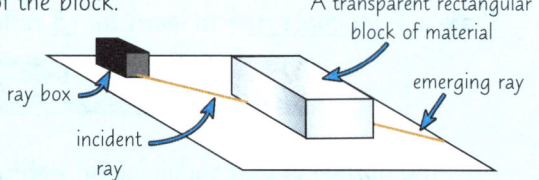

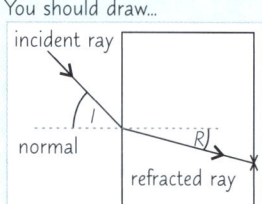
You should draw... incident ray, normal, refracted ray

Different Materials Reflect Light Differently

Method

1) Take a piece of paper and draw a straight line across it. Place an object so one of its sides lines up with this line.
2) Use a ray box to shine a ray of light at the object's surface.
3) Trace the incoming and reflected light beams.
4) Draw the normal at the point where the ray hits the object.
5) Use a protractor to measure the angle of incidence and the angle of reflection. Record these values in a table (see p.101).
6) Repeat this experiment for a range of objects.

- You should find that smooth surfaces (like mirrors) give clear reflections.
- Rough surfaces (like paper) give diffuse reflections. The reflected beam could be wider and dimmer than the incident beam, or you might not be able to see a reflected beam at all.
- You should also find that the angle of incidence ALWAYS equals the angle of reflection.

Time to reflect...

These experiments aren't the trickiest, but you still have to be able to describe how to do them and what they show.

Q1 Describe an experiment you could do to measure how light is refracted by different materials. [4 marks]

Electromagnetic (EM) Waves

Quick Quiz

The light waves that we see are just one small part of a big group of electromagnetic waves...

Electromagnetic Waves Transfer Energy

- Electromagnetic (EM) waves are transverse waves (p.69).
- They transfer energy from a source to an absorber. For example:

   1) A campfire is a source.
   2) It transfers energy to its surroundings by giving out infrared radiation.
   3) Infrared radiation is a type of EM wave.
   4) These infrared waves are absorbed by objects.
   5) Energy is transferred to the objects' thermal energy stores.
   6) This causes the objects to warm up.

- All EM waves travel at the same speed through air or a vacuum (space).
- This speed is much faster than the speed of sound in air.

There's a Continuous Spectrum of EM Waves

- EM waves vary in wavelength and frequency.
- There are EM waves of every wavelength within a certain range.
- This is known as a continuous spectrum.
- The spectrum is split into seven groups based on wavelength and frequency.

Our eyes can only detect a small part of this spectrum — visible light.

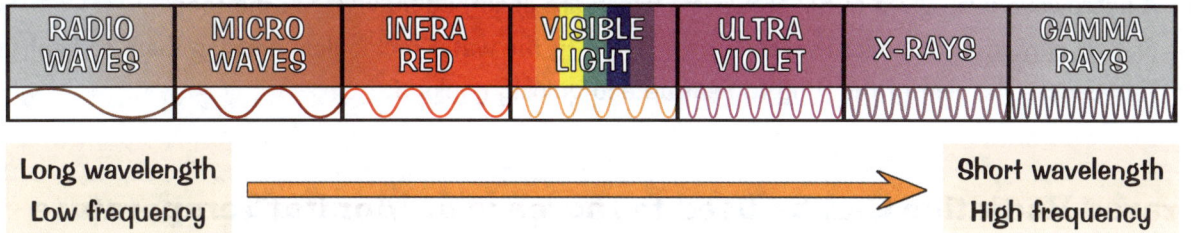

RADIO WAVES | MICRO WAVES | INFRA RED | VISIBLE LIGHT | ULTRA VIOLET | X-RAYS | GAMMA RAYS

Long wavelength, Low frequency → Short wavelength, High frequency

Changes In Atoms Produce EM Waves

1) EM radiation can be absorbed or produced by changes in atoms and their nuclei.
2) There are lots of different changes that can happen in atoms. For example:
   - Electrons can move between energy levels in atoms (see p.39).
   - Changes in the nucleus of an atom can create gamma rays (see p.41).
3) Each different change produces or absorbs a different frequency of EM wave.
4) This is why atoms can generate (create) EM waves over a large range of frequencies.
5) It is also why atoms can absorb a range of frequencies.

Learn about the EM spectrum and wave goodbye to exam stress...

Nothing too difficult here, just a lot of facts to remember. Here's a handy way to remember the order of EM waves: 'Rock Music Is Very Useful for eXperiments with Goats'.

Q1   State the type of electromagnetic wave that has the lowest frequency.   [1 mark]

Q2   Name the section of the electromagnetic spectrum that humans can see.   [1 mark]

Quick Quiz

Uses of EM Waves

EM waves are used for all sorts of stuff — and radio waves are definitely the most entertaining. They transfer energy to your car radio and your TV — what would you do without them?

Radio Waves are Used Mainly for Communication

- Radio and TV signals can be sent by radio waves.
- Very short wavelength signals are used for FM radio and TV.
- They have to be in direct sight of the receiver when they're sent, with nothing in the way, so they can't travel very far.
- Longer wavelength radio waves can travel further.
- They can be used to send radio signals around the world.

Bluetooth® uses even shorter wavelengths to send data over very short distances between devices without wires (e.g. wireless headphones).

Microwaves are Used for Satellites and Cooking

Satellite communication

1) A microwave signal is sent into space to a satellite dish high above Earth's atmosphere.
2) The satellite sends the signal back to Earth in a different direction.
3) A satellite dish on the ground receives the signal.

Things like satellite TVs use microwaves in this way.

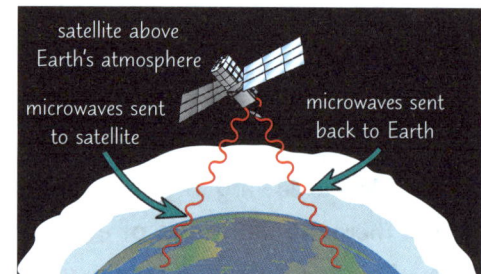

Microwave ovens

1) A microwave oven gives out microwaves, which are absorbed by water in the food.
2) Energy carried by the microwaves is transferred to the water molecules, causing them to heat up.
3) This causes the rest of the food to heat up and quickly cooks it.

Infrared Radiation Can be Used to Increase or Monitor Temperature

Infrared (IR) radiation is given out by all objects. The hotter the object, the more infrared radiation it gives out. When an object absorbs infrared radiation, energy is transferred to the object's thermal energy store. This makes it warm up.

Infrared cameras

- They can be used to detect IR radiation and monitor temperature.
- This is useful for seeing where energy is being lost from a house.
- It can also allow you to see hot objects in the dark.

The different colours show different amounts of IR radiation being detected. Here, the redder the colour, the more infrared radiation is being detected.

Heating

- Electric heaters release lots of IR radiation to warm a room.
- And food can be cooked using infrared radiation, e.g. from a toaster's heating element.

Revision time — adjust depending on brain wattage...

Who knew we used microwaves for more than cooking chips in less than 3 minutes? Turns out, they're dead handy.

Q1   State one use of radio waves.   [1 mark]

More Uses of EM Waves

Haven't had enough uses of EM waves? Good, because here's a few more. Get learning.

Fibre Optic Cables Use Visible Light to Send Data

1) Optical fibres are thin glass or plastic tubes that can carry data over long distances.
2) They're often used to send information to telephones or computers.
3) Information is sent from one end of the fibre to the other as pulses of visible light.
4) The light rays are reflected back and forth along the fibre until they reach the other end.

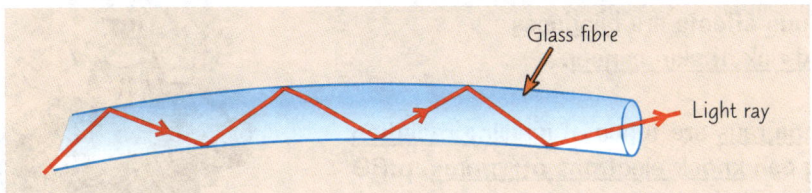

Ultraviolet (UV) Radiation — Fluorescent Lights and Suntans

1) When some materials absorb UV light, they give off visible light.
2) This can be pretty useful:

- Fluorescent lights use UV radiation to produce visible light. They are energy-efficient.
- Security pens can be used to mark property with your name.
- Under UV light the ink will glow, but it's invisible otherwise.
- This can help the police identify stolen property.

3) Ultraviolet radiation is also produced by the Sun. It's what gives you a suntan.
4) Some people use UV lamps to get a suntan without the Sun, but this can be dangerous.

X-rays and Gamma Rays are Used in Medicine

X-RAY IMAGES
- X-rays pass easily through flesh but not through bones or metal.
- This can be used to create an X-ray image to check for broken bones.

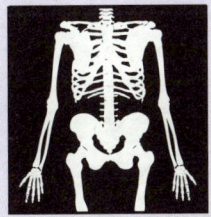

RADIOTHERAPY
- X-rays and gamma rays (see p.40) can both be used to treat people with cancer.
- This is because X-rays and gamma rays can kill living cells.
- The radiation is aimed carefully at the cancer cells, to avoid killing too many healthy cells.

MEDICAL TRACERS
- Gamma rays pass through the body easily.
- That's why small amounts of them are used in 'medical tracers' (see p.45).
- Their movement around the body can be tracked.
- This can tell doctors if organs are working as they should.

Don't lie to an X-ray — they can see right through you...

I hate to say it, but go back to page 76 and read all of the uses for EM waves again to really learn them.

Q1   State two uses of X-rays.   [2 marks]

Find the CGP RevisionHub at cgpbooks.co.uk/Mass

Dangers of EM Waves

Okay, so you know how useful electromagnetic radiation can be — well, it can also be pretty dangerous.

Some EM Radiation Can be Harmful to People

- When EM radiation enters living tissue — like you — it can be dangerous.
- High frequency waves like UV, X-rays and gamma rays can all cause lots of damage:

UV radiation damages surface cells, which can lead to sunburn and cause skin to age faster than it should. Some more serious effects are blindness and an increased risk of skin cancer.

X-rays and gamma rays are types of ionising radiation. This means they can knock electrons off atoms, p.39. This can destroy cells or mutate (change) genes. This can cause cancer.

You Can Measure Risk Using the Radiation Dose in Sieverts

1) Whilst UV radiation, X-rays and gamma rays can all be harmful, they are also very useful (see page 77).
2) Before these types of EM radiation are used, people weigh-up the benefits and health risks.

For example, the risk of a person involved in a car accident developing cancer from having an X-ray image taken is much smaller than the potential health risk of not finding and treating their injuries.

3) Radiation dose (measured in sieverts) is a measure of the risk of harm from the body being exposed to radiation.
4) The risk depends on the total amount of radiation absorbed and how harmful the type of radiation is.
5) A sievert is pretty big, so millisieverts (mSv) are often used.

1000 mSv = 1 Sv

Risk can be Different for Different Parts of the Body

- A CT scan uses X-rays to create a detailed picture of the inside of a patient's body.
- The table shows the radiation dose received by two different parts of a patient's body when having CT scans.

	Radiation dose (mSv)
Head	2.0
Chest	8.0

- You can see that the radiation dose from a chest scan is 4 times larger than from a head scan — (2.0 mSv × 4 = 8.0 mSv).
- Remember, radiation dose measures the risk of harm.
- This means that if a patient has a CT scan on their chest, they are four times more likely to be harmed than if they have a head scan.

This is not an excuse to stay in bed all day...

A small dose of radiation every now and then is very low risk — so X-rays are nothing to worry about.

Q1 Give two effects of a person being exposed to too much UV radiation. [2 marks]

Q2 What property of gamma rays and X-rays makes them dangerous to humans? [1 mark]

78 Topic 6a — Wave Basics and EM Waves

Revision Summary Test for Topic 6a

Make yourself useful like an EM wave and answer these questions to help you master topic 6a:
- Tackle the revision summary test below, or scan the QR code to do it online.
  The questions are hard, but they'll show you how well you really know your stuff.
- Track your progress online and see which areas need more work.
- Compare your answers with sample answers for the test here: www.cgpbooks.co.uk/Mass

Wave Properties (p.69-71)

1) Do waves cause matter to travel with them? Give an example to explain your answer.
2) What's the difference between transverse and longitudinal waves?
3) Give an example of a transverse wave. What about a longitudinal wave?
4) What is the amplitude, wavelength, frequency and time period of a wave?
5) What does each symbol in the formula $v = f\lambda$ mean?
6) Describe an experiment you could do to measure the speed of sound in air.
7) How can you measure the wavelength of water ripples in a wave tank by looking at their shadow?
8) Describe a method you could use to measure the speed of waves on a vibrating string.

Refraction and Reflection (p.72-74)

9) What is refraction?
10) Draw a ray diagram for a light ray that is refracted at a boundary, where the angle of refraction is smaller than the angle of incidence. Label the angle of incidence (I) and the angle of refraction (R).
11) What three things can happen when waves arrive at a boundary between two different materials?
12) Describe what the 'normal' is when drawing ray diagrams.
13) What rule is true for all reflected waves?
14) What is the difference between specular reflection and diffuse reflection?
15) Give a method that could be used to investigate how each of the following are affected by different materials: a) refraction,   b) reflection.

Electromagnetic (EM) Waves (p.75)

16) Give an example of how EM waves transfer energy from a source to an absorber.
17) True or false? Different EM waves travel at different speeds through a vacuum.
18) List the seven basic types of EM wave in order from longest to shortest wavelength.
19) Give two ways that an atom can produce EM waves.

Uses and Dangers of EM Waves (p.76-78)

20) What are three uses of radio waves?
21) Describe how microwaves are used in: a) satellite communication,   b) microwave ovens.
22) Give two things that use IR radiation for heating.
23) What type of EM radiation do fibre optic cables use? How do they work?
24) List three uses of UV lamps.
25) What is radiotherapy? Why are X-rays and gamma rays used?
26) Other than radiotherapy, what is one way gamma rays are used in medicine? What about X-rays?
27) How can the following types of EM waves cause harm to people: a) UV, b) X-rays and gamma rays?
28) What is radiation dose? What are three things that it depends on?

Topic 6b — Light and Radiation

Lenses and Images

Quick Quiz

These next few pages are about how light acts when it hits a lens. Be ready for lots of diagrams.

All Lenses Have Some Common Features

Lenses form images by refracting light (p.72) and changing its direction. Here are some features of lenses:

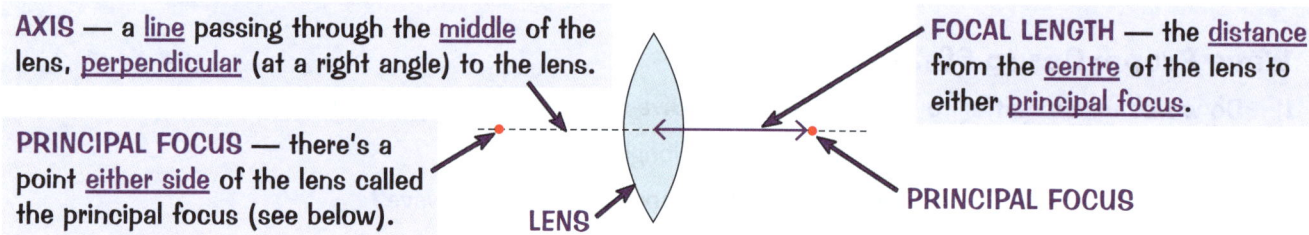

AXIS — a line passing through the middle of the lens, perpendicular (at a right angle) to the lens.

FOCAL LENGTH — the distance from the centre of the lens to either principal focus.

PRINCIPAL FOCUS — there's a point either side of the lens called the principal focus (see below).

There are two main types of lens. They have different shapes and do opposite things to light rays:

Convex (or Converging) Lens

- Bulges outwards.
- Causes parallel rays of light to be brought together (converge).
- The principal focus of a convex lens is where rays hitting the lens parallel to the axis all meet.

Concave (or Diverging) Lens

- Caves inwards.
- Causes rays of light to spread out (diverge).
- Rays hitting the lens parallel to the axis appear to come from the principal focus — you can trace them back to this point, where they all appear to meet.

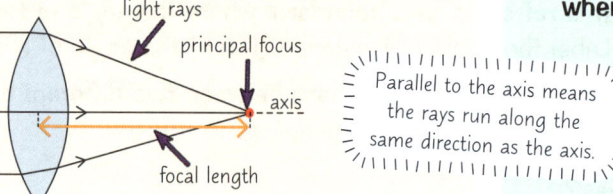

Parallel to the axis means the rays run along the same direction as the axis.

Lenses can Produce Real and Virtual Images

1) A real image is where the light rays from an object actually come together. This can form an image on a screen.
2) A virtual image happens when the light rays only seem like they come together.
3) The light rays are actually diverging (spreading out from each other).
4) So the light from the object appears to be coming from a completely different place.
5) When you look in a mirror, you see a virtual image of your face. The object (your face) appears to be behind the mirror.
6) You can't display a virtual image on a screen.

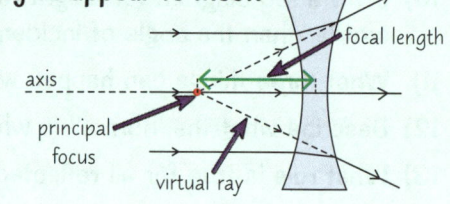
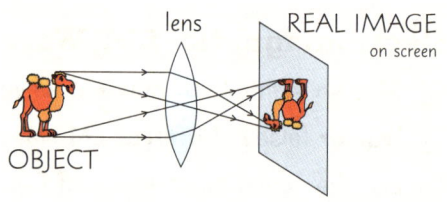

Virtual images — they're not just in video games...

Don't forget which lens is which — convex lenses bulge outwards and concave lenses cave inwards.

Q1 Light rays parallel to the axis pass through a convex lens. What happens at the principal focus? [1 mark]

Q2 Copy and complete the diagram on the right to show the path of the light rays when they emerge from the lens. Include any virtual rays in your diagram. The principal focus is shown by the grey dot. [2 marks]

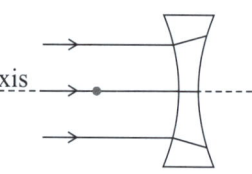

80   Topic 6b — Light and Radiation

Convex Lenses and Ray Diagrams

Believe it or not, ray diagrams have absolutely nothing to do with sea creatures painting pretty pictures...

You Can Draw a Ray Diagram for an Image Through a Convex Lens

① Draw a ray going from the top of the object to the lens, parallel to the axis of the lens.

② This ray is refracted through the principal focus (F) on the other side of the lens. Draw a refracted ray passing through F.

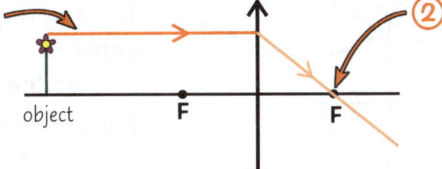

③ Draw another ray going from the top of the object, right through the middle of the lens.

④ This ray doesn't bend — it just goes straight through.

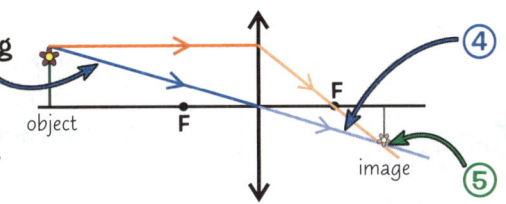

⑤ Mark where the rays meet. This is the top of the image.

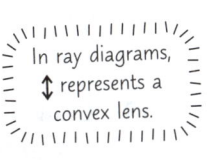

In ray diagrams, ↕ represents a convex lens.

⑥ When the bottom of the object is on the axis, the bottom of the image is also on the axis.

Distance from the Lens Affects the Image

To describe an image properly, you need to say 3 things:
- Whether it's real or virtual.
- Whether it's upright or inverted (upside down) compared to the object.
- How big it is compared to the object.

How near to or far from the lens an object is changes the type of image that is formed:

An object or image at 2F is at a distance of two focal lengths from the lens.

Object is further than 2F
The image is:
- Real
- Inverted
- Smaller than the object

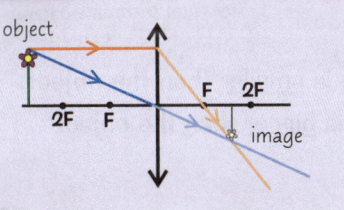

Object is at 2F
The image is:
- Real
- Inverted
- The same size as the object

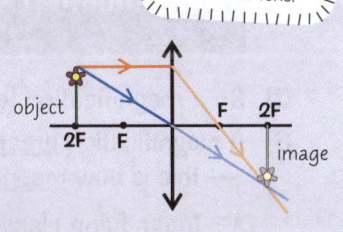

Object is between F and 2F
The image is:
- Real
- Inverted
- Bigger than the object

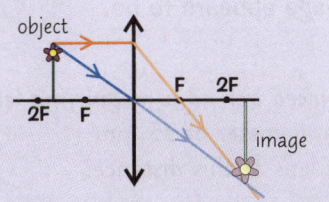

Object is nearer than F
The image is:
- Virtual
- Upright
- Bigger than the object

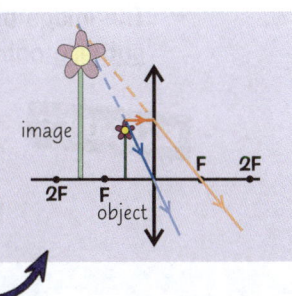

When the image is virtual, it forms on the same side of the lens as the object.

Warning — too much revision can cause a loss of focus...

Ray diagrams are great for figuring out what images look like, so make sure you know how to draw them.

Q1 Draw a ray diagram for an object at a distance of 2F in front of a convex lens. [3 marks]

Find the CGP RevisionHub at cgpbooks.co.uk/Mass   Topic 6b — Light and Radiation

Concave Lenses and Magnification

Now for concave lenses. Then you'll get up close and personal with the handy magnification equation.

You Can Draw a Ray Diagram for an Image Through a Concave Lens

① Draw a ray going from the top of the object to the lens, parallel to the axis of the lens.

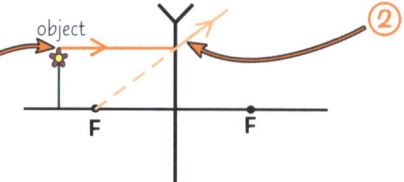

② This ray is refracted so it appears to have come from the principal focus on the same side as the object. Draw a ray from this principal focus. Make it dashed when it's on the same side of the lens as the object.

③ Draw a ray going straight through the middle of the lens.

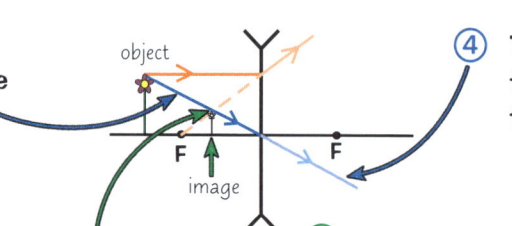

④ The ray passing through the middle of the lens doesn't bend.

In ray diagrams, ⟩⟨ represents a concave lens.

⑤ Mark where the rays meet — this is the top of the image.

⑥ When the bottom of the object is on the axis, the bottom of the image is also on the axis.

- A concave lens always produces a virtual image (see p.80).
- The image is always the right way up and smaller than the object.
- The further an object is from the concave lens, the smaller the image produced.
- The image is always on the same side of the lens as the object — no matter where the object is.

Magnification Compares Object Size and Image Size

1) You can use the magnification formula to work out the magnification produced by a lens at a given distance:

$$\text{magnification} = \frac{\text{image height}}{\text{object height}}$$

Magnification is a ratio, so it doesn't have any units. As long as the units for both heights are the same, you can measure them in whatever units you like (e.g. mm or cm).

2) So a magnification less than 1 means the image is smaller than the object.
3) A magnification greater than 1 means the image is bigger than the object — this is how magnifying glasses work:

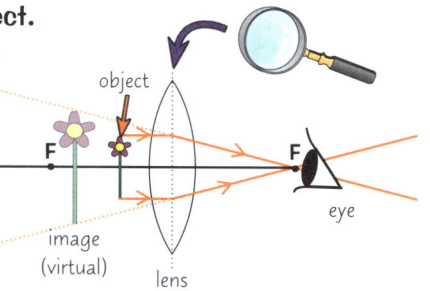

- Magnifying glasses use a convex lens.
- The object must be closer to the lens than the focal length.
- The image produced is a virtual image. So the light rays don't actually come from the place where the image appears to be.

EXAMPLE A coin with diameter 14 mm is placed behind a magnifying lens. The virtual image produced has a diameter of 35 mm. What is the magnification of the lens at this distance?

magnification = image height ÷ object height = 35 ÷ 14 = 2.5

If you ask me, lenses are magnificent...

Congratulations, you've reached the end of lenses. Why not celebrate with these practice questions?

Q1 Find the magnification of a lens if a 12 cm tall object produces a 6 cm high image. [2 marks]

Q2 Calculate the height of an image if the object is 10 cm tall and the magnification is 2.5. [3 marks]

Visible Light

Ah, light. That stuff we see all of the time. But it's a bit more complicated than you might have thought.

Visible Light is Made Up of a Range of Colours

1) As you saw on page 75, electromagnetic waves cover a very large spectrum.
2) We can only see a tiny part of this spectrum — the visible light spectrum.
3) The visible light spectrum has a range of different wavelengths.
4) We see these wavelengths as different colours. Each colour has its own narrow range of wavelengths (and frequencies).
5) The visible light spectrum ranges from violets down at 400 nm up to reds at 700 nm.   Remember, 1 nm = 1×10^{-9} m
6) Colours can also mix together to make other colours.
7) The only colours you can't make by mixing are the primary colours: pure red, green and blue.
8) Putting all of the different colours together creates white light.

These are the primary colours of light. Don't confuse green with yellow — yellow is a primary colour of paint.

Opaque Objects Do Not Let Light Through

How you see an object depends on how the light from it reaches your eyes. Light can be:

ABSORBED	The light wave enters the object, but does not leave the object again.
TRANSMITTED	The light wave enters the object, moves through it and passes out the other side.
REFLECTED	The light wave bounces back off the object.

- Opaque objects do not transmit (let through) light.
- Opaque means you can't see through it.
- When visible light hits an opaque object, some of the wavelengths of light are reflected.
- The rest of the wavelengths are absorbed.

The light reflected from an opaque object won't always give a nice clear reflection. If the reflection is diffuse, the light is scattered in all different directions (see p.73).

Colour Depends On The Wavelengths An Object Absorbs

1) The colour of an opaque object depends on which wavelengths of light are most strongly reflected.

- A red apple looks red because of the wavelengths of light that are reaching your eyes. These are from the red part of the visible spectrum.
- This happens because the red wavelengths are the most strongly reflected.
- The other wavelengths of light are absorbed.

2) White objects reflect all of the wavelengths of visible light equally.
3) Black objects absorb all wavelengths of visible light.

Your eyes see black as the lack of any visible light (i.e. the lack of any colour).

Have you seen my white shirt? It's red and green and blue...

Remember that the colour of an opaque object depends on the wavelengths of visible light it most strongly reflects.

Q1   Explain why an opaque blue object appears blue.   [1 mark]

Quick Quiz

Transmitting Visible Light

Some objects let light through. Good job — reading glasses might not work very well otherwise.

Objects That Aren't Opaque are Either Transparent or Translucent

1) You can see through a transparent object, like a window.
2) You can partially see through translucent objects, like tracing paper.
3) Both transparent and translucent objects transmit light. Some light passes through.
4) Some wavelengths of light may be absorbed or reflected.
5) The colour of a transparent or translucent object depends on the wavelengths of light it reflects and transmits:

- A stained glass window is made up of lots of different panels of glass.
- The panels appear to be different colours because each one transmits different wavelengths of light.
- A green pane of glass appears green because it transmits wavelengths of green light.
- It also reflects some wavelengths of green light. It absorbs all other colours.

Colour Filters Only Let Through Particular Wavelengths

1) Colour filters are used to filter out different wavelengths of light.
2) This means that only certain wavelengths (colours) are transmitted.
3) The rest of the wavelengths are absorbed.
4) A primary colour filter will only transmit one particular colour. E.g. if white light is shone at a blue colour filter, only blue light will be let through. The rest of the light will be absorbed.

If you look at a blue object through a blue colour filter, it will still look blue. Blue light is reflected from the object's surface and is transmitted by the filter.

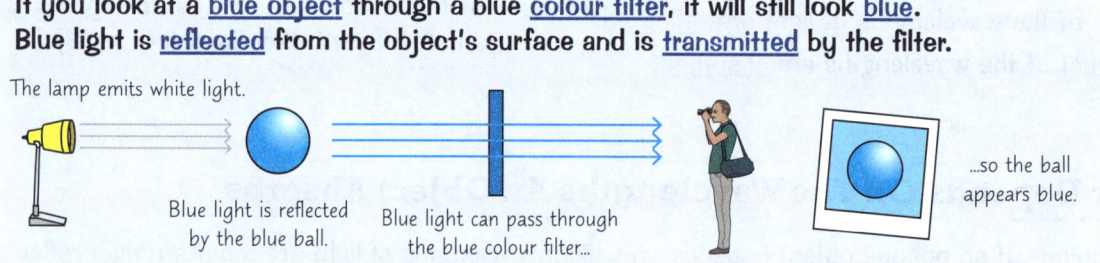

If the object was red (or any colour not made from blue light), the object would appear black when viewed through a blue filter. All of the wavelengths of light reflected by the object will be absorbed by the filter.

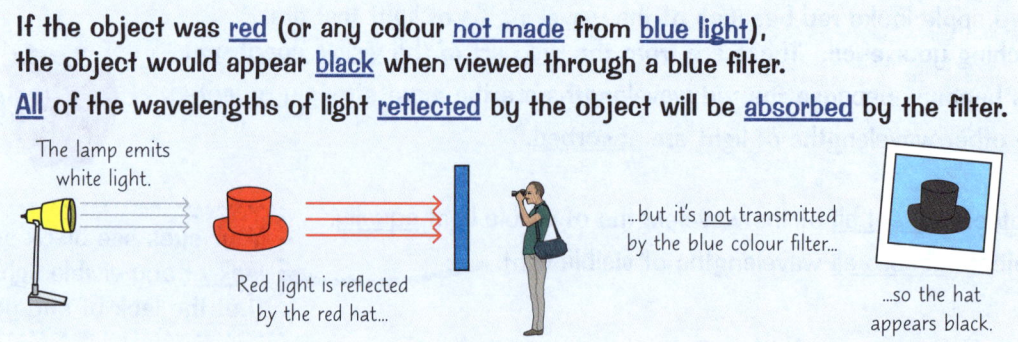

Have I made myself perfectly clear?

The colour of translucent or transparent objects depends on the wavelengths of light reflected AND transmitted.

Q1   What colour would a green bag appear when it is viewed through a red filter?   [1 mark]

Black Body Radiation and Temperature

Quick Quiz

This page isn't as bad (or as sci-fi) as it sounds. Just take some time to really absorb all the info.

Every Object Absorbs and Emits Infrared Radiation

1) All objects constantly emit (give out) infrared (IR) radiation.
2) Infrared radiation is emitted from the surface of objects.
3) As well as emitting IR radiation, all objects constantly absorb it (take it in).
4) No matter what temperature an object is, it will emit and absorb some IR radiation.
5) But the hotter an object is, the more infrared radiation it emits in a given time.

You can also say an object 'radiates' infrared. This means the same thing as 'emits'.

- The mug of hot chocolate is warmer than the cold glass of chocolate milk.
- So the mug emits more IR radiation in a given time than the glass of milk.

Black Bodies are the Ultimate Emitters

> A PERFECT BLACK BODY is an object that ABSORBS ALL of the radiation that hits it.
> NO radiation is REFLECTED or TRANSMITTED.

1) A good absorber of radiation is also a good emitter of radiation.
2) So perfect black bodies are the best possible emitters of radiation.
3) The intensity of the wavelengths emitted by an object (including black bodies) depends on its temperature.
4) You can plot a black body curve for an object at a certain temperature.

Intensity is a measure of how much energy is transferred by the radiation.

All objects emit electromagnetic (EM) radiation. This radiation isn't just in the infrared part of the spectrum — it covers a range of wavelengths and frequencies from the EM spectrum (see p.75).

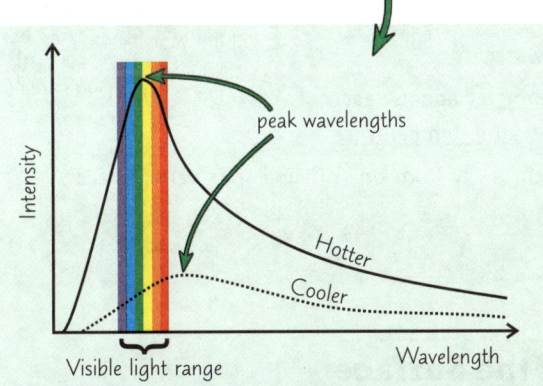

580 nm to peak

- The black body curve of an object shows the intensity of the different wavelengths emitted at that temperature.
- The peak in the curve happens at the wavelength that has the highest intensity. This is the peak wavelength for that temperature.
- Hotter objects have a shorter peak wavelength and a higher intensity.

- The black body curves above are for the same object at two different temperatures.
- When the object is cooler, it emits all wavelengths with a lower intensity, and the peak wavelength is in the infrared part of the spectrum.
- As the object gets hotter, the intensity of all radiation increases and the peak wavelength decreases.

Don't let this get you hot under the collar...

Everything around us emits radiation. Including you — at a peak wavelength of about 10 μm. Pretty cool.

Q1 The peak wavelength of light from the Sun is about 500 nm.
The peak wavelength of light from a second star is at about 850 nm.
Which star is cooler? Explain your answer. [2 marks]

Q1 Video Solution

Find the CGP RevisionHub at cgpbooks.co.uk/Mass Topic 6b — Light and Radiation

Investigating IR Radiation — PRACTICAL

Now it's time to see how the surface of an object affects how much infrared radiation it gives out. I know, you can hardly contain your excitement. Neither can I.

Different Surfaces Emit Different Amounts of IR Radiation

1) The amount of infrared radiation an object gives out depends on its temperature — see p.85.
2) It also depends on its surface.
3) This includes how rough or shiny it is, and its colour.
4) One way to investigate how much IR radiation different surfaces emit is by using a Leslie cube.
5) A Leslie cube is a hollow, metal cube.
6) The four side faces have different surfaces.
7) For example, matt (dull) black paint, matt white paint, shiny metal and dull metal.

You Can Investigate Emission With a Leslie Cube

- As well as the Leslie cube, you'll need a heat-proof mat, an infrared detector, a pencil and a kettle.
- Set up the equipment like this:

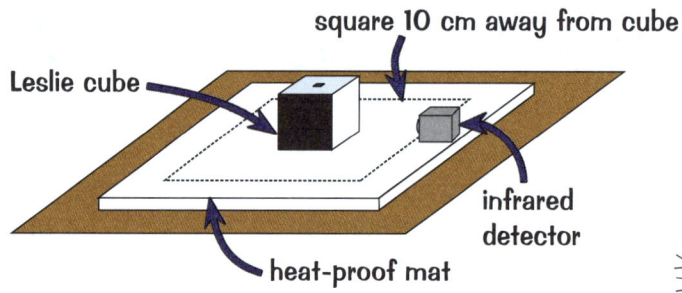

Method

1) Draw a square around the cube, 10 cm from all faces of the cube.
2) Boil water in a kettle. Fill the Leslie cube with the boiling water.
3) Wait a while for the cube to warm up. Then hold a thermometer against each of the four vertical faces — you should find that they're all the same temperature.
4) Use the square you drew to place an infrared detector 10 cm away from one of the cube's vertical faces.
5) Record the amount of IR radiation it detects.
6) Repeat steps 4) and 5) for each of the four faces.

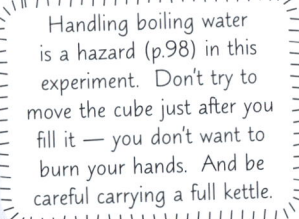

Handling boiling water is a hazard (p.98) in this experiment. Don't try to move the cube just after you fill it — you don't want to burn your hands. And be careful carrying a full kettle.

Results Will Depend on the Properties of the Surface

- The face that had the highest reading is giving off the most IR radiation.
- You should find that the black surface is radiating more IR radiation than the white one.
- Matt surfaces should give off more than shiny ones.
- As always, you should repeat the experiment to check your results.

And don't forget to give Leslie his cube back when you're done...

When doing this experiment, you could also place your hand near each surface of the cube (but not touching, it'll be super hot). You'll be able to feel which surface is giving off more infrared radiation.

Q1 What surface is the better emitter of infrared radiation out of:
 a) a black surface and a white surface?   b) a shiny surface and a matt surface?   [2 marks]

Topic 6b — Light and Radiation

PRACTICAL — **Investigating IR Absorption**

Have you ever noticed that wearing black clothes on a hot day can make you feel really warm? Turns out there's some science behind it...

You Can Investigate Absorption with the Melting Wax Trick

- The amount of infrared radiation absorbed by different materials also depends on the surface.
- You can do an experiment to show this.
- You'll need a Bunsen burner, candle wax, metal plates and metal balls.
- The metal plates should be identical except their back surface.
- E.g. one plate will have a black back, and the other will have a white back.
- Set up the equipment like this:

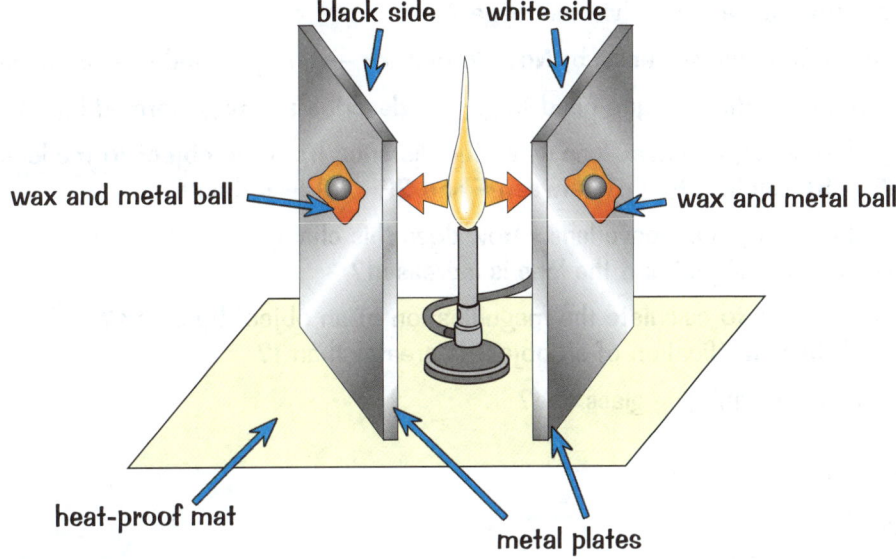

Method

1) Place a Bunsen burner on a heat-proof mat.
2) Stick a metal ball to each identical side of the metal plates with hot candle wax.
3) Leave the candle wax to cool. The wax will harden and hold the ball in place.
4) Then face the back of these plates towards the flame.
5) They should both be the same distance away from the flame.
6) Record which ball falls first.

Black Surfaces are Good Absorbers of IR

1) The plates absorb infrared radiation given out by the Bunsen burner.
2) Energy is transferred to the thermal energy stores of the candle wax.
3) The candle wax starts to melt, causing the balls to fall.
4) The ball will fall quicker from the plate that is better at absorbing IR radiation.
5) You should find that the ball on the plate with the black back falls first.
6) This means the black surface was better at absorbing infrared radiation than the white surface.

> The results from the experiment on the last page should show that black surfaces are better emitters of IR radiation than white surfaces. This experiment should show that black surfaces are also better absorbers of IR radiation.

Wear a black hat to help your brain absorb this information...

...probably best not to rely on that for the exam, though. There's nothing for it — get learning.

Q1 Give two ways in which the experiment above is made a fair test. [2 marks]

Revision Summary Test for Topic 6b

Use this page to test your knowledge of Topic 6b and you'll be radiating confidence in the exams.
- Tackle the revision summary test below, or scan the QR code to do it online. The questions are hard, but they'll show you how well you really know your stuff.
- Track your progress online and see which areas need more work.
- Compare your answers with sample answers for the test here: cgpbooks.co.uk/Mass

Lenses (p.80-82)

1) What do these lens terms mean?   a) axis   b) focal length
2) True or false? There is a principal focus on each side of a lens.
3) Describe two differences between convex and concave lenses.
4) What is meant by a 'real image' and a 'virtual image'?
5) a) Draw a ray diagram for a convex lens. b) Now do one for — you guessed it — a concave lens.
6) What three pieces of information do you need to give to describe an image formed by a lens?
7) Describe the image formed by a convex lens when the distance from the object to the lens is:
   a) greater than 2F,   b) exactly 2F,   c) between F and 2F,   d) less than F.
8) Describe the image formed by a concave lens. How does this change as the distance between the object and the lens is increased?
9) What formula could you use to calculate the magnification of an object by a lens? What does it mean if the magnification of an object is greater than 1?
10) What type of lens does a magnifying glass use?

Visible Light (p.83-84)

11) What is visible light?
12) Name the primary colours of light.
13) What is an opaque object? What happens to light when it hits an opaque object?
14) How do different wavelengths of light behave when they hit an opaque object that is:
    a) black,   b) white,   c) blue?
15) How are transparent and translucent objects different from opaque objects?
16) Give an example of: a) a transparent object, and b) a translucent object.
17) Explain why a red apple appears black when it's looked at through a green colour filter.

Black Body Radiation and IR Radiation (p.85-87)

18) True or false? The cooler an object is, the more infrared radiation it emits in a given time.
19) What is a 'perfect black body'?
20) What is a black body curve? What is the 'peak wavelength' of a black body curve?
21) How would the black body curve for an object change if its temperature decreased?
22) a) What is a Leslie cube? How could you use one to investigate the IR radiation emitted by different surfaces?
    b) What results would you expect for this experiment?
23) a) How could you use the melting wax trick to investigate the absorption of IR radiation by different surfaces?
    b) Explain the results and what they tell you about IR absorption by different surfaces.

Topic 7 — Magnetism and Electromagnetism

Permanent and Induced Magnets

I think magnetism is an attractive subject, but don't get repelled by the exam — revise.

Magnets Exert Forces on Each Other

- All magnets have a north (or north seeking) pole and south (or south seeking) pole.
- All magnets produce a magnetic field — an area where other magnets or magnetic materials feel a force.
- The force felt in a magnetic field is a non-contact force (p.48).
- If two poles are put near each other, they will each exert a force on the other.
- Two like poles (poles that are the same) will repel each other.
- Two unlike poles will attract each other.

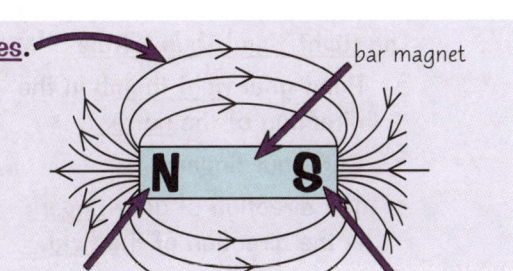

Iron, steel, nickel and cobalt are examples of magnetic materials.

1) You can show a magnetic field by drawing magnetic field lines.
2) The lines go from north to south. They show which way the force would push a north pole at that point.
3) Lines closer together mean a stronger magnetic field.
4) The closer to a magnet you are, the stronger the field is.
5) The magnetic field is strongest at the poles.
6) This means the magnetic force is strongest there too.

A Compass Shows the Direction of a Magnetic Field

- The needle of a compass is a tiny bar magnet. It points in the direction of any magnetic field that it's in.
- So you can use a compass to plot magnetic field patterns:

  1) Draw around a magnet on a piece of paper and put a compass by the magnet.
  2) Draw a dot at each end of the compass needle.
  3) Move the compass so that the tail end of the needle is where the tip of the needle was before.
  4) Repeat this lots of times. Join up all the marks. You will end up with a drawing of one field line.

- When they're not near a magnet, compasses always point north.
- This is because they point in the direction of the Earth's magnetic field.
- So the inside (core) of the Earth must be magnetic.

Magnets Can be Permanent or Induced

There are two types of magnet.

For induced magnets:
- When you take an induced magnet away from the magnetic field, it quickly stops being a magnet. It loses all (or most) of its magnetism.
- Permanent and induced magnets are always attracted to one another — there is always a force of attraction between them.

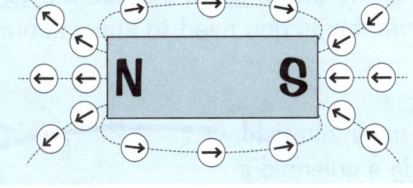

PERMANENT	Produce their own magnetic field.
INDUCED	Magnetic materials that turn into a magnet when they're put into a magnetic field.

Magnets are like farmers — surrounded by fields...

Magnetism is tricky and takes a while to make sense. Learn these basics — you'll need them.

Q1 What will happen when the north poles of two magnets are brought close together? [1 mark]

Electromagnetism

A magnetic field is also created around a wire that has a current passing through it. Fascinating stuff...

A Current Creates a Magnetic Field

1) A current flowing through a wire creates a magnetic field.
2) The field is made up of circles around the wire (see below).
3) You can see this by placing a compass near to the wire. The compass needle will move to point in the direction of the field.
4) You can use this to draw the field, just like on the previous page.
5) You can also use the right-hand thumb rule to quickly work out which way the field goes:

The Right-Hand Thumb Rule
- Point your right thumb in the direction of the current.
- Curl your fingers.
- The direction of your fingers is the direction of the field.

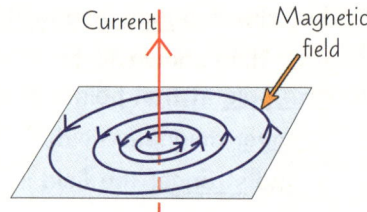
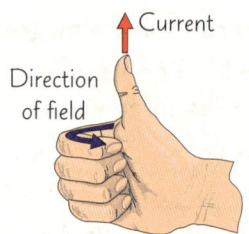

6) Reversing (swapping) the direction of the current reverses the direction of the magnetic field.
7) The closer to the wire you are, the stronger the magnetic field gets (the field lines are closer together nearer to the wire).
8) And the larger the current through the wire is, the stronger the field is.

A Solenoid is a Coil of Wire

If you wrap a wire into a coil it's called a solenoid.
Here are some things you need to know about solenoids when a current passes through them:

The magnetic field inside a solenoid is strong and uniform. A uniform field has the same strength and direction everywhere.

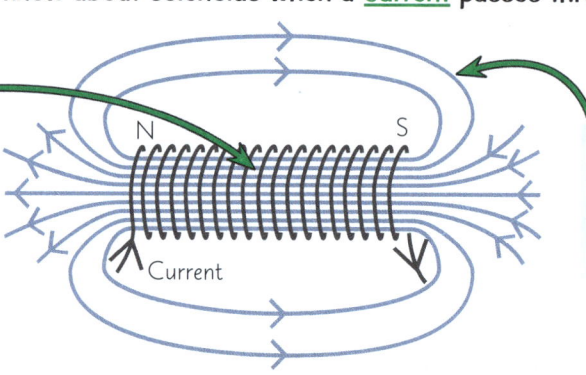

The magnetic field outside a coil is just like the one around a bar magnet.

- Wrapping a wire into a solenoid increases the strength of the magnetic field produced by the current in the wire.
  1) This is because the field lines around each loop of wire line up with each other.
  2) So lots of field lines end up close to each other and pointing in the same direction.
  3) The closer together field lines are, the stronger the field is.
- You can increase the field strength even more by putting a block of iron in the coil.
- A solenoid with an iron core is called an ELECTROMAGNET.

Strong, in uniform and a magnetic personality — I'm a catch...

There isn't a whole lot to learn, but this can be a fairly difficult topic. Have another read of this page.

Q1 Draw the magnetic field for a current-carrying wire. [2 marks]

Topic 7 — Magnetism and Electromagnetism

Electromagnetic Devices

Electromagnets are different from permanent magnets, and they have lots of helpful uses.

Electromagnets Have Lots of Uses

- Electromagnets only work when a current is flowing through the coil.
- This means they can be switched on and off (unlike permanent magnets, which are always magnetic).
- An electromagnet can be made stronger by increasing the current that flows through it.
- This means electromagnets can be made to be a lot stronger than permanent magnets.
- Electromagnets have a lot of uses...

They're Used to Lift Heavy Magnetic Loads...

Electromagnets can be used in cranes to pick up things made from magnetic materials, like iron and steel.

1) The cranes are used in scrapyards to separate magnetic material from material that isn't magnetic.
2) The crane has a large electromagnetic disc on the end of its arm.

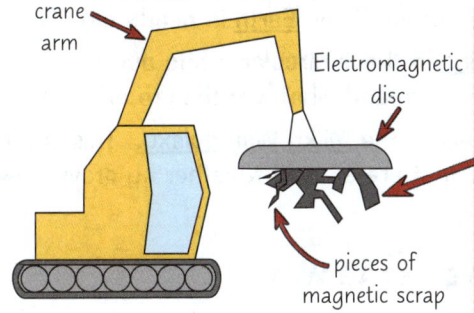

3) When a current flows, it becomes a powerful electromagnet and the magnetic scrap metal becomes attracted to the disc.
4) To drop the metal, the current is switched off. The disc is no longer an electromagnet and the metal falls.

...And They're Also Used to Start Other Circuits

- Electromagnets can also be used within other circuits to act as switches.
- The diagrams show an electromagnet being used to turn on a motor.

1) When the switch in circuit one is closed, it turns on the electromagnet.
2) The electromagnet is now magnetic and attracts the iron contact on the rocker (an arm that can move around a point).

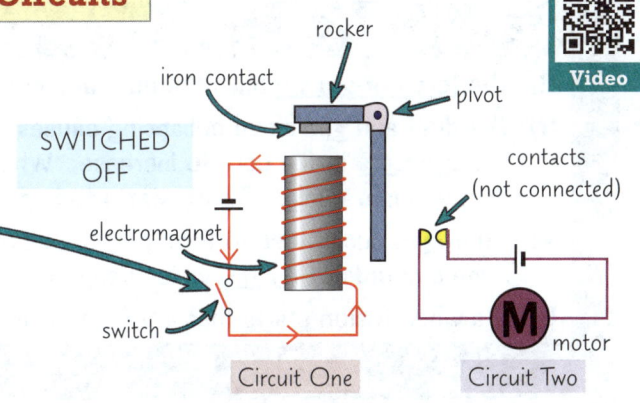

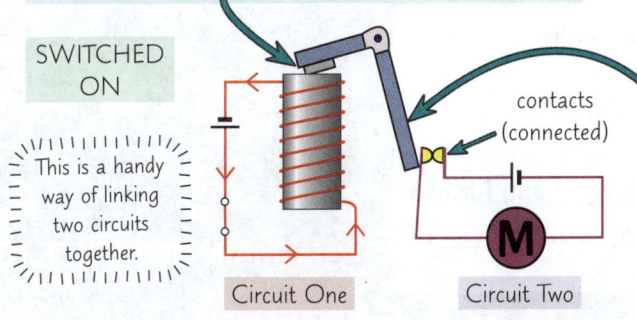

This is a handy way of linking two circuits together.

3) The rocker pivots (turns) towards the electromagnet.
4) The other end of the arm of the rocker presses against the contacts in circuit two.
5) This causes the contacts to touch, completing circuit two.
6) The motor turns on.

I tried to think of something IRONic — but nothing really stuck...

Electromagnets are used in everyday things such as alarms and trains, so you'd better learn how they work.

Q1   Name one advantage of using an electromagnet over a permanent magnet.   [1 mark]

Topic 8 — Space Physics

The Solar System and Stars

The Sun is the centre of our solar system. It's orbited by eight planets, along with a bunch of other objects.

Our Solar System has One Star — The Sun

- The solar system is the Sun and all the stuff that orbits it (moves round and round it). This includes:

PLANETS	Large objects that orbit a star. There are eight in our solar system — Mercury, Venus, Earth, Mars, Jupiter, Saturn, Uranus and Neptune.
DWARF PLANETS	Planet-like objects that orbit stars, but don't meet all of the rules for being a planet (like our pal, Pluto).
MOONS	Natural satellites (i.e. not man-made) that orbit planets.
ARTIFICIAL SATELLITES	Satellites built by humans — most of them orbit the Earth.

A satellite is an object that orbits a second, bigger object.

- The planets move around the Sun in almost circular orbits. The Moon and many artificial satellites also orbit the Earth in nearly circular orbits.
- These objects are kept moving in these circular orbits due to the force of gravity between them and whatever they're orbiting.
- Our solar system is a tiny part of the Milky Way galaxy. This is a massive collection of billions of stars that are all held together by gravity.

You are here.

All Stars Are Born in the Same Way

All stars go through a life cycle. This begins in the same way for all stars:

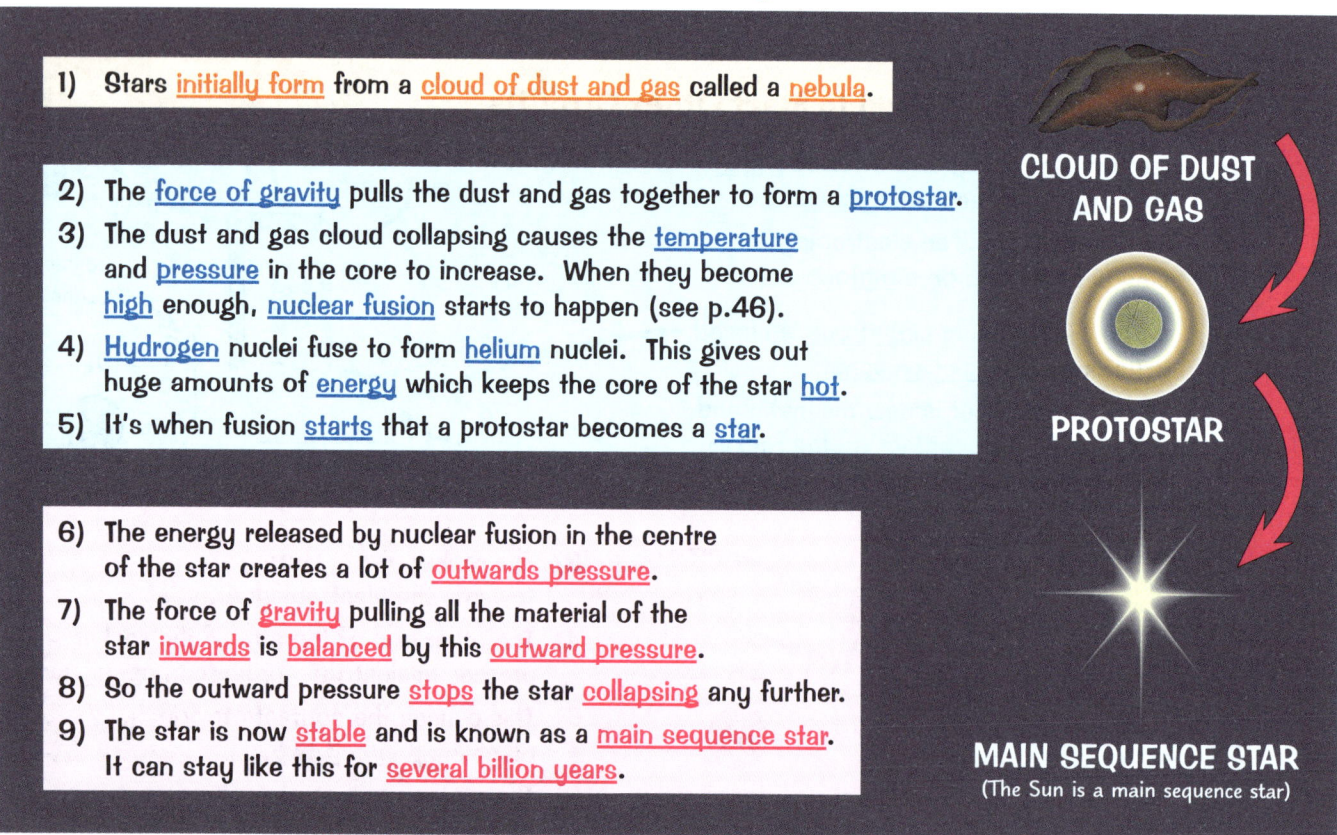

1) Stars initially form from a cloud of dust and gas called a nebula.

2) The force of gravity pulls the dust and gas together to form a protostar.
3) The dust and gas cloud collapsing causes the temperature and pressure in the core to increase. When they become high enough, nuclear fusion starts to happen (see p.46).
4) Hydrogen nuclei fuse to form helium nuclei. This gives out huge amounts of energy which keeps the core of the star hot.
5) It's when fusion starts that a protostar becomes a star.

6) The energy released by nuclear fusion in the centre of the star creates a lot of outwards pressure.
7) The force of gravity pulling all the material of the star inwards is balanced by this outward pressure.
8) So the outward pressure stops the star collapsing any further.
9) The star is now stable and is known as a main sequence star. It can stay like this for several billion years.

CLOUD OF DUST AND GAS

PROTOSTAR

MAIN SEQUENCE STAR
(The Sun is a main sequence star)

Revision's hard work — you've got to plan et...

Gravity is really the key to how stars form and why nearly everything in the solar system moves in orbits.

Q1   What provides an outwards pressure that is balanced by gravity in main sequence stars?   [1 mark]

The Life Cycle of Stars

Quick Quiz

Stars may all begin the same way, but how they end their life cycle depends on how big they are.

The Life Cycle of Main Sequence Stars Depends on Their Size and Mass

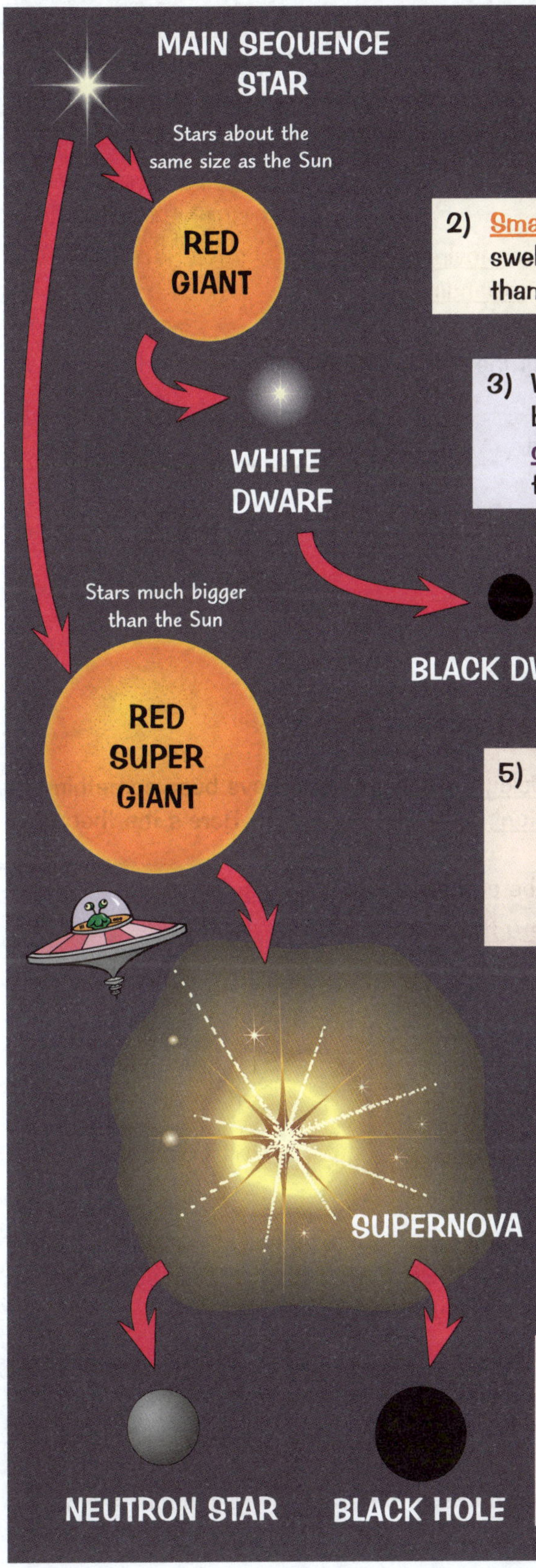

MAIN SEQUENCE STAR

Stars about the same size as the Sun → **RED GIANT** → **WHITE DWARF** → **BLACK DWARF**

Stars much bigger than the Sun → **RED SUPER GIANT** → **SUPERNOVA** → **NEUTRON STAR** / **BLACK HOLE**

1) Eventually the hydrogen in the core of a main sequence star begins to run out. The star then comes to the end of that stage of its life.

2) Small-to-medium-sized stars (with masses similar to our Sun) will swell up into red giants. A red giant will fuse elements heavier than hydrogen in nuclear fusion reactions to form other elements.

3) When all the fuel inside a red giant runs out, it becomes unstable. It ejects (throws out) its outer layers of dust and gas. This leaves behind the dense, solid core — known as a white dwarf.

4) White dwarfs start off very hot but they cool down over time. As they cool, they emit less and less energy. When they no longer emit much energy, they are called black dwarfs.

5) When really big stars (with a much larger mass than the Sun) run out of hydrogen, they will form red super giants. The star swells up and glows brightly again. Red super giants have enough energy to form elements as heavy as iron through nuclear fusion.

6) Eventually red super giants become unstable and blow up in a huge explosion called a supernova. The exploding supernova throws the outer layers of dust and gas into space. Supernovae form elements heavier than iron, and eject and scatter these elements across the universe. Stars and supernovae form all the natural elements in the universe.

Supernovae is the plural of supernova.

7) A supernova can leave behind a very dense core called a neutron star. Some stars have too much mass to become neutron stars. Instead, they become black holes. Black holes have such a strong gravitational pull that not even light can escape from them.

It's the end of the world as we know it...

Even our Sun will eventually come to the end one day. Don't worry though, we've got ages yet (billions of years).

Q1   Describe the steps of our Sun's life cycle after it becomes a red giant.   [3 marks]

Red-Shift and the Big Bang

'How it all began' is a tricky question that we just can't answer. Was it the chicken or the egg...

The Universe Seems to Be Expanding

1) All galaxies emit light. The wavelengths of light coming from far away galaxies have increased by the time the light reaches Earth. They've been shifted to the red end of the visible light spectrum (see p.83).
2) This is known as red-shift. When a galaxy moves away from us, the light from it gets red-shifted.
3) The faster a galaxy moves away from us, the greater the red-shift.
4) The more distant a galaxy is, the more the light from it is red-shifted. So the faster it is moving away from us.
5) Red-shift is good evidence that galaxies in the universe are moving away from each other and so the universe (and space itself) is expanding.

A greater red-shift just means the increase in wavelength of the light is bigger.

A good way to model the expansion of the universe is the balloon model:
- Imagine a balloon covered with pompoms.
- As you blow into the balloon, it stretches and the pompoms move further away from each other.
- The balloon is the universe and each pompom is a galaxy.
- As time goes on, space stretches and expands, moving the galaxies away from each other.

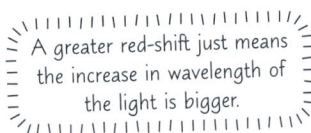

This Evidence Suggests the Universe Started with a Bang

So all the galaxies are moving away from each other very quickly. But there must have been something that got them going. That 'something' was probably a big 'explosion' called the Big Bang. Here's the theory...

- All the matter in the universe used to be crammed into a very small space.
- This tiny space was very dense and very hot.
- Then it 'exploded' — space started expanding and the expansion is still going on.

New Evidence Might Change Our Theories

There's more on scientific theories on p.96.

1) The Big Bang theory is the best idea we have to explain the universe so far.
2) When scientists discover new evidence that doesn't fit with their theory, they have to change their theories to explain what they've seen.
3) Scientists have been making observations of supernovae since 1998. What they've seen suggests that the furthest galaxies aren't just moving away from us quickly, they are actually speeding up.
4) This suggested that the expansion of the universe is getting faster.
5) Scientists now think that the reason for this expansion is because of something called dark energy. We now think the universe is mostly made up of dark energy and something else called dark matter (or dark mass).
6) No-one really knows what these things are yet, but there are lots of different theories about them.

There is still a lot we don't know about the universe.

And it all started with the Big Bang...

Or at least, that's what we currently think is most likely. Remember that theories change depending on evidence.

Q1 Briefly explain what the Big Bang theory is. [2 marks]

Topic 8 — Space Physics

Revision Summary Test for Topics 7 & 8

Space physics — the final ~~frontier~~ topic. Now it's time to test your knowledge of Topics 7 & 8:
- Tackle one of the revision summary tests below, or scan the QR code to do it online. The questions are hard, but they'll show you how well you really know your stuff.
- Track your progress online and see which areas need more work.
- Compare your answers with sample answers for the tests here: cgpbooks.co.uk/Mass

Topic 7

Permanent and Induced Magnets (p.89)

1) What is a magnetic field? Is the force felt in a magnetic field a contact or non-contact force?
2) Why do magnetic field lines point from north to south? How do the lines show how strong a field is?
3) Are the magnetic forces between these pairs attractive or repulsive? a) like poles, b) unlike poles.
4) Describe how you could use a compass to plot a magnetic field line of a bar magnet.
5) What is the difference between a permanent magnet and an induced magnet?

Electromagnetism (p.90-91)

6) What happens to the strength of the magnetic field at a point around a wire carrying a current when you: a) move closer to the wire, b) increase the current through the wire?
7) Describe the magnetic field inside and outside a solenoid when a current flows through it.
8) What is an electromagnet? Give two things electromagnets can do that permanent magnets can't.
9) Describe how an electromagnet in one circuit can be used to switch on a motor in another circuit.

Topic 8

The Solar System and the Life Cycle of Stars (p.92-93)

1) How many stars are there in our solar system? And how many planets?
2) What do planets and dwarf planets orbit?
3) Is a moon an artificial satellite or a natural satellite? What do moons orbit?
4) What shape is the orbit of a planet around the Sun? What force keeps the planet in this orbit?
5) What is a nebula? How is a protostar formed from a nebula?
6) What causes a protostar to turn into a main sequence star?
7) How long is a main sequence star typically stable for? What makes it stable?
8) A main sequence star that is a similar size to the Sun starts to run out of hydrogen. What happens inside the core of this star when this happens?
9) What kind of size do stars have to be to turn into: a) red giants,   b) red super giants.
10) Describe what happens to a red giant once it has run out of fuel. What does it turn into?
11) How does a black dwarf form from a white dwarf?
12) At what stage in the life cycle of a star are elements heavier than iron made?
13) What two things can be left behind by a star after a supernova?

Red-Shift and the Big Bang (p.94)

14) What is red-shift?
15) How can red-shift tell us how fast galaxies are moving? How does it tell us the universe is expanding?
16) Describe the ideas that make up the Big Bang theory.
17) What have scientists discovered from the observation of supernovae since 1998?

Working Scientifically

The Scientific Method

This section <u>isn't</u> about how to 'do' science — but it does show you the way <u>most scientists</u> work.

Science is All About Testing Hypotheses

1) Scientists make an observation

- Scientists <u>observe</u> (look at) something they don't understand, e.g. the structure of the atom (see pages 38 and 39).
- They come up with a <u>possible explanation</u> for what they've observed.
- This explanation is called a <u>hypothesis</u>.

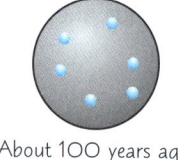

About 100 years ago, scientists had a hypothesis that atoms looked like this.

2) They test their hypothesis

- They do this by making a <u>prediction</u> — a statement based on the hypothesis that can be tested.
- They then <u>test</u> this prediction by carrying out <u>experiments</u>.
- If their prediction is <u>right</u>, this is <u>evidence</u> that their <u>hypothesis might be right</u> too.

3) Other scientists test the hypothesis too

- Other scientists <u>check</u> the evidence — for example, they check that the experiment was carried out in a <u>sensible</u> way. This is called <u>peer-review</u>.
- Scientists then <u>share their results</u>, e.g. in scientific papers.
- Other scientists carry out <u>more experiments</u> to test the hypothesis.
- Sometimes these scientists will find more evidence that the <u>hypothesis is right</u>.
- Sometimes they'll find evidence that shows the <u>hypothesis is wrong</u>.

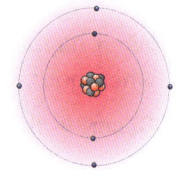

After gathering more evidence, scientists thought they looked more like this.

4) The hypothesis is accepted or rejected

- If <u>all the evidence</u> that's been found <u>supports</u> the hypothesis, it becomes the basis of an <u>accepted theory</u>. It might go into <u>textbooks</u> for people to learn.
- Our currently accepted theories are ones that have survived <u>lots</u> of rounds of <u>testing</u> over many <u>years</u>.
- If the <u>evidence</u> shows that the hypothesis is <u>wrong</u>, scientists must:
  a) <u>change</u> the hypothesis, OR b) come up with a <u>new hypothesis</u>.

Now they think it's more like this.

Theories Can Involve Different Types of Models

1) A <u>model</u> is a <u>simple way</u> of <u>describing</u> or <u>showing</u> what's going on in <u>real life</u>.
2) Models can be used to <u>explain ideas</u> and <u>make predictions</u>.
3) All models have <u>limits</u> — a single model <u>can't explain</u> everything about an idea.

Example — The Big Bang Model

- The <u>Big Bang Model</u> is used to describe the <u>start</u> of the <u>universe</u>.
- It can be used to explain why everything in the universe is <u>moving away</u> from us (p.94).
- But it doesn't explain what happened in the moments <u>before</u> the Big Bang.

There are different types of models, including:
- <u>Representational models</u> — simplified descriptions or pictures, e.g. the <u>Bohr model</u> of an atom (see p.38).
- <u>Mathematical models</u> — equations and numerical explanations, e.g. $pV = $ <u>constant</u> for gases, (p.37).

I'm off to the zoo to test my hippo-thesis...

You can see just how much testing has to be done before an idea gets accepted as a theory. If scientists aren't busy testing their own, then they're busy testing someone else's. Or just playing with their models.

Communication & Issues Created by Science

Scientific developments can be great, but they can sometimes raise more questions than they answer...

It's Important to Tell People About Scientific Discoveries

1) Scientists should tell the world about their discoveries, as they can make a big difference to people's lives.
2) They might need to advise people to change their habits, e.g. stop smoking to protect against lung cancer.
3) They might also need to tell people about new technologies. For example:

- Radioactive materials are widely used in medicine (see p.45).
- Doctors need to be given information about these materials so they can use them.
- Patients need information so they can make an informed decision about their treatment.

Scientific Evidence can be Presented in a Biased Way

1) Reports about scientific discoveries in the media (e.g. newspapers or TV) can sometimes be misleading.
2) The data might be presented in a way that's not quite right. Or it might be oversimplified.
3) This means that people may not properly understand what the scientists found out.
4) People who want to make a point can also sometimes present data in a biased way (in a way that's unfair or ignores one side of the argument). For example:

People can sometimes present data in a biased way by accident.

- A scientist may talk a lot about one particular relationship in the data (and not mention others).
- A newspaper article might report data supporting an idea without giving any evidence against it.

Scientific Developments are Great, but they can Raise Issues

Economic (money) issues	Society can't always afford to do what scientists recommend, like spending money on green energy resources.
Social (people) issues	Decisions based on scientific evidence affect people. For example, should fossil fuels be taxed more highly? These decisions can affect some groups of people more than others, which can be unfair.
Personal issues	Some decisions will affect individuals. For example, people may be upset if a wind farm is built next to their house.
Environmental issues	Human activity often affects the environment. For example, building a dam to produce electricity can change the habitat for wildlife.

Science Can't Answer Every Question — Especially Ethical Ones

1) At the moment scientists don't agree on some things — like what the universe is made of.
2) This is because there isn't enough data yet to support the scientists' hypotheses.
3) Eventually, we probably will be able to answer these questions once and for all.
4) But experiments can't tell us whether something is ethically right or wrong. E.g. whether it's right for people to use new drugs to help them do better in exams.
5) The best we can do is make a decision that most people are more or less happy to live by.

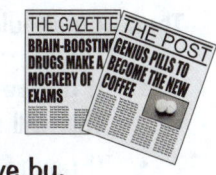

Tea to milk or milk to tea? — Totally unanswerable by science...

Science can't tell you whether or not you should do something. That's for you and society to decide. But there are tons of questions science might be able to answer, like where life came from and where my superhero socks are.

Risk

WARNING — by reading this page you are agreeing to the risk of a paper cut...

Every Hazard has a Risk Attached to it

HAZARD — something that could cause harm.
RISK — the chance that the hazard will cause harm.

To make a decision about activities that involve hazards, we need to think about:
- the chance of the hazard causing harm,
- how bad the outcome (consequences) would be if it did.

New technology can bring new risks. E.g. scientists are creating technology to capture and store carbon dioxide. But if the carbon dioxide leaked out it could damage soil or water supplies. These risks need to be considered alongside the benefits of the technology, e.g. lower greenhouse gas emissions.

A good way to estimate the size of a risk is to look at data. E.g. you could estimate the risk of a driver crashing by recording how many people in a group of 100 000 drivers crashed their cars over a year.

People Have Different Opinions on Taking Risks

There are lots of factors that can affect how people feel about taking different risks:

Familiarity

People tend to think familiar activities are low-risk. They tend to think unfamiliar activities are high-risk. But this isn't always true. For example:
- Cycling on roads is often high-risk. But it's a familiar activity, so many people are happy to do it.
- Air travel is actually pretty safe, but a lot of people think it is high-risk.

Choice

People tend to be more willing to accept a risk if they choose to do something, compared to having the risk imposed on them (e.g. having a nuclear power station built next door).

Visibility

People may underestimate the risk of things with long-term or invisible effects, e.g. using tanning beds.

Investigations Can Have Hazards

Hazards from science experiments include things like:

LASERS 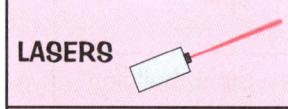	A laser directed into someone's eye can cause blindness.	ELECTRICITY 	Faulty electrical equipment could give you a shock.
GAMMA RADIATION 	Gamma-emitting radioactive sources can cause cancer.	FIRE 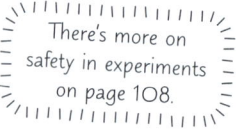	An unattended Bunsen burner is a fire hazard.

When you plan an investigation you need to make sure that it's safe. You should identify all the hazards that you might come across. Then you should think of ways of reducing the risks. For example:

There's more on safety in experiments on page 108.

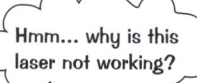

- If you're working with springs, always wear safety goggles. This will reduce the risk of the spring hitting your eye if the spring snaps.
- If you're using a Bunsen burner, stand it on a heat proof mat. This will reduce the risk of starting a fire.

Not revising — an unacceptable exam hazard...

The world is a dangerous place. You need to look out for hazards and find ways to reduce their risks.

Designing Investigations

Dig out your lab coat and dust down your badly-scratched safety goggles... it's investigation time.

Investigations Produce Evidence to Support or Disprove a Hypothesis

1) Like all great scientists, you'll need to be able to come up with a hypothesis to explain an observation (see p.96).
2) To find out if a hypothesis is right, you need to do an investigation to gather evidence.
3) To do this, you need to use your hypothesis to make a prediction — something you think will happen and can test.
4) Investigations are used to see if there are patterns or relationships between two variables. E.g. to see if there's a relationship between the variables 'number of spots' and 'size of feet'.

❶ Observation: People have big feet and spots.

❷ Hypothesis: Having big feet causes spots.

❸ Prediction: People who have bigger feet will have more spots.

To Make an Investigation a Fair Test You Have to Control the Variables

1) In a lab experiment you usually change one thing (a variable) and measure how it affects another thing (another variable).
2) Everything else (all other variables) that could affect the results needs to stay the same. Then you know that the thing you're changing is the only thing that's affecting the results.

The different kinds of variables are:

INDEPENDENT	The variable that you change
DEPENDENT	The variable that you measure
CONTROL	The variables you keep the same

EXAMPLE: you might change the current through a circuit component and see how it affects the pd:
- Independent variable = current
- Dependent variable = pd
- Control variables = temperature of the component, pd of the power supply, etc.

3) Because you can't always control all the variables, you often need to use a control experiment.
4) This is an experiment that's kept under the same conditions as the rest of the investigation, but doesn't have anything done to it.
5) Control experiments let you see what happens when you don't change anything at all.

Evidence Needs to be Repeatable, Reproducible and Valid

REPEATABLE — if the same person does the experiment again, they'll get similar results. To check your results are repeatable, repeat the readings at least three times. Then check the repeat results are all similar.

REPRODUCIBLE — if someone else does the experiment, the results will still be similar. To make sure your results are reproducible, get another person to do the experiment too.

VALID RESULTS — results that are both repeatable and reproducible, and that answer the original question. They have come from experiments designed to be a fair test.

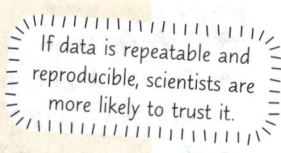
If data is repeatable and reproducible, scientists are more likely to trust it.

This is no high street survey — it's a designer investigation...

You need to be able to plan your own investigations. You should also be able to look at someone else's plan and decide whether anything needs to be changed to make it better. Those examiners are pretty demanding.

Collecting Data

So you've designed the perfect investigation — now it's time to get your hands mucky and collect some data.

The Bigger the Sample Size the Better

1) Sample size is the number of observations or measurements you make in an investigation, e.g. 500 people or 20 different lengths of wire.
2) A bigger sample size reduces the chance of any weird results.
3) But scientists have to be realistic when choosing how big their sample should be. For example:

> If you were studying the effects of living near a nuclear power plant, it'd be great to study everyone who lived near a nuclear power plant (a huge sample), but it'd take ages and cost loads.
> Instead, it'd be more realistic to study 1000 people, with a range of ages, genders and races. This sample would be representative of the population as a whole.

Your Data Should be Precise and Accurate

> PRECISE RESULTS — where the data is all really close to the mean (average) of your repeated results (i.e. not spread out).
> ACCURATE RESULTS — results that are really close to the true answer.

- The accuracy of your results usually depends on your method.
- E.g. estimating the volume of an irregularly shaped solid by measuring the sides isn't very accurate — it doesn't account for any gaps in the object. It's more accurate to measure the volume using a eureka can (see p.34).

Repeat	Data set 1	Data set 2
1	12	11
2	14	17
3	13	14
Mean	13	14

Data set 1 is more precise than data set 2.

Your Equipment has to be Right for the Job

1) The measuring equipment you use has to be sensitive enough to measure accurately.

   E.g. if you need to measure out 11 cm³ of a liquid, use a measuring cylinder that can measure in steps of 1 cm³ — not steps of 5 or 10 cm³.

2) You also need to set up the equipment properly.

   For example, make sure your mass balance is set to zero before you start weighing things.

Look out for Errors and Anomalous Results

Systematic errors

- This is when a measurement is wrong by the same amount every time.
- E.g. if you measure from the very end of your ruler instead of from the 0 cm mark every time, all your measurements would be a bit small.
- If you know you've made a systematic error, you might be able to correct it. For example, by adding a bit on to all your measurements.

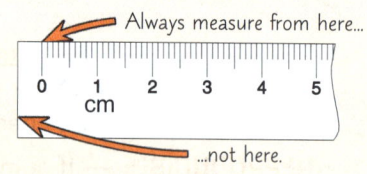
Always measure from here...
...not here.

Random errors

- The results of an experiment will always vary a bit because of random errors, e.g. an inaccuracy in your measuring.
- To reduce the effect of random errors, take repeat readings and find the mean.

Anomalous results

- A result that doesn't fit with the rest.
- You should try to find what caused it.
- Then you can ignore it when processing your results (next page).

The bigger the better — what's true for cakes is true for samples...

Make sure you take lots of care when collecting data — there's plenty to watch out for, as you can see.

Processing and Presenting Data

As I always say, trust the process, and read on to see how you can go about making your data more useful...

Tables are Useful for Organising Data

When you draw a table, use a ruler and make sure each column has a heading (including the units).

Test tube	Repeat 1 (cm^3)	Repeat 2 (cm^3)
A	28	37
B	47	51

Mean, Median and Mode are Types of Average

1) When you've done repeats of an experiment you should always calculate the mean.
2) The median is the middle value when you write your data from smallest to largest.
3) The number that appears most often is the mode.
4) You might also need to calculate the range (how spread out the data is).

When people say to calculate 'the average', they're usually talking about the mean.

If you have an even number of values, the median is halfway between the middle two values.

EXAMPLE

The results in the table show the extension of two springs when a force is applied to both of them. Calculate the mean extension and the range.

Extension (cm)		
Repeat 1	Repeat 2	Repeat 3
18	26	22

1) To calculate the mean, add together all the values. Then divide by the number of values in the sample. $(18 + 26 + 22) \div 3 = 22$ cm
2) To calculate the range, subtract the smallest number from the largest number. $26 - 18 = 8$ cm

Round to the Lowest Number of Significant Figures

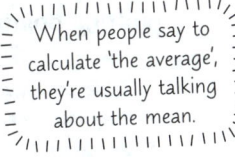
1st significant figure
0.0307
2nd 3rd

1) The first significant figure of a number is the first digit that's not zero.
2) The second and third significant figures come straight after (even if they're zeros).
3) In any calculation, you should round the answer to the lowest number of significant figures (s.f.) given.
4) If your calculation has more than one step, only round the final answer.

EXAMPLE

The mass of a solid is 0.24 g and its volume is 0.715 cm^3. Calculate the density of the solid.

Density = mass ÷ volume
= 0.24 g ÷ 0.715 cm^3 = 0.33566... = 0.34 g/cm^3 (2 s.f.)
2 s.f.   3 s.f.

Final answer should be rounded to 2 s.f.

If Your Data Comes in Categories, Present it in a Bar Chart

If the independent variable comes in clear categories (e.g. solid, liquid, gas) or can be counted exactly (e.g. number of protons) you should use a bar chart to display the data:

The UK's Top 40 Bar Charts
1. The Leaky Tap ↑2
2. Benny's Barstool —○
3. The Regal Eagle ↓2
4. The Chic Saloon ↑1

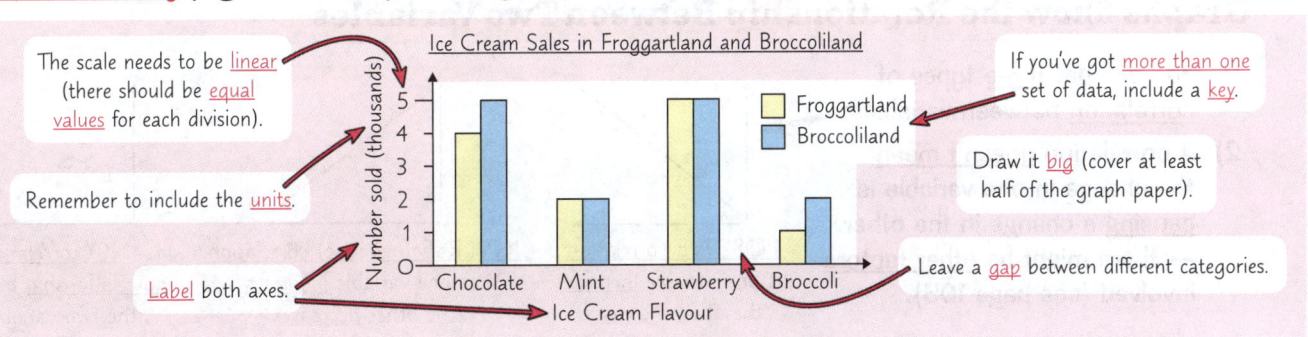

The scale needs to be linear (there should be equal values for each division).

Remember to include the units.

Label both axes.

If you've got more than one set of data, include a key.

Draw it big (cover at least half of the graph paper).

Leave a gap between different categories.

I figured this page would be pretty significant to you...

Mode, median, mean — that's a lot of M's. It can be really easy to get them mixed up, so try to remember: the mode is the MOst common number, the median is the MiDdle number and the mean just means 'the average'.

More on Processing and Presenting Data

You see, I'd make a joke about the gradient of graphs here — but that can become quite the slippery slope...

If Your Data is Continuous, Plot a Graph

If both variables can have any value within a range (e.g. length, volume) use a graph to display the data.

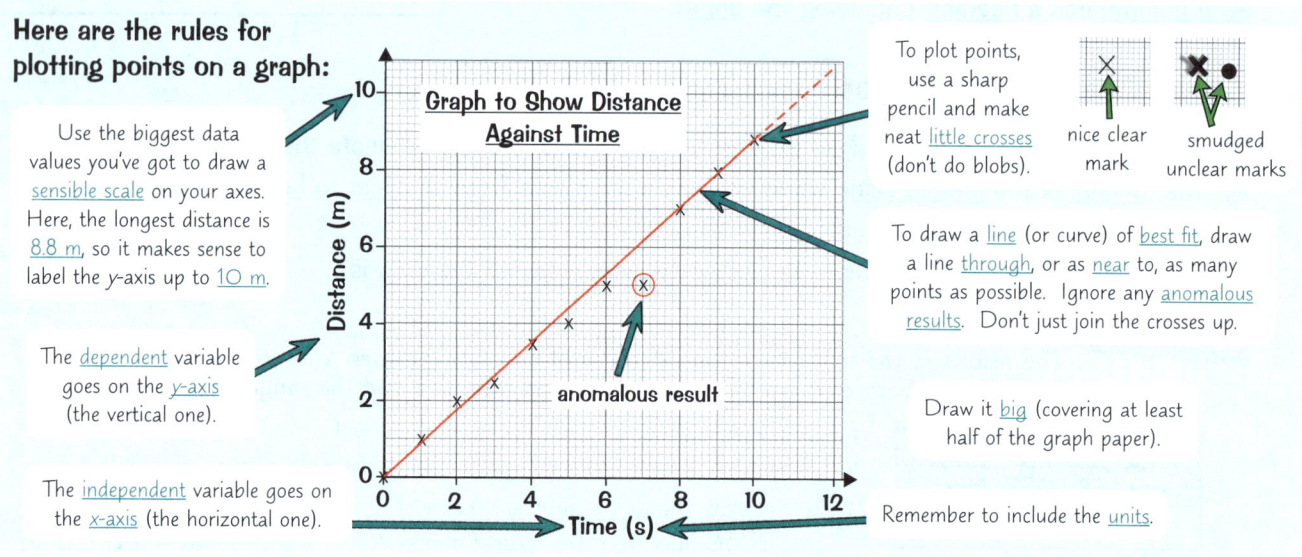

Here are the rules for plotting points on a graph:

Use the biggest data values you've got to draw a sensible scale on your axes. Here, the longest distance is 8.8 m, so it makes sense to label the y-axis up to 10 m.

The dependent variable goes on the y-axis (the vertical one).

The independent variable goes on the x-axis (the horizontal one).

To plot points, use a sharp pencil and make neat little crosses (don't do blobs). — nice clear mark / smudged unclear marks

To draw a line (or curve) of best fit, draw a line through, or as near to, as many points as possible. Ignore any anomalous results. Don't just join the crosses up.

Draw it big (covering at least half of the graph paper).

Remember to include the units.

You Need to be Able to Calculate the Gradient of a Graph

The gradient (slope) of a graph tells you how quickly the dependent variable changes if you change the independent variable.

$$\text{gradient} = \frac{\text{change in } y}{\text{change in } x}$$

You can use the gradient to find different things, depending on what variables are on the axes.

This graph shows the distance walked by a person against time. The graph is linear (it's a straight line). You can calculate the gradient of the line to find out the speed of the person.

1) To calculate the gradient, pick two points on the line that are easy to read and a good distance apart.

2) Draw a line down from the top point and a line across from the bottom point to make a triangle. The line drawn down the side of the triangle is the change in y and the line across the bottom is the change in x.

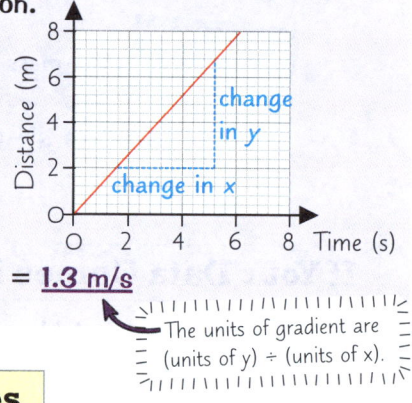

$$\text{Speed} = \frac{\text{distance}}{\text{time}} = \text{gradient} = \frac{\text{change in } y}{\text{change in } x} = \frac{6.8 - 2}{5.2 - 1.6} = \frac{4.8 \text{ m}}{3.6 \text{ s}} = 1.3 \text{ m/s}$$

The units of gradient are (units of y) ÷ (units of x).

Graphs Show the Relationship Between Two Variables

1) You can get three types of correlation between variables:

2) A correlation doesn't mean the change in one variable is causing a change in the other — there might be other factors involved (see page 105).

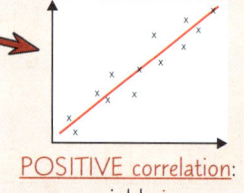
POSITIVE correlation: as one variable increases the other increases.

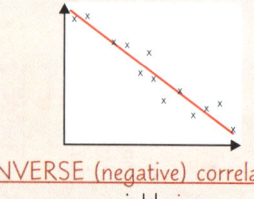
INVERSE (negative) correlation: as one variable increases the other decreases.

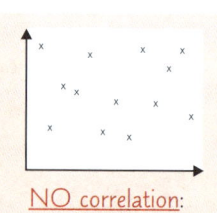
NO correlation: no relationship between the two variables.

I love eating apples — I call it core elation...

Science is all about finding relationships between things. And I don't mean that scientists gather together in corners to discuss whether or not Devini and Sebastian might be a couple... though they probably do that too.

Units

Drawing graphs is all very well, but the data doesn't mean much if you can't get the units right.

S.I. Units Are Used All Round the World

- All scientists use the same units to measure their data.
- These are standard units, called S.I. units.
- Here are some S.I. units you might come across:

Quantity	S.I. Base Unit
mass	kilogram, kg
length	metre, m
time	second, s
temperature	kelvin, K

Different Sized Units Help You Write Large and Small Quantities

- Quantities come in a huge range of sizes.
- To make the size of numbers easier to handle, larger or smaller units are used.
- Larger and smaller units are written as the S.I. base unit with a little word in front (a prefix). Here are some examples of prefixes and what they mean:

Kilogram is an exception. It's an S.I. unit with the prefix already on it.

Prefix	mega (M)	kilo (k)	deci (d)	centi (c)	milli (m)	micro (μ)	nano (n)
How it compares to the base unit	1 000 000 times bigger	1000 times bigger	10 times smaller	100 times smaller	1000 times smaller	1 000 000 times smaller	1 000 000 000 times smaller

E.g. 1 kilometre is 1000 metres.   E.g. there are 1000 millimetres in 1 metre.

You Need to be Able to Convert Between Units

Here are some conversions that'll be useful for GCSE physics:

Mass can have units of kg and g.

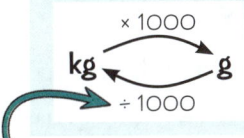

Volume can have units of m^3 and cm^3.

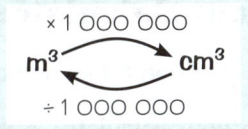

Length can have lots of units, including m, mm and μm.

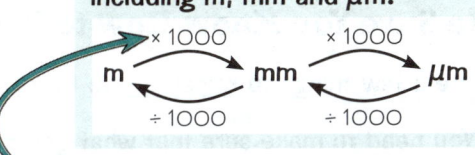

DIVIDE to go from a smaller unit to a bigger unit.   MULTIPLY to go from a bigger unit to a smaller unit.

EXAMPLE   A car has travelled 0.015 kilometres. How many metres has it travelled?

1 km = 1000 m. So to convert from km (a bigger unit) to m (a smaller unit) you need to multiply by 1000.

0.015 km × 1000 = 15 m

Always Check the Values Used in Equations Have the Right Units

You may have to convert a value into different units before you can put it into the formula.

To make sure your units are right, it can help to write them down on each line of your calculation.

EXAMPLE   In an experiment to find the average speed of a trolley, the trolley travels 30 cm in 3 seconds. Calculate the average speed of the trolley in m/s.

1) Convert the distance measurement from cm into m by dividing by the correct conversion factor.

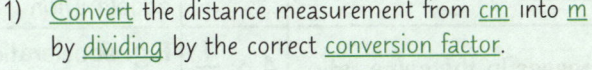

30 cm →(÷100)→ 0.3 m

2) Find the speed using speed = distance ÷ time.

$v = s ÷ t = 0.3 ÷ 3 = 0.1$ m/s

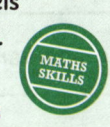

I wasn't sure I liked units, but now I'm converted...

If you're moving from a smaller unit to a larger unit (e.g. g to kg) the number should get smaller, and vice versa.

Maths Skills

No, you haven't opened a maths book. Maths comes up all the time in physics, so get comfortable using it.

Standard Form Can be Used For Really Big or Really Small Numbers

You need to know how to deal with numbers in standard form. They always look like this:

A is a number between 1 and 10, but not including 10.

$A \times 10^n$

n is the number of places the decimal point would move if you wrote the number out fully. It's negative for numbers less than 1, and positive for numbers greater than 1.

So 200 000 Pa is 2×10^5 Pa in standard form. And 0.0000038 m is 3.8×10^{-6} m.

To Rearrange a Formula, do the Same Thing to Both Sides

- You might need to rearrange a formula to be able to solve for the variable (thing) you want.
- You need to do the same thing to each side until you get that variable on its own.

EXAMPLE

Rearrange $E_e = \frac{1}{2} ke^2$ to solve for k.

1) You're trying to get k on its own. $E_e = \frac{1}{2} ke^2$
2) Multiply both sides by 2 to get rid of the fraction. $2 \times E_e = 2 \times \frac{1}{2} ke^2$
3) Simplify the right-hand side to tidy things up. $2E_e = ke^2$
4) Divide both sides by e^2. $\frac{2E_e}{e^2} = \frac{ke^2}{e^2}$
5) Simplify the right-hand side again. Then flip things around so k is on the left. $k = \frac{2E_e}{e^2}$

You can put simple formulas into formula triangles if you find them helpful:

$A = B \times C$ 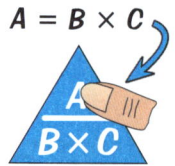 $D = E \div F$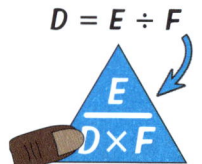

To use them, cover up what you want to find and write down what's left showing.

Make Sure You Know How to Use Your Calculator Correctly

Here are a few things to remember to make sure you don't lose marks for calculator mistakes:

- You need to make sure that what you put in your calculator is the same calculation as is on the page, even if it looks a bit different.
- For example, to put $\frac{11.5 + 6.8}{3}$ into any standard calculator, you type (11.5 + 6.8) ÷ 3. Don't forget the brackets. You could also use the fraction button on a scientific calculator.

Your calculator will follow the order of operations for what you've typed. If you forget the brackets, it won't do the calculation you want and you'll get 13.766... instead of 6.1.

Use exact values from previous calculations in your calculator rather than rounding (p.101). Make sure you know how to find these values on your calculator — e.g. by using the 'Ans' button or scrolling up.

Proportionality is a Way to Describe How Two Variables are Related

There are two types of proportionality:

This symbol means 'is proportional to'.

DIRECT	As one variable increases, the other increases in the same ratio.	$A \propto B$	E.g. force and acceleration
INVERSE	As one variable increases, the other decreases in the same ratio.	$A \propto \frac{1}{B}$	E.g. acceleration and mass

> Some people love formula triangles, some people not so much. You can use them as a tool if you want to, but you need to know how to rearrange formulas properly, not least because complicated formulas don't work in triangles.
>
> ## This tip box is in non-standard form...

Drawing Conclusions

Congratulations — you're nearly at the end of a gruelling investigation. Time to draw some conclusions.

You Can Only Conclude What the Data Shows and NO MORE

1) To come to a conclusion, look at your data and say what you see.

EXAMPLE: The table on the right shows the current through a light bulb for three different pds across the bulb:

Potential difference (V)	Current (A)
6	4
9	10
12	13

CONCLUSION: When the pd across the bulb is higher, the current through the bulb is higher.

2) It's important that your conclusion matches the data you've got and doesn't go any further.

EXAMPLE continued: You can't conclude that a higher potential difference than 12 V gives a higher current.

3) You also need to be able to use your results to justify your conclusion (i.e. back it up).

EXAMPLE continued: The current through the bulb was 9 A higher with a pd of 12 V compared to the current at 6 V.

4) When writing a conclusion you need to say whether the data supports the original hypothesis.

EXAMPLE continued: The hypothesis might have been that the current through the bulb is higher when the pd across the bulb is higher. If so, the data supports the hypothesis.

Correlation DOES NOT Mean Cause

1) If two things are correlated, there's a relationship between them — see page 102.
2) But a correlation doesn't always mean that a change in one variable is causing the change in the other.
3) There are three possible reasons for a correlation:

1 CHANCE

The results happened by chance. Other scientists wouldn't get a correlation if they carried out the same investigation.

E.g. a study might find a correlation between people's hair colour and their frisbee skills. But other scientists don't get a correlation — the results of the first study are just a fluke.

2 LINKED BY A 3rd VARIABLE

There's another factor involved.

E.g. there's a correlation between seawater temperature and shark attacks. They're linked by a third variable — the number of people swimming (more people swim when the water's warmer, which means you get more shark attacks).

3 CAUSE

Sometimes a change in one variable does cause a change in the other. You can only conclude this when you've controlled all the variables that could be affecting the result.

E.g. there's a correlation between smoking and lung cancer. This is because chemicals in tobacco smoke cause lung cancer. This conclusion was only made once other variables had been controlled. This allowed the effect of smoking to be isolated and shown to increase the risk of someone getting lung cancer.

I conclude that this page is a bit dull...

In the exams you could be given a conclusion and asked whether some data supports it — so make sure you understand how far conclusions can go. And remember, correlation does not (necessarily) mean cause.

Uncertainties and Evaluations

Hurrah! The end of another investigation. Well, now you have to work out all the things you did wrong.

Uncertainty is the Amount of Error Your Measurements Might Have

1) Measurements you make will have some uncertainty in them (i.e. they won't be completely perfect).
2) This can be due to random errors (see page 100).
   It can also be due to limits in what your measuring equipment can measure.
3) Random errors cause some uncertainty in the mean of your results.
4) You can calculate the uncertainty of a mean result using this equation:
5) The less precise your results are, the higher the uncertainty will be.
6) Uncertainties are shown using the '±' symbol.

The range is the largest value minus the smallest value (p.101).

$$\text{uncertainty} = \frac{\text{range}}{2}$$

EXAMPLE

The table below shows the results of an experiment to find the speed of a trolley. Calculate the uncertainty of the mean.

1) First work out the range:
   Range = 2.02 − 1.98
   = 0.04 m/s

Repeat	1	2	3	mean
Speed (m/s)	2.02	1.98	2.00	2.00

2) Use the range to find the uncertainty: Uncertainty = range ÷ 2 = 0.04 ÷ 2 = 0.02 m/s
   So, uncertainty of the mean = 2.00 ± 0.02 m/s

Evaluations — Describe How it Could be Improved

1) In an evaluation you look back over the whole investigation:

   - You should comment on the method — was it valid?
     Did you control all the other variables to make it a fair test?
   - Comment on the quality of the results — was there enough evidence to reach a valid conclusion?
     Were the results repeatable, reproducible, accurate and precise?
   - Were there any anomalous results? If there were none then say so.
     If there were any, try to explain them — were they caused by errors in measurement?
   - You should comment on the level of uncertainty in your results too.

I'd value this E somewhere in the region of 250-300k

2) Thinking about these things lets you say how confident you are that your conclusion is right.
3) Then you can suggest any changes to the method that would improve the quality of the results, so you could have more confidence in your conclusion.
4) For example, taking measurements at narrower intervals could give you a more accurate result:

   - Say you do an experiment to find the limit of proportionality of a spring (see p.52).
   - You apply forces of 1 N, 2 N, 3 N, 4 N and 5 N.
     The results show that the limit of proportionality is somewhere between 4 N and 5 N.
   - To get a more accurate result, you could repeat the experiment and take more measurements between 4 N and 5 N. You might then find that the limit of proportionality is 4.6 N.

5) You could also make more predictions based on your conclusion.
   You could then carry out further experiments to test the new predictions.

Evaluation — next time, I'll make sure I don't burn the lab down...

So there you have it — Working Scientifically. Make sure you know this stuff like the back of your hand. It's not just in the lab that you'll need to know how to work scientifically. You can be asked about it in the exams as well.

Practical Skills

Apparatus and Techniques

Get your lab coat on, it's time to find out about the skills you'll need in experiments...

Measure the Mass of Solids and Liquids Using a Balance

FOR A LIQUID...
1) Put an empty container onto the balance.
2) Reset the balance to zero.
3) Pour your liquid into the container.
4) Read off the mass.

FOR A SOLID...
1) Set the balance to zero.
2) Place your object onto the scale.
3) Read off the mass.

Measure Most Lengths with a Ruler

1) Make sure you choose the right ruler to measure length:
   - In most cases a centimetre ruler can be used.
   - Metre rulers are handy for large distances.
   - Micrometers are used for measuring tiny things (e.g. the diameter of a wire).

2) The ruler should always be alongside what you want to measure.

3) You might need to take lots of measurements of the same object (e.g. a spring). Always measure from the same point on the object — you can put a small marker onto the object to line your ruler up against.

4) It may be tricky to measure just one of something (e.g. water ripples, p.71). Instead, you can measure the length of ten of them together. Then divide your measurement by ten to find the length of one.

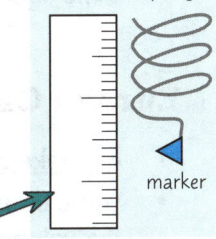

The ruler and the object should always be at eye level when you take a reading.

Use a Protractor to Find Angles

1) Place the middle of the protractor on the pointy bit of the angle.
2) Line up the base line of the protractor with one line of the angle.
3) Use the scale on the protractor to measure the angle of the other line.

Use a sharp pencil to draw lines at an angle (e.g. in ray diagrams). This helps to reduce errors when measuring the angles.

Measure Temperature Using a Thermometer

- Make sure the bulb of your thermometer is completely under the surface of the substance.
- If you're taking a starting temperature, you should wait for the temperature to stop changing.
- Read your measurement off the scale at eye level.

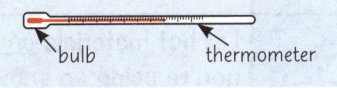

You May Have to Measure the Time Taken for a Change

- You should use a stopwatch to time most experiments.
- They are more accurate than regular watches.
- Always make sure you start and stop the stopwatch at exactly the right time.
- You might be able to use a light gate instead (p.109).

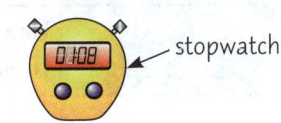

Experimentus apparatus...

You need to know the right kit to use, and how to use it. Speaking of which, that's a thermometer, not a magic wand.

Find the CGP RevisionHub at cgpbooks.co.uk/Mass

More Apparatus and Techniques

More bits of equipment on this page and how to use them accurately. Then a bit on how to work safely in the lab.

Measuring Cylinders Measure Liquid Volume

Measuring cylinders come in all different sizes.
Make sure you choose one that's the right size for the measurement you want to make.
- It's no good using a huge 1 litre cylinder to measure out 2 cm³ of a liquid — the gaps between the scale markers will be too big and you'll end up with massive errors.
- It'd be much better to use one that measures up to 10 cm³.

Always read the volume from the bottom of the meniscus (the curved upper surface of the liquid) when it's at eye level.

You might also use a pipette in the lab. They are used to suck up and transfer liquid between containers, or to measure small amounts of liquid accurately.

Eureka Cans Measure the Volumes of Solids

- A eureka can is a beaker with a spout.
- You can use one (along with a measuring cylinder) to find the volume of an irregularly shaped solid object (p.34).

How to use a eureka can

1) Fill the eureka can with water so the water level is above the spout.
2) Let the water drain from the spout, leaving the water level just at the height of the spout (this will help make sure your results are accurate).
3) Put a measuring cylinder under the end of the spout. When you place an object in the beaker, it causes the water level to rise and water to flow out of the spout.
4) Wait until the spout has stopped dripping before you measure the volume of the water in the measuring cylinder. And eureka! You know the object's volume.

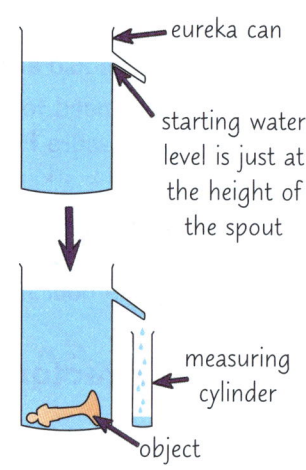

eureka can

starting water level is just at the height of the spout

measuring cylinder

object

Every Experiment has Hazards

Make sure you know what safety measures you should be taking before you start an experiment. Here are some tips for working with equipment safely...

You also need to be aware of general safety in the lab. E.g. handle glassware carefully.

CLAMP STANDS AND MASSES	Use clamp stands to stop masses and equipment falling. Make sure masses aren't too heavy (so they don't break any other equipment). Use pulleys that aren't too long (so hanging masses don't hit the floor).
HEATING EQUIPMENT	Let hot materials cool before moving them, or wear insulated gloves to handle them. If you're using an immersion heater to heat liquids, always let it dry out in air. This is just in case any liquid has leaked inside the heater. You might also need to wear eye protection.
LASERS	Always wear laser safety goggles. Never look directly into the laser or shine it towards another person. Turn the laser off when it's not needed.
ELECTRONICS	Use a low voltage and current. This prevents wires from overheating. It also stops damage to components.

What did the left foot say to the right foot? Eureka...

I know — lab safety isn't the most exciting topic. But it's very important. Not only will it stop you from blowing your eyebrows off, it'll help you pick up more marks in the exam. And that IS worth getting excited about...

Working with Electronics

Electrical devices are used in loads of experiments. Make sure you know how to use them.

There Are a Couple of Ways to Measure Potential Difference and Current

Voltmeters Measure Potential Difference

1) Connect the voltmeter in parallel (p.24) across the component you want to test.
2) The wires that come with a voltmeter are usually red (positive) and black (negative). These go into the red and black coloured ports on the voltmeter.
3) Then read the potential difference from the scale (or from the screen if the voltmeter is digital).

Ammeters Measure Current

1) Connect the ammeter in series (p.23) with the component you want to test.
2) Ammeters usually have red and black ports to show you where to connect your wires.
3) Read off the current shown on the scale (or screen).

Turn your circuit off between readings. This stops wires overheating and affecting your results (page 20).

Multimeters Measure Both

- A multimeter is a single device that can measure potential difference, current and (usually) resistance.
- To find potential difference, connect the multimeter in parallel. Make sure the red wire is plugged into the port that has a 'V' (for volts).
- To find the current, connect the multimeter in series. Use the port labelled 'A' (for amps).
- The dial on the multimeter should then be turned to the relevant section — for example, to measure the current in amps, turn the dial to 'A'.
- The screen will display the value you're measuring.

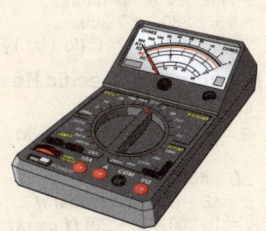

Light Gates Measure Time, Speed and Acceleration

- A light gate sends a beam of light from one side of the gate to a detector on the other side.
- When something passes through the gate, the light beam is interrupted.
- The gate measures when the beam was interrupted and how long it was interrupted for.
- Light gates can be connected to a computer.
- To find the speed of an object, type the length of the object into the computer. The computer will calculate the speed of the object as it passes through the beam.
- To measure acceleration, use an object that interrupts the signal twice, e.g. a piece of card with a gap cut into the middle.
- The light gate measures the speed for each section of the object. It uses this to calculate the object's acceleration. This can then be read from the computer screen.
- Light gates can be used instead of a stopwatch. This will reduce the errors in your experiment.

Have a look at page 63 for an example of a light gate being used.

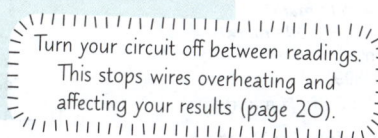

Light gate

Beam of light

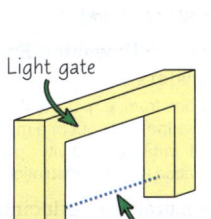

Piece of card

That's not a gate — where are the hinges...

After finishing this page, you should be able to take on any electrical experiment that they throw at you... ouch.

Answers

Topic 1 — Energy

p.3 — Energy Stores and Systems
Q1 Any four from: kinetic, thermal, chemical, gravitational potential, elastic potential, electrostatic, magnetic, nuclear *[4 marks]*.

p.4 — Conservation of Energy and Energy Transfers
Q1 Energy is transferred mechanically *[1 mark]* from the kinetic energy store of the wind *[1 mark]* to the kinetic energy store of the windmill *[1 mark]*.

p.5 — Kinetic and Potential Energy Stores
Q1 The change in height is 5.0 m. So the energy transferred from the gravitational potential energy store is:
$E_p = mgh = 2.0 \times 9.8 \times 5.0 = 98$ J *[1 mark]*
This is transferred to the kinetic energy store of the object, so $E_k = 98$ J *[1 mark]*
$E_k = \tfrac{1}{2}mv^2$
so $v^2 = 2E_k \div m$ *[1 mark]*
$= (2 \times 98) \div 2.0$ *[1 mark]*
$= 98$ m²/s²
$v = \sqrt{98} = 9.899...$
$= 9.9$ m/s (to 2 s.f.) *[1 mark]*

p.6 — Energy Transfers by Heating
Q1 $\Delta E = mc\Delta\theta$
so $\Delta\theta = \Delta E \div (m \times c)$ *[1 mark]*
$= 50\,000 \div (5 \times 4200)$
$= 2.380...$ °C *[1 mark]*
So the new temperature
$= 5 + 2.380... = 7.380...$
$= 7$ °C (to 1 s.f.) *[1 mark]*

p.7 — Investigating Specific Heat Capacity
Q1 $E = P \times t = 80 \times 200$ *[1 mark]*
$= 16\,000$ J *[1 mark]*
$\Delta E = mc\Delta\theta$, so
$c = \Delta E \div (m \times \Delta\theta)$ *[1 mark]*
$= 16\,000 \div (2 \times 20)$ *[1 mark]*
$= 400$ J/kg°C *[1 mark]*

p.8 — Power
Q1 $P = E \div t$
$t = 2 \times 60 = 120$ s *[1 mark]*
$P = 4800 \div 120$ *[1 mark]*
$= 40$ W *[1 mark]*

p.9 — Reducing Unwanted Energy Transfers
Q1 Any one from: e.g. make the walls thicker / make the walls out of a material with a low thermal conductivity / put in thermal insulation (e.g. loft insulation) *[1 mark]*.

p.10 — Investigating Reducing Energy Transfers
Q1 E.g. the volume/mass of water used / the initial temperature of the water / the time between temperature measurements *[1 mark]*.

p.11 — Efficiency
Q1 efficiency = useful output energy transfer ÷ total input energy transfer
$= 225 \div 300$ *[1 mark]*
$= 0.75$ *[1 mark]*

Q2 efficiency = useful power output ÷ total power input
$= 900 \div 1200 = 0.75$ *[1 mark]*
useful output energy transfer
= efficiency × total input energy transfer *[1 mark]*
$= 0.75 \times 72\,000$ *[1 mark]*
$= 54\,000$ J *[1 mark]*

p.12 — Energy Resources and Their Uses
Q1 a) renewable *[1 mark]*
b) non-renewable *[1 mark]*
c) non-renewable *[1 mark]*
d) renewable *[1 mark]*

p.13 — Wind, Solar and Geothermal
Q1 E.g. wind power can be unreliable as it doesn't provide a constant supply of energy because sometimes there's no wind / the turbines have to be stopped because the wind is too strong *[1 mark]*. Geothermal power plants are reliable because the hot rocks are always hot *[1 mark]*.

p.14 — Hydro-electricity, Waves and Tides
Q1 E.g. it disturbs the seabed / it disturbs the habitats of animals *[1 mark]*.

p.15 — Bio-fuels and Non-renewables
Q1 E.g. they're reliable / they can respond quickly to changes in demand. *[2 marks — 1 mark for each correct answer]*

Q2 E.g. burning oil releases carbon dioxide, which contributes to global warming. / It produces sulfur dioxide which causes acid rain, which is harmful to trees and animals. / Oil spills can occur when transporting oil, which can harm/kill animals that live in and around the sea *[3 marks — 1 mark for each correct answer]*.

p.16 — Trends in Energy Resource Use
Q1 Any two from: e.g. building new renewable power plants is expensive / people don't want to live near new power plants / renewable energy resources are less reliable than non-renewable energy resources / electric cars are more expensive than petrol cars. *[2 marks — 1 mark for each correct answer]*

Topic 2 — Electricity

p.18 — Current and Circuit Symbols
Q1 $Q = It$ so $t = Q \div I$ *[1 mark]*
$= 28\,800 \div 8$ *[1 mark]*
$= 3600$ s *[1 mark]*
$t = 3600 \div 60 = 60$ minutes *[1 mark]*

p.19 — Resistance and V = IR
Q1 $V = IR$ so $R = V \div I$ *[1 mark]*
$= 230 \div 5.0$ *[1 mark]*
$= 46$ Ω *[1 mark]*

p.20 — Investigating Resistance
Q1 E.g.

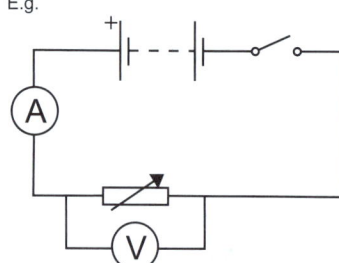

[1 mark for all circuit symbols correct, 1 mark for battery, variable resistor (test wire) and ammeter connected in series, 1 mark for voltmeter connected in parallel with the variable resistor (test wire)]

You'll still get the marks if you didn't include a switch in your circuit — but it's useful to help you control your experiment.

p.21 — I-V Characteristics
Q1 As the current through the lamp increases, the temperature of its filament increases *[1 mark]* causing its resistance to increase *[1 mark]*. A larger resistance means less current can flow per unit potential difference, and so the graph gets shallower *[1 mark]*.

p.22 — Circuit Devices
Q1 E.g.

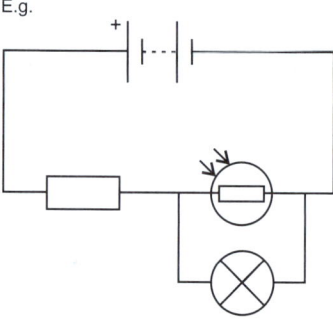

[1 mark for all symbols correct, 1 mark for the LDR connected in series with a resistor and a source of potential difference, 1 mark for the bulb connected in parallel with the LDR]

p.23 — Series Circuits
Q1 $R_{total} = 4 + 5 + 6 = 15$ Ω *[1 mark]*
$V = I \times R = 0.6 \times 15$ *[1 mark]* $= 9$ V *[1 mark]*

p.24 — Parallel Circuits
Q1 The total current through the circuit decreases *[1 mark]* as there are fewer paths for the current to take *[1 mark]*. The total resistance of the circuit increases *[1 mark]* as, using $V = IR$, a decrease in the total current means an increase in the total resistance *[1 mark]*.

p.25 — Investigating Circuits
Q1

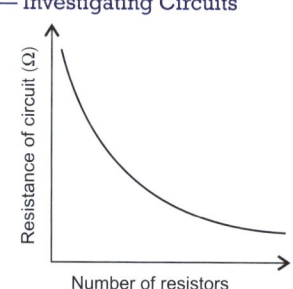

[1 mark for correct axes, 1 mark for correctly drawn curve]

p.26 — Electricity in the Home
Q1 a) 230 V *[1 mark]*
b) (around) 0 V *[1 mark]*
c) 0 V *[1 mark]*

p.27 — Power of Electrical Appliances
Q1 $E = P \times t$ so $P = E \div t$ *[1 mark]*
$= 6000 \div 30$ *[1 mark]*
$= 200$ W *[1 mark]*

Q2 $E = P \times t$ *[1 mark]*
$= 250 \times (2 \times 60 \times 60)$
$= 1\,800\,000$ J *[1 mark]*
$E = 375 \times (2 \times 60 \times 60)$
$= 2\,700\,000$ J *[1 mark]*
So change in energy is
$2\,700\,000 - 1\,800\,000$
$= 900\,000$ J *[1 mark]*

p.28 — More on Energy Transfers and Power
Q1 $E = Q \times V$
$= 10\,000 \times 200$ *[1 mark]*
$= 2\,000\,000$ J *[1 mark]*

Q2 $P = V \times I$
$= 12 \times 4.0$ *[1 mark]*
$= 48$ W *[1 mark]*

Q3 $R = P \div I^2$ *[1 mark]*
$= 2300 \div 10.0^2$ *[1 mark]*
$= 23$ Ω *[1 mark]*

p.29 — The National Grid
Q1 The National Grid is a system of cables and transformers linking power stations to consumers *[1 mark]*.

p.30 — Static Electricity
Q1 E.g. when you touch the car, a charge travels through you giving you a shock *[1 mark]*.

p.31 — Electric Fields
Q1

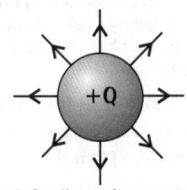

[1 mark for lines drawn at right angles and evenly spaced, 1 mark for arrows pointing away from the sphere]

Topic 3 — Particle Model of Matter

p.33 — The Particle Model and Density
Q1 a) When the substance is liquid, the particles are quite close together in an irregular pattern *[1 mark]*.
   b) When the substance is solid, the particles are held closely together in a regular, fixed pattern *[1 mark]*.
Q2 $\rho = m \div V$, so $m = \rho \times V$ *[1 mark]*
    $m = 2.5 \times 0.0048$ *[1 mark]*
    $= 0.012$ kg *[1 mark]*

p.34 — Investigating Density
Q1 Gemstone's mass = 0.019 kg
    $= 0.019 \times 1000$
    $= 19$ g *[1 mark]*
    Gemstone's volume = volume of water pushed out of eureka can = 7.0 cm^3
    $\rho = m \div V$
    $= 19 \div 7.0$ *[1 mark]*
    $= 2.714...$
    $= 2.7$ g/cm^3 (to 2 s.f.) *[1 mark]*

p.35 — Internal Energy and Changes of State
Q1 a) melting *[1 mark]*
   b) boiling / evaporating *[1 mark]*
   c) condensing *[1 mark]*

p.36 — Specific Latent Heat
Q1 $E = m \times L = 0.25 \times 120\,000$ *[1 mark]*
    $= 30\,000$ J *[1 mark]*

p.37 — Particle Motion and Pressure in Gases
Q1 pV = constant
    When $V = 3.5$ m^3,
    $pV = 520 \times 3.5 = 1820$ *[1 mark]*
    So when $V = 1$ m^3, $p \times 1 = 1820$ *[1 mark]*
    So $p = 1820$ Pa
    $= 1800$ Pa (to 2 s.f.) *[1 mark]*

Topic 4 — Atomic Structure

p.38 — Developing the Model of the Atom
Q1 The plum pudding model describes the atom as a ball of positive charge with electrons scattered in it *[1 mark]*.

p.39 — The Structure of the Atom
Q1 a) neutrons *[1 mark]*, protons *[1 mark]*
   b) The radius of an atom is around 1×10^{-10} m *[1 mark]*. The radius of a nucleus is over 10 000 times smaller than this *[1 mark]*.

p.40 — Isotopes and Nuclear Radiation
Q1 E.g. Alpha would not be suitable because it is stopped by a few cm of air or a sheet of paper *[1 mark]*. It would not be able to pass through the packaging to sterilise the equipment *[1 mark]*.

p.41 — Nuclear Equations
Q1 a beta particle / beta radiation *[1 mark]*
Q2 $^{219}_{86}\text{Rn} \rightarrow {}^{215}_{84}\text{Po} + {}^{4}_{2}\text{He}$
    [1 mark for correct layout, 1 mark for correct symbol for an alpha particle, 1 mark for total atomic and mass numbers being equal on both sides]

p.42 — Half-life
Q1 The rate at which a source decays *[1 mark]*.
Q2 Initial count-rate = 168 cps
    After 1 half-life,
    count-rate = 168 ÷ 2 = 84 cps
    After 2 half-lives,
    count-rate = 84 ÷ 2 = 42 cps
    After 3 half-lives,
    count-rate = 42 ÷ 2 = 21 cps *[1 mark]*.
    So, it took 3 half-lives for the count-rate to drop to 21 cps. This means that 60 minutes is equal to 3 half-lives *[1 mark]*.
    So, the half-life of the sample
    = 60 ÷ 3 = 20 minutes *[1 mark]*.

p.43 — Background Radiation and Radiation Dose
Q1 Any three from: e.g. air / food / building materials / rocks / space or cosmic rays / nuclear waste / fallout from nuclear explosions. *[3 marks — 1 mark for each correct answer]*

p.44 — Irradiation and Contamination
Q1 Gamma rays can penetrate through skin and can get to internal organs *[1 mark]* whereas alpha particles are stopped by skin *[1 mark]*.

p.45 — Uses and Risk
Q1 Radioactive isotopes are swallowed by or injected into a person *[1 mark]*. The gamma radiation the isotope gives off is detected outside the body *[1 mark]*. How the isotope moves around the body can show how the body is working *[1 mark]*.

p.46 — Fission and Fusion
Q1 Two lighter nuclei *[1 mark]*, two or three neutrons *[1 mark]*, gamma rays *[1 mark]*.

Topic 5a — Forces, Moments and Pressure

p.48 — Contact and Non-Contact Forces
Q1 a) Any two from: e.g. speed / distance / mass / temperature / time *[2 marks]*
   b) Any two from: e.g. displacement / force / acceleration / velocity *[2 marks]*
Q2 Contact force: air resistance *[1 mark]*
    Non-contact force: gravitational force *[1 mark]*

p.49 — Weight, Mass and Gravity
Q1 a) $W = mg = 5 \times 9.8$ *[1 mark]* $= 49$ N *[1 mark]*
   b) $W = 5 \times 1.6$ *[1 mark]* $= 8$ N *[1 mark]*

p.50 — Resultant Forces and Work Done
Q1 20 cm = 0.2 m *[1 mark]*
    $W = Fs = 20 \times 0.2$ *[1 mark]* $= 4$ J *[1 mark]*

p.51 — Forces and Elasticity
Q1 2 cm = 0.02 m *[1 mark]*
    $F = ke$ so $k = F \div e$ *[1 mark]*
    $= 1 \div 0.02$ *[1 mark]*
    $= 50$ N/m *[1 mark]*

p.52 — Investigating Springs
Q1 4.0 cm = 0.040 m *[1 mark]*
    $E_e = \tfrac{1}{2}ke^2 = \tfrac{1}{2} \times 25 \times (0.040)^2$ *[1 mark]*
    $= 0.020$ J *[1 mark]*

p.53 — Moments
Q1 6.0 cm = 6.0 ÷ 100 = 0.060 m *[1 mark]*
    $M = Fd$ so $F = M \div d$ *[1 mark]*
    $F = 1.44 \div 0.060$ *[1 mark]*
    $= 24$ N *[1 mark]*

p.54 — More on Moments
Q1 For forces to balance, anticlockwise moment = clockwise moment *[1 mark]*
    Let your distance = y
    So $300 \times 2 = 600 \times y$ *[1 mark]*
    $y = 600 \div 600 = 1$ m *[1 mark]*

p.55 — Fluid Pressure and Atmospheric Pressure
Q1 $p = F \div A$
    so $A = F \div p$ *[1 mark]*
    $= 220\,000 \div 120\,000$ *[1 mark]*
    $= 1.833...$
    $= 1.8$ m^2 (to 2 s.f.) *[1 mark]*

Topic 5b — Forces and Motion

p.57 — Distance, Displacement, Speed and Velocity
Q1 $s = vt$ so $v = s \div t$ *[1 mark]*
    $= 200 \div 25$ *[1 mark]*
    $= 8$ m/s *[1 mark]*

p.58 — Acceleration
Q1 $u = 0$ m/s, $v = 7.0$ m/s, $a = g = 9.8$ m/s^2,
    $s = (v^2 - u^2) \div 2a$ *[1 mark]*
    $= (49 - 0) \div (2 \times 9.8)$ *[1 mark]*
    $= 2.5$ m *[1 mark]*

p.59 — Distance-Time Graphs
Q1 E.g.

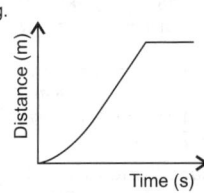

[1 mark for a curved line with an increasing positive gradient, 1 mark for the line becoming a straight line with a positive gradient, 1 mark for the line then becoming horizontal]

p.60 — Velocity-Time Graphs and Terminal Velocity
Q1 E.g.

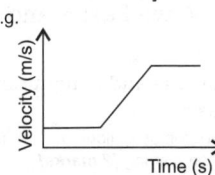

[1 mark for a straight, horizontal line representing constant speed, 1 mark for a straight line with a positive gradient representing constant acceleration, 1 mark for a straight, horizontal line at a different velocity to the initial velocity to represent a different constant speed]

Q2

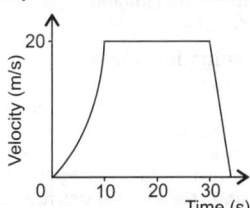

[1 mark for an upwards curved acceleration line to 20 m/s, 1 mark for a straight line representing steady speed, 1 mark for a straight line representing deceleration]

p.61 — Newton's First and Second Laws
Q1 $F = ma = (70 + 10) \times 0.25$ *[1 mark]*
    $= 20$ N *[1 mark]*

p.62 — Newton's Third Law
Q1 Any one from: e.g the gravitational force of the Earth attracts the car and the gravitational force of the car attracts the Earth *[1 mark]* / the car exerts a normal contact force down against the ground and the normal contact force from the ground pushes up against the car *[1 mark]* / the car (tyres) pushes the road backwards and the road pushes the car (tyres) forwards *[1 mark]*.

p.63 — Investigating Motion
Q1 The weight of the hook and the masses attached to it *[1 mark]*.

p.64 — Stopping Distance and Thinking Distance
Q1 E.g. speed / reaction time / tiredness / drugs / alcohol / distractions *[1 mark]*

p.65 — Braking Distance
Q1 Energy in car's kinetic energy store
= ½ × m × v²
= ½ × 1000 × 10² *[1 mark]*
= 50 000 J *[1 mark]*
To stop the car, the brakes must do work to transfer all the energy away from the car's kinetic energy store:
½ × m × v² = F × d *[1 mark]*
So F × d = 50 000
Rearrange for F:
F = 50 000 ÷ d
= 50 000 ÷ 50 *[1 mark]*
= 1000 N *[1 mark]*

p.66 — More on Stopping Distances
Q1 Thinking distance increases linearly with speed, so thinking distance
= 3 × 6 = 18 m *[1 mark]*
Braking distance increases with speed by 3² times.
So braking distance = 3² × 6 *[1 mark]*
= 54 m *[1 mark]*
Stopping distance = 18 + 54 = 72 m *[1 mark]*

p.67 — Reaction Times
Q1 a) In the afternoon *[1 mark]* because the ruler had fallen a smaller distance in the early afternoon than at night *[1 mark]*.
b) His reaction time is longer at night *[1 mark]* so whilst driving, he may take longer to react to a hazard, meaning his thinking distance would be longer *[1 mark]*.

Topic 6a — Wave Basics and EM Waves

p.69 — Transverse and Longitudinal Waves
Q1 Any two from: e.g. light / ripples on water / waves on a string *[2 marks]*

p.70 — Frequency, Period and Wave Speed
Q1 7.5 ÷ 100 = 0.075 m *[1 mark]*
wave speed = frequency × wavelength,
so frequency = wave speed ÷ wavelength *[1 mark]*
= 0.15 ÷ 0.075 *[1 mark]*
= 2 Hz *[1 mark]*

p.71 — Investigating Waves
Q1 E.g. attach a signal generator to a dipper and place it in a ripple tank filled with water to create some waves *[1 mark]*. Place a screen under the ripple tank, then turn on a lamp and dim the other lights in the room *[1 mark]*. Measure the distance between shadow lines that are 10 wavelengths apart on the screen under the tank. Divide this number by 10 to get the average wavelength of the water waves *[1 mark]*.

p.72 — Refraction
Q1 E.g.

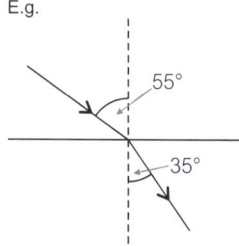

[1 mark for correctly drawing the boundary and the normal, 1 mark for drawing an incident ray at the correct angle, 1 mark for drawing the refracted ray at the correct angle]

p.73 — Reflection
Q1

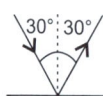

[1 mark for correct diagram showing rays and the normal, 1 mark for correct angle of incidence, 1 mark for correct angle of reflection]

p.74 — Investigating Light
Q1 E.g. draw around a transparent block on a piece of paper. Shine a light ray from a ray box into the block *[1 mark]*. Trace the incident ray and mark where the ray leaves the block with a cross. Remove the block and join these up with a straight line *[1 mark]*. Measure the angle of incidence and angle of refraction *[1 mark]*. Repeat this experiment for different materials. Keep the angle of incidence the same and see how the angle of refraction changes with the material *[1 mark]*.

p.75 — Electromagnetic (EM) Waves
Q1 Radio waves *[1 mark]*
Q2 Visible light *[1 mark]*

p.76 — Uses of EM Waves
Q1 E.g. TV / radio signals *[1 mark]*

p.77 — More Uses of EM Waves
Q1 E.g. seeing broken bones *[1 mark]* treating cancer *[1 mark]*

p.78 — Dangers of EM Waves
Q1 Any two from: e.g. damage to surface cells / sunburn / faster ageing of the skin / blindness / increased risk of skin cancer *[2 marks]*.
Q2 E.g. they are both ionising (they can knock electrons off atoms) *[1 mark]*.

Topic 6b — Light and Radiation

p.80 — Lenses and Images
Q1 The light rays converge (come together) *[1 mark]*.
Q2 E.g.

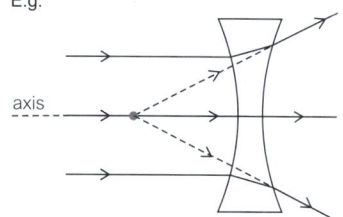

[1 mark for all three light rays continued correctly, 1 mark for virtual rays drawn to show that the light rays appear to have all come from the principal focus on the same side of the lens as the incident rays]

p.81 — Convex Lenses and Ray Diagrams
Q1

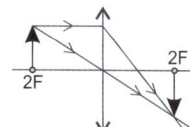

[1 mark for an image at a distance 2F from the lens, 1 mark for an inverted image, 1 mark for two correct light rays]

p.82 — Concave Lenses and Magnification
Q1 magnification
= image height ÷ object height
= 6 ÷ 12 *[1 mark]* = 0.5 *[1 mark]*
Q2 magnification
= image height ÷ object height
so image height
= magnification × object height *[1 mark]*
= 2.5 × 10 *[1 mark]* = 25 cm *[1 mark]*

p.83 — Visible Light
Q1 The wavelengths of light that come from the blue part of the visible spectrum are most strongly reflected (and other wavelengths are absorbed) by the object *[1 mark]*.

p.84 — Transmitting Visible Light
Q1 Black *[1 mark]*

p.85 — Black Body Radiation and Temperature
Q1 The second star is cooler *[1 mark]* because it has the longer peak wavelength, and the colder an object is, the longer its peak wavelength *[1 mark]*.

p.86 — Investigating IR Radiation
Q1 a) a black surface *[1 mark]*
b) a matt surface *[1 mark]*

p.87 — Investigating IR Absorption
Q1 Any two from: e.g. the plates are an equal distance from the Bunsen burner / the same wax is used / the same amount of wax is used / identical metal balls are used / the plates are identical (except for their different coloured sides) *[2 marks]*.

Topic 7 — Magnetism and Electromagnetism

p.89 — Permanent and Induced Magnets
Q1 They'll repel each other *[1 mark]*.

p.90 — Electromagnetism
Q1 E.g. for current out of the page, looking down along the length of the wire:

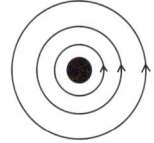

[1 mark for concentric circles around a central wire getting further apart, 1 mark for arrows on field lines with correct direction]

p.91 — Electromagnetic Devices
Q1 E.g. electromagnets can easily be switched on and off / you can change how strong an electromagnet is by changing how much current flows through it / electromagnets can be stronger than permanent magnets *[1 mark]*.

Topic 8 — Space Physics

p.92 — The Solar System and Stars
Q1 Nuclear fusion *[1 mark]*.

p.93 — The Life Cycle of Stars
Q1 E.g. the red giant fuses elements heavier than hydrogen in nuclear fusion reactions *[1 mark]*. When the red giant runs out of fuel, it will eject its outer layers and become a white dwarf *[1 mark]*. Eventually, the white dwarf will cool to become a black dwarf *[1 mark]*.

p.94 — Red-shift and the Big Bang
Q1 All the matter in the universe used to all be crammed into a tiny and very hot, dense space *[1 mark]*. The universe began expanding from this point (and is still expanding today) *[1 mark]*.

Glossary

A

Absorption When a wave transfers energy to the energy stores of a material.

Acceleration A change in velocity in a certain amount of time.

Accurate result A result that is very close to the true answer.

Activity (radioactive) The number of nuclei of a sample that decay per second.

Air resistance The frictional force caused by air on a moving object.

Alpha decay A type of radioactive decay in which an alpha particle is given out from a decaying nucleus.

Alpha particle A positively-charged particle made up of two protons and two neutrons (a helium nucleus).

Alpha particle scattering experiment An experiment in which alpha particles were fired at gold foil to see if they were deflected. It led to the plum pudding model being abandoned in favour of the nuclear model of the atom.

Alternating current (ac) Current that is constantly changing direction.

Ammeter A component used to measure the current through a component. It is always connected in series with the component.

Amplitude The maximum displacement of a point on a wave from its undisturbed position.

Angle of incidence The angle the incident ray of a wave makes with the normal at a boundary.

Angle of reflection The angle a reflected ray makes with the normal at a boundary.

Angle of refraction The angle a refracted ray makes with the normal when a wave refracts at a boundary.

Anomalous result A result that doesn't seem to fit with the rest of the data.

Artificial satellite A man-made satellite (normally orbiting the Earth).

Atmosphere A relatively thin layer of air that surrounds the Earth.

Atmospheric pressure The pressure felt by any surface within the atmosphere, due to air molecules colliding with the surface.

Atom A particle that makes up matter.

Atomic number The number of protons in the nucleus of an atom.

Axis (of a lens) A line passing through the middle of a lens, perpendicular to the lens.

B

Background radiation The radiation which surrounds us at all times, arising from both natural and man-made sources.

Beta decay A type of radioactive decay in which a beta particle is given out from a decaying nucleus.

Beta particle A high-speed electron emitted in beta decay.

Bias Unfairness in the way data is presented, possibly because the presenter is trying to make a particular point (sometimes without knowing they're doing it).

Big Bang theory The idea that the universe began from a small, very hot and dense region of space, which exploded and has been expanding ever since.

Bio-fuel A renewable energy resource made from plant products or animal dung.

Black body An object that absorbs all the electromagnetic radiation that hits it. A black body is also the best possible emitter of radiation.

Black dwarf The remains of a star that are left behind when a white dwarf cools.

Black hole A super dense region of space that light cannot escape from.

Braking distance The braking distance is the distance a vehicle travels after the brakes are applied until it comes to a complete stop, as a result of the braking force.

C

Categoric data Data that comes in distinct categories, e.g. metals (copper, zinc, etc.).

Chain reaction A reaction which keeps going (without any outside input) because the products of the reaction cause further reactions (e.g. nuclear fission).

Closed system A system where neither matter nor energy can enter or leave. The net change in total energy in a closed system is always zero.

Concave lens A lens that curves inwards and causes rays of light parallel to the axis to diverge (spread out) so they appear to have come from the principal focus.

Conservation of energy principle Energy can be transferred usefully from one energy store to another, stored or dissipated — but it can never be created or destroyed.

Contamination (radioactive) The presence of unwanted radioactive atoms on or inside an object.

Continuous data Numerical data that can have any value within a range (e.g. length, volume or temperature).

Control experiment An experiment that's kept under the same conditions as the rest of the investigation, but where the independent variable isn't altered.

Control variable A variable in an experiment that is kept the same.

Convex lens A lens that bulges outwards and causes rays of light parallel to the axis to converge (come together) at the principal focus.

Correlation A relationship between two variables.

Cosmic ray Radiation from space.

Current The flow of electric charge. The size of the current is the rate of flow of charge. Measured in amperes (A).

D

Density A substance's mass per unit volume.

Dependent variable The variable in an experiment that is measured.

Diffuse reflection When parallel waves are reflected by a rough surface (e.g. a piece of paper) and the reflected rays are scattered in lots of different directions.

Diode A circuit component that only allows current to flow through it in one direction. It has a very high resistance in the other direction.

Direct current (dc) Current that always flows in the same direction.

Glossary

Displacement The straight-line distance and direction from an object's starting position to its finishing position.

Distance-time graph A graph showing how the distance travelled by an object changes over a period of time.

Drag The frictional force caused by any fluid (a liquid or gas) on a moving object.

Dwarf planet A planet-like object in space that orbits a star but which doesn't match all of the rules for being a planet.

E

Earth wire The green and yellow wire in an electrical cable that only carries current when there's a fault. It stops exposed metal parts of an appliance from becoming live.

Efficiency The proportion of input energy transfer which is usefully transferred. Also the proportion of input power which is usefully output.

Elastic deformation An object undergoing elastic deformation will return to its original shape and length once any forces being applied to it are removed.

Elastic object An object which can be elastically deformed.

Elastic potential energy store Anything that has been stretched or compressed, e.g. a spring, has energy in its elastic potential energy store.

Electric field A region in which an electrically charged object experiences an electrostatic force.

Electromagnet A solenoid with an iron core.

Electromagnetic (EM) spectrum A continuous spectrum of all the possible wavelengths of electromagnetic waves.

Electron A negatively charged particle that orbits the nucleus of an atom.

Electrostatic attraction/repulsion The non-contact force which acts to bring together opposite charges (attraction) / push apart like charges (repulsion).

Energy store A means by which an object stores energy. There are 8 different types of energy store: thermal, kinetic, gravitational potential, elastic potential, chemical, magnetic, electrostatic and nuclear.

Equilibrium A state in which all the forces acting on an object are balanced, so the resultant force is zero.

F

Fair test A controlled experiment where the only thing being changed is the independent variable.

Fluid A substance that can flow — either a liquid or a gas.

Focal length (of a lens) The distance from the centre of a lens to the principal focus.

Force A push or a pull on an object caused by it interacting with something.

Fossil fuel The fossil fuels are coal, oil and natural gas. They're non-renewable energy resources that we burn to generate electricity.

Frequency The number of complete waves passing a certain point per second. Measured in hertz (Hz).

Friction A force that opposes an object's motion. It acts in the opposite direction to motion.

G

Gamma decay A type of radioactive decay in which a gamma ray is given out from a decaying nucleus.

Gamma ray A high-frequency, short-wavelength electromagnetic wave.

Gear A circular disc with teeth round its edge. It can be used to transmit the rotational effect of a force.

Geiger-Müller tube A particle detector that is used with a counter to measure count rate.

Geothermal power A renewable energy resource where energy is transferred from the thermal energy stores of hot rocks underground and is used to generate electricity or to heat buildings.

Gradient The slope of a line graph. It shows how quickly the variable on the y-axis changes with the variable on the x-axis.

Gravitational potential energy (g.p.e) store Anything that has mass and is in a gravitational field has energy in its gravitational potential energy store.

H

Half-life The time it takes for the number of nuclei of a radioactive isotope in a sample to halve.
OR
The time it takes for the count rate (or activity) of a radioactive sample to fall to half its initial level.

Hazard Something that has the potential to cause harm (e.g. fire, electricity, etc.).

Hypothesis A possible explanation for a scientific observation.

I

Independent variable The variable in an experiment that is changed.

Induced magnet An object that becomes a magnet when it is placed inside another magnetic field.

Inelastic deformation An object undergoing inelastic deformation will not return to its original shape and length once the forces being applied to it are removed.

Infrared (IR) radiation A type of electromagnetic wave continually emitted and absorbed by all objects.

Internal energy The total energy that a system's particles have in their kinetic and potential energy stores.

Ionising radiation Radiation that has enough energy to knock electrons off atoms.

Irradiation Exposure to radiation.

Isotopes Different forms of the same element, which have atoms with the same number of protons (atomic number), but different numbers of neutrons (and so different mass numbers).

I-V characteristic A graph of current against potential difference for a component.

K

Kinetic energy store Anything that's moving has energy in its kinetic energy store.

Glossary

L

Latent heat The energy required to change the state of a substance without changing its temperature.

Law of reflection The angle of reflection of a reflected ray is always equal to the angle of incidence.

Lever A device that increases the distance between an applied force and a pivot, making it easier to do work.

Light-dependent resistor (LDR) A resistor whose resistance is dependent on light intensity. The resistance decreases as light intensity increases.

Limit of proportionality The point beyond which the force applied to an elastic object is no longer directly proportional to the extension of the object.

Line of action (of a force) A straight line passing through the point at which the force is acting in the same direction as the force.

Linear graph A straight line graph.

Live wire The brown wire in an electrical cable that carries an alternating potential difference from the mains.

Longitudinal wave A wave in which the vibrations are along the same line as the direction of energy transfer.

Lubricant A substance used between two objects to reduce friction between surfaces.

M

Magnetic field A region where magnetic materials (like iron and steel) experience a force.

Magnetic material A material (such as iron, steel, cobalt or nickel) which is attracted to magnets.

Magnification The ratio of the size of the image to the size of the object.

Main sequence star A star in the main sequence of its life, which is stable because the nuclear fusion in the star provides an outward pressure that balances the inward pull of gravity.

Mass number The number of neutrons and protons in the nucleus of an atom.

Mean (average) A measure of average found by adding up all the data and dividing by the number of values there are.

Median (average) A measure of average found by selecting the middle value from a data set arranged in ascending order.

Medical tracer A radioactive isotope that can be injected into or swallowed by people. Their progress around the body can be followed using an external detector and can diagnose medical conditions.

Microwave A type of electromagnetic wave that can be used for cooking and satellite communications.

Mode (average) A measure of average found by selecting the most frequent value from a data set.

Model Used to describe or display how an object or system behaves in reality.

Moment The turning effect of a force.

Moon A natural satellite which orbits a planet.

N

National Grid The network of transformers and cables that distributes electrical power from power stations to consumers.

Nebula A cloud of dust and gas in space.

Neutral wire The blue wire in an electrical cable that current in an appliance normally flows through. It is around 0 V.

Neutron A particle found in the nucleus of an atom. It has no charge.

Neutron star The very dense core of a star that is left behind when a red super giant explodes in a supernova.

Newton's First Law An object will remain at rest or travelling at a constant velocity unless it is acted on by a resultant force.

Newton's Second Law The acceleration of an object is directly proportional to the resultant force acting on it, and inversely proportional to its mass.

Newton's Third Law When two objects interact, they exert equal and opposite forces on each other.

Non-contact force A force that can act between objects that are not touching.

Non-renewable energy resource An energy resource that is non-renewable cannot be made at the same rate as it's being used.

Normal (at a boundary) A line that's perpendicular (at 90°) to a surface at the point of incidence (where a wave hits the surface).

Nuclear fission When an atomic nucleus splits up to form two smaller nuclei.

Nuclear fusion When two nuclei join to create a heavier nucleus.

Nuclear model A model of the atom that says that the atom has a small, central positively-charged nucleus with negatively-charged electrons moving around the nucleus, and that most of the atom is empty space. The nucleus is made up of protons and neutrons.

Nucleus (atom) The centre of an atom, containing protons and neutrons.

O

Ohmic conductor A conductor with resistance that is constant at a constant temperature. It has a linear I-V characteristic.

P

Parallel circuit A circuit in which every component is connected separately to the positive and negative ends of the battery.

Peer-review The process in which other scientists check the results and explanations of an investigation before they are published.

Period (of a wave) The time taken for one complete wave to pass a certain point.

Permanent magnet An object that always has its own magnetic field around it.

Glossary

Physical change A change where you don't end up with a new substance — it's the same substance as before, just in a different form. (A change of state is a physical change.)

Planet A natural object in space which orbits a star.

Potential difference The driving force that pushes electric charge around a circuit, measured in volts (V). Also known as pd or voltage.

Power The rate of transferring energy (or doing work). Normally measured in watts (W).

Precise result When all the data is close to the mean.

Prediction A statement that can be tested and is based on a hypothesis.

Pressure The force per unit area exerted on a surface.

Principal focus of a concave lens The point where rays hitting the lens parallel to the axis appear to have come from.

Principal focus of a convex lens The point where rays hitting the lens parallel to the axis all meet.

Proton A positively charged particle found in the nucleus of an atom.

Protostar The earliest stage in the life cycle of a star. Protostars are formed when the force of gravity causes clouds of dust and gas to pull together.

R

Radiation dose A measure of the risk of harm to your body due to exposure to radiation.

Radio wave A type of electromagnetic wave mainly used for radio and TV signals.

Radioactive decay The random process of a radioactive substance giving out radiation from the nuclei of its atoms.

Radioactive substance A substance that spontaneously gives out radiation from the nuclei of its atoms.

Radiotherapy A treatment of cancer that uses ionising radiation (such as gamma rays and X-rays) to kill cancer cells.

Random error A difference in the results of an experiment caused by unpredictable events, e.g. human error in measuring.

Range The difference between the smallest and largest values in a set of data.

Ray A straight line showing the path along which a wave moves.

Ray diagram A diagram that shows the path of light waves.

Reaction time The time taken for a person to react after an event (e.g. seeing a hazard).

Real image An image formed when light rays from a point on an object come together at another point — the light rays actually pass through that point.

Red giant A type of star that is formed when a star around the same size as the Sun expands as it starts to run out of hydrogen.

Red super giant A type of star that is formed when a large star (much bigger than the Sun) expands as it starts to run out of hydrogen.

Red-shift The shift in observed wavelength of light from a source moving away from a stationary observer. The wavelength is shifted towards the red end of the electromagnetic spectrum.

Reflection When a wave bounces back as it meets a boundary between two materials.

Refraction When a wave changes direction as it passes across the boundary between two materials at an angle to the normal.

Renewable energy resource An energy resource that is renewable is one that is being, or can be, made at the same rate (or faster) than it's being used.

Repeatable result A result that will come out the same if the experiment is repeated by the same person using the same method and equipment.

Reproducible result A result that will come out the same if someone different does the experiment.

Resistance Anything in a circuit that reduces the flow of charge. Measured in ohms (Ω).

Resultant force A single force that can replace all the forces acting on an object to give the same effect as the original forces acting altogether.

Right-hand thumb rule The rule to work out the direction of the magnetic field around a current-carrying wire. Your thumb points in the direction of the current, and your fingers curl in the direction of the magnetic field.

Risk The chance that a hazard will cause harm.

S

Satellite An object which orbits a second more massive object.

Scalar A quantity that has magnitude but no direction.

Series circuit A circuit in which every component is connected in a line, end to end.

S.I. unit A unit recognised as standard by scientists all over the world.

Significant figure The first significant figure of a number is the first non-zero digit. The second, third and fourth significant figures follow on immediately after it.

Solar cell A device that generates electricity directly from the Sun's radiation.

Solenoid A coil of wire often used in the construction of electromagnets.

Spark The passage of electrons across a (usually) small gap between a static charge and an earthed conductor.

Specific heat capacity The amount of energy (in joules) needed to raise the temperature of 1 kg of a material by 1 °C.

Specific latent heat (SLH) The amount of energy needed to change 1 kg of a substance from one state to another without changing its temperature. (For cooling, it is the energy released by a change in state.)

Specific latent heat of fusion The specific latent heat for changing between a solid and a liquid (melting or freezing).

Specific latent heat of vaporisation The specific latent heat for changing between a liquid and a gas (evaporating, boiling or condensing).

Specular reflection When parallel waves are reflected in a single direction by a smooth surface.

Standard form A number written in the form $A \times 10^n$, where A is a number between 1 and 10.

State of matter The form which a substance can take — e.g. solid, liquid or gas.

Glossary

Static charge An electric charge that cannot move. It often forms on electrical insulators, where charge cannot flow freely.

Stopping distance The distance covered by a vehicle in the time between the driver spotting a hazard and the vehicle coming to a complete stop. It's the sum of the thinking distance and the braking distance.

Supernova The explosion of a red super giant.

System The object, or group of objects, that you're considering.

Systematic error An error that is consistently made throughout an experiment.

T

Terminal velocity The maximum velocity a falling object can reach without any added driving forces. It's the velocity at which the resistive forces (drag) acting on the object match the force due to gravity (weight).

Theory An explanation or system of ideas that has been accepted by the scientific community because there is good evidence to back it up.

Thermal conductivity A measure of how quickly an object transfers energy by heating through conduction.

Thermal insulator A material with a low thermal conductivity.

Thermistor A resistor whose resistance is dependent on the temperature. The resistance decreases as temperature increases.

Thinking distance The distance a vehicle travels during the driver's reaction time (before the brakes have been applied).

Three-core cable An electrical cable containing a live wire, a neutral wire and an earth wire.

Transformer A device which can change the potential difference of an ac supply.

Transmission (of a wave) When a wave passes through a boundary from one material into another and continues travelling.

Transverse wave A wave in which the vibrations are perpendicular (at 90°) to the direction of energy transfer.

U

Ultraviolet (UV) radiation A type of electromagnetic wave, the main source of which is sunlight.

Uncertainty The amount by which a given result may differ from the true value.

V

Valid result A result that is repeatable and reproducible, and comes from an experiment that was designed to be a fair test (so that it answers the original question).

Vector A quantity which has both magnitude (size) and a direction.

Velocity The speed and direction of an object.

Velocity-time graph A graph showing how the velocity of an object changes over a period of time.

Virtual image An image that is formed when light rays appear to have come from one point, but have actually come from another — the light rays don't actually pass through that point.

Visible light The part of the electromagnetic spectrum that we can see with our eyes.

Voltmeter A component used to measure the potential difference across a component. Always connected in parallel with the component.

W

Wave A vibration that transfers energy without transferring any matter.

Wavelength The length of a full cycle of a wave, e.g. from a crest to the next crest.

Weight The force acting on an object due to gravity.

White dwarf The hot, dense core left behind when a red giant becomes unstable and ejects its outer layer of dust and gas.

Work done The energy transferred when a force moves an object through a distance, or by a moving charge.

X

X-ray A high-frequency, short-wavelength electromagnetic wave. It is mainly used in medical imaging and treatment.

Index

A
acceleration 58-61, 63
   estimating 58
accuracy 100
activity (radioactivity) 42, 43
air resistance 60
alpha radiation 40, 41
   dangers 44
alternating currents (ac) 26
altitude 55
ammeters 18, 109
amplitude (waves) 69
angles
   measuring 107
   of incidence 72-74
   of reflection 73, 74
   of refraction 72, 74
anomalous results 100
apparatus 107, 108
atmosphere 55
atomic models 38, 39
atomic numbers 40, 41
atoms 38-41
average speeds 57

B
background radiation 43
balances 107
balancing equations 41
bar charts 101
beta radiation 40, 41, 44, 45
   dangers 44
bias 97
Big Bang theory 94
bio-fuels 15
black bodies 85
black dwarfs 93
black holes 93
Bohr model of the atom 38
boiling 35, 36
brakes 65
braking distance 64-66

C
calculating gradients 59, 102
cancer 45, 77, 78
centre of mass 49
chain reactions 46
changes of state 35, 36
charge
   in circuits 18, 27, 28, 31
   ions 39
   of a nucleus 40, 41
   of an atom 39
   static 30, 31
circuit symbols 18
circuits 18-25
   investigating *I-V* characteristics 21
   investigating resistance 20, 25
   parallel 24
   sensing 22
   series 23
climate change 15
closed systems 3
coal 12, 15
colours 83, 84
communication of ideas 97
compasses 89
compressions (waves) 69
concave lenses 80, 82
conclusions 105
condensing 35, 36
conservation of energy 4
conservation of mass 35
contact forces 48
contamination (radioactivity) 44
control experiments 99
control rods 46
control variables 99
converting units 103
convex lenses 80-82
cooling 35, 36
correlations 102, 105
count-rate 42, 43
current (electrical) 18, 19
   alternating 26
   direct 26
   energy transferred 27, 28
   I-V characteristics 21
   in parallel circuits 24, 25
   in series circuits 23, 25
   magnetic field around a current-carrying wire 90
   mains supply 26
   National Grid 29

D
dangers of ionising radiation 44, 45, 78
dark energy 94
dark matter 94
decay (radioactive) 40-44
deceleration 58, 65
density 33, 34
dependent variables 99
diffuse reflection 73, 74
diodes 18, 19, 21
direct currents (dc) 26
displacement 57
dissipated energy 4, 9-11
distance 57, 59
distance-time graphs 59
drag 60
dwarf planets 92

E
earth wires 26
efficiency 11
elastic deformation 51, 52
elastic objects 51
elastic potential energy stores 5, 51, 52
electric charge 18, 27, 28, 31
electric fields 31
electric heaters 12
electric shocks 26, 30
electrical energy transfers 3, 27, 28
electricity 18-31
   supply and demand 29
electromagnetic spectrum 75
electromagnetic waves 75-78, 83-87
   black body radiation 85
   dangers 45, 78
   uses 45, 76, 77
electromagnetism 90, 91
   uses 91
electrons 30, 38-41
electrostatic force 30, 31
energy 3-16, 27, 28, 50
   conservation of 4
   internal 35, 36
   stores 3-7, 52
energy levels (atoms) 38, 39
energy resources 12-16
   generating electricity 13-16
   heating 12
   non-renewables 12, 15
   renewables 12-15
   transport 12, 16
   trends in use 16
energy transfers 3, 4
   by heating 3, 6, 7, 35, 36
   by waves 3, 69, 75
   efficiency 11
   electrical 3, 27, 28
   mechanical 3, 4, 50, 52, 65
   rate of 8, 27, 28
   reducing 9, 10
   work done 3, 4, 50, 65
equilibrium (forces) 62
estimating
   accelerations 58
   forces 61
   stopping distances 66
ethical issues 97
eureka cans 34, 108
evaluations 106
evaporation 35, 36
expansion of the universe 94
experimental safety 98, 108
extension (of objects) 51, 52

F
field lines 31, 89, 90
fields
   electric 31
   gravitational 49
   magnetic 89, 90
filament lamps 18, 19, 21
fission 46
fluids 55
focal length 80-82
force-extension graphs 51, 52
forces
   contact 48
   electrostatic 30, 31
   frictional 9, 50, 65
   gravitational 4, 48, 49, 60, 92, 93
   interaction pair 48, 62
   magnetic 89
   moments 53, 54
   Newton's laws 61, 62
   non-contact 48
   pressure 37, 55
   resultant 50, 61
   weight 49
formation of stars 92
formulas 104
fossil fuels 12, 15
freezing 35, 36
frequency 69, 70, 71
   of EM waves 75
   of mains supply 26
friction 9, 50, 65
fusion 46, 92, 93

G
galaxies 92, 94
gamma rays 40, 41, 46, 75
   dangers 44, 45, 78
   uses 45, 77
gases 37
   gas pressure 37
   natural gas 15
   particle motion 37
   states of matter 33, 35
   temperature 37
   volume 37
gears 54
Geiger-Muller tube 42
geothermal power 13
global warming 15
gradients 59, 60, 102
graphs 102
   distance-time 59
   force-extension 51, 52
   gradients 59, 102
   heating and cooling 36
   I-V characteristics 21
   radioactive decay 42
   resistance 20, 25
   stopping distances 66
   terminal velocity 60
   velocity-time 60
gravitational field strength 5, 49
gravitational force 4, 48, 49
   star formation 92, 93
gravitational potential energy stores 4, 5
greenhouse gases 15

H
half-life 42, 43
hazards (experiments) 98, 108
heating 6, 7, 35, 36
hydroelectric power 14
hypotheses 96, 99

I
images (types of) 80
independent variables 99
induced magnets 89
inelastic deformation 51, 52
infrared cameras 76
infrared radiation 75, 76, 85-87
insulation 9, 10
intensity (of waves) 85
interaction pairs 48, 62
internal energy 35, 36
ionisation 31, 39, 40
ionising power 40
ionising radiation 40, 41, 44, 45, 78
   alpha 40, 41, 44
   background 43
   beta 40, 41, 44, 45
   dangers 44, 45, 78
   gamma 40, 41, 44, 45, 75
   uses 45
ions 39
irradiation (radioactivity) 44
isotopes 40, 43
I-V characteristics 21

K
kinetic energy stores 5, 65, 66

L
latent heat 36
laws of motion 61, 62
LDRs 18, 22
lenses 80-82
   concave 80, 82
   convex 80-82
Leslie cubes 86
levers 54
life cycle of stars 92, 93
light 74, 83, 84
light gates 63, 109
limit of proportionality 51, 52
linear components (of circuits) 21
liquids 33, 35
   density of 34
   measuring volume 108
live wires 26
longitudinal waves 69
lubricants 9

Index

M
magnetic
 field of the Earth 89
 fields 89, 90
 forces 89
 materials 89
magnets 89, 90
magnification 82
main sequence stars 92, 93
mass 35, 49, 61
 in fusion reactions 46
 mass balances 107
mass numbers 40, 41
mean (average) 101
measuring cylinders 108
mechanical energy transfers 3, 4, 50, 52, 65
medical tracers 45
melting 35, 36
micrometers 107
microwaves 75, 76
models 96
moments 53, 54
moons 92

N
National Grid 29
natural gas 15
nebulae 92
neutral wires 26
neutron stars 93
neutrons 38, 39, 40, 46
Newton's First Law 61
Newton's Second Law 61, 63
Newton's Third Law 62
non-contact forces 48
non-linear components (of circuits) 21, 22
non-renewables 12, 15
north poles (magnets) 89
nuclear equations 41
nuclear fission 46
nuclear fuels 15, 46
nuclear fusion 46, 92, 93
nuclear model (of the atom) 38, 39
nuclear power 15
nuclear radiation 40-42, 44
nuclear weapons 46
nuclei 38-41, 46

O
ohmic conductors 19, 21
oil 15
opaque 83
optical fibres 77
orbits 92
oscilloscopes 70

P
parallel circuits 24, 25
particle model of matter 33, 35-37
peer review 96
period (waves) 69, 70
permanent magnets 89
physical changes 35
planets 92
plugs 26
plum pudding model 38
plutonium 46

potential difference 18, 19
 alternating 26
 direct 26
 energy transferred 28
 in parallel circuits 24
 in series circuits 23
 I-V characteristics 21
 measuring 109
 National Grid 29
power 8, 11
 electrical 27, 28
 ratings 27
precision 100
predictions 96, 99
pressure 37, 55, 92
 atmospheric 55
 fluids 55
 gases 37
principal focus 80, 82
proportionality 104
protons 38-40
protostars 92

R
radiation 40-46, 75-78, 85-87
 energy transfers 3, 75, 86, 87
 sickness 45
radiation dose 43, 78
radio waves 75, 76
radioactive decay 40-42, 44, 45
 alpha 40, 41
 background 43
 beta 40, 41, 45
 gamma 40, 41, 44, 45, 75
radioactivity
 count-rate 42, 43
 natural sources 43
radiotherapy 45
random errors 100
range (of data) 101
rarefactions (waves) 69
ray boxes 74
ray diagrams
 concave lenses 80, 82
 convex lenses 80-82
 reflection 73, 74
 refraction 72, 74
reaction times 64, 67
real images 80, 81
red giants 93
red super giants 93
red-shift 94
reducing energy transfers 9, 10
reflection 73, 74
refraction 72, 74, 80-82
renewables 12-15
repeatable results 99
reproducible results 99
resistance (electrical) 18-22
 in parallel circuits 24, 25
 in series circuits 23, 25
 wire length 20
resultant force 50, 61
right-hand thumb rule 90
ripple tanks 71
risks 98
 and radiation 44, 45, 78
ruler drop test 67

S
safety
 driving 64-66
 during experiments 98, 108
 radioactive 44, 45
sampling 100

satellites 76, 92
scalars 48
sensing circuits 22
series circuits 23, 25
sieverts 43, 78
significant figures 101
S.I. units 103
skin cancer 78
solar power 13
solar system 92
solenoids 90
solids 33, 35
sound waves 69, 70
sources (of background radiation) 43
south poles (magnets) 89
space 92, 93, 94
sparks 30, 31
specific heat capacity 6, 7
specific latent heat 36
spectrum
 electromagnetic 75
 visible light 83, 84
specular reflection 73, 74
speed 57, 59, 60
 braking distances 65, 66
 of sound in air 57
 of waves 70, 71, 75
 typical speeds 57
speed limits 64
spring constant 51, 52
springs 51, 52
standard form 39, 104
stars 92, 93
states of matter 33, 35
 gases 33, 37
 liquids 33
 solids 33
static electricity 30
step-down transformers 29
step-up transformers 29
stopping distances 64-66
 graphs 66
stopwatches 107
sublimation 35
Sun 93
sunburn 78
supernovae 93, 94
systematic errors 100
systems 3

T
tables (of data) 101
taking measurements 107-109
temperature 85
 internal energy 35, 36
 measuring 107
 monitoring with IR 76
 specific heat capacity 6, 7
 specific latent heat 36
terminal velocity 60
theories 96
thermal conductivity 9, 10
thermal energy stores 4, 6, 7, 9, 27, 50
thermal insulation 9,10
thermistors 22
thermometers 107
thinking distance 64, 66
three-core cables 26
tidal barrages 14
timing 107
tracers 45
transformers 29
translucent 84
transparent 84

transverse waves 69
trends
 in electricity use 29
 in energy use 16
turning effects 53, 54
TV signals 76
typical
 car stopping distances 66
 reaction times 67
 speeds 57
 vehicle masses 61

U
UK mains supply 26
ultraviolet (UV) 75, 77, 78
uncertainties 106
uniform acceleration 58
uniform magnetic fields 90
units 103
universe 94
uranium 46

V
validity 99
variables 99
vectors 48
velocity 57, 60
velocity-time graphs 60
virtual images 80-82
visible light 75, 77, 83, 84
 refraction and reflection 74
voltage 18, 19
 alternating 26
 direct 26
 energy transferred 28
 in parallel circuits 24
 in series circuits 23
 I-V characteristics 21
 measuring 109
 National Grid 29
voltmeters 109
volume (measuring) 34, 108

W
wasted energy 4, 9, 11
wave equation 70
wave power 14
wave speed 70, 71
wavelength 69, 83-85
 measuring 70, 71
 of EM waves 75
 peak 85
 red-shift 94
waves 69-88
 absorption 83-85
 at a boundary 73
 electromagnetic 75-78, 83-87
 longitudinal 69
 on a string 71
 reflection 73, 83, 84
 refraction 72
 scattering 83, 84
 speed 70, 71
 transmission 83, 84
 transverse 69, 75
 wavelength 69, 70, 71
weight 49
white dwarfs 93
wind power 13
work done
 by charges 27, 28
 by forces 4, 8, 50, 52, 65

X
X-rays 75, 77, 78

Formulas

In your GCSE Physics exams, you'll be given an <u>equations sheet</u> listing the formulas you might need. That means you <u>don't</u> have to <u>learn them all</u> (hurrah), but you do need to be able to <u>pick out</u> the right formulas to use and be really confident <u>using</u> them. Here are the formulas that you'll be given:

---

kinetic energy = 0.5 × mass × (speed)² $E_k = ½mv^2$

elastic potential energy = 0.5 × spring constant × (extension)² $E_e = ½ke^2$

gravitational potential energy = mass × gravitational field strength × height $E_p = mgh$

change in thermal energy = mass × specific heat capacity × temperature change $\Delta E = mc\Delta\theta$

efficiency = useful output energy transfer / total input energy transfer

efficiency = useful power output / total power input

power = energy transferred / time $P = \dfrac{E}{t}$

power = work done / time $P = \dfrac{W}{t}$

---

charge flow = current × time $Q = It$

potential difference (pd) = current × resistance $V = IR$

power = pd × current $P = VI$

energy transferred = power × time $E = Pt$

energy transferred = charge flow × pd $E = QV$

power = (current)² × resistance $P = I^2R$

---

weight = mass × gravitational field strength $W = mg$

force = spring constant × extension $F = ke$

pressure = force normal to surface / area of surface $p = \dfrac{F}{A}$

work done = force × distance (along the line of action of the force) $W = Fs$

moment of a force = force × distance (normal to direction of force) $M = Fd$

---

distance = speed × time $s = vt$

force = mass × acceleration $F = ma$

acceleration = change in velocity / time taken $a = \dfrac{\Delta v}{t}$

(final velocity)² − (initial velocity)² = 2 × acceleration × distance $v^2 - u^2 = 2as$

---

density = mass / volume $\rho = \dfrac{m}{V}$

thermal energy for a change of state = mass × specific latent heat $E = mL$

pressure (of a gas) × volume (of a gas) = constant $pV = $ constant

period = 1 / frequency $T = \dfrac{1}{f}$

magnification = image height / object height

wave speed = frequency × wavelength $v = f\lambda$